Praise for *Applied Value Investing*

"Calandro's clever application of value investing principles to corporate decision-making could transform how businesses operate and what business school students are taught. This thought-provoking work takes value investing to the next level."

—Seth A. Klarman, president, The Baupost Group, L.L.C.; lead editor of Graham and Dodd's *Security Analysis*, Sixth Edition; and author of *Margin of Safety*

"After seventy-five years, Graham and Dodd remains the true North Star for those seeking the Rosetta Stone to unlock values. Professor Joseph Calandro adopts Graham and Dodd's fundamental premises and uses them to focus on new dynamics."

—Mario J. Gabelli, CFA, chairman and CEO, GAMCO Investors, Inc.

"Calandro's application of Graham and Dodd principles outside the traditional realm of value investing involves multi-disciplinary thinking, a necessary skill for constructively framing and reframing the investment landscape in today's chaotic world. Particularly interesting is Calandro's chapter on the relationship between Graham and Dodd's discussion of the market valuation cycle of greed and fear, and the top down macro ideas of George Soros. In essence, Calandro shows how Mr. Market's bipolar psychology can be linked to Soros' concepts of reflexivity and feedback between conditions on Wall Street and Main Street. Given the wild downward oscillations we have experienced over the last year, every value investor should be able to weave these two investment approaches together to understand when and why a cycle develops, and where market behavior diverges significantly from the fundamentals."

—Mitchell R. Julis, co-chairman and co-CEO, Canyon Partners, L.L.C.

"Joseph Calandro's *Applied Value Investing* is the most important business book of our time. Today our global economy is in the throes of major readjustment, and this book's analysis is a critical navigation tool to help executives and investors find and create value. Calandro extends the classic work of Graham and Dodd to evaluate mergers and acquisitions, catastrophe-based alternative investment, and most importantly integrates it with a strategic framework for managers to determine if they are truly creating value above their cost of capital, risk adjusted. It is also well written, practical, and an enjoyable read."

　　—Dr. John J. Sviokla, vice chairman, Diamond Management
　　& Technology Consultants, and former associate professor of
　　Harvard Business School

"For anyone interested in the interface between strategy and finance—CEOs, CFOs, operations executives, planners, investors, analysts, and risk managers—*Applied Value Investing* by Joseph Calandro, Jr. offers two key lessons that are potentially extremely rewarding. One is that business leaders can find new sources of competitive advantage if they learn to think like highly successful investors. The other is that investors and analysts can gain valuable insights if they study how a company achieves the creative interaction of strategy, resource allocation, performance management, and risk management. In other words, investors should learn to think like astute business leaders. Calandro's groundbreaking book integrates these two lessons into a holistic and practical business framework, which can be used to either assess or manage a business."

　　—Robert M. Randall, editor, *Strategy & Leadership*, and
　　coauthor of *The Portable MBA in Strategy*

"This is an extremely smart book. The three chapters on M&A alone are worth the price of admission. If executives will adopt the discipline that Joseph Calandro lays out, they will avoid many, many costly mistakes."

—Paul B. Carroll, coauthor of *Billion-Dollar Lessons: What You Can Learn from the Most Inexcusable Business Failures of the Last 25 Years*

"Joseph Calandro successfully applies the modern approach to Graham and Dodd's investment valuation. The book is a 'must read' for all Graham and Dodd followers, and valuation practitioners."

—Patrick Terrion, principal, Founders Capital Management, and author of *The Company You Keep: A Commonsense Guide to Value Investing*

"A useful addition to every value investor's library."

—Bruce Greenwald, Robert Heilbrunn Professor of Finance and Asset Management, Columbia Business School

"You will enjoy learning from real world cases how to apply the investment principles of the legendary Benjamin Graham and Warren Buffett. Because of outstanding writing and some fascinating corporate and financial history, this book is an excellent way to learn how to be a successful investor."

—Dr. Thomas J. O'Brien, professor of finance, University of Connecticut, and author of *International Finance: Corporate Decisions in Global Markets*

APPLIED
VALUE
INVESTING

APPLIED VALUE INVESTING

THE PRACTICAL APPLICATIONS OF
BENJAMIN GRAHAM'S AND
WARREN BUFFETT'S
VALUATION PRINCIPLES TO
ACQUISITIONS, CATASTROPHE PRICING,
AND BUSINESS EXECUTION

JOSEPH CALANDRO, JR.

New York   Chicago   San Francisco   Lisbon   London   Madrid
Mexico City   Milan   New Delhi   San Juan   Seoul
Singapore   Sydney   Toronto

The *McGraw-Hill* Companies

4 5 6 7 8 9 0   QVS/QVS   0 1 5 4

ISBN: 978–0–07–162818–1
MHID: 0–07–162818–5

This publication is designed to provide accurate and authoritative information in regard to the subject matter covered. It is sold with the understanding that neither the author nor the publisher is engaged in rendering legal, accounting, futures/securities trading, or other professional service. If legal advice or other expert assistance is required, the services of a competent professional person should be sought.

> —*From a Declaration of Principles jointly adopted*
> *by a Committee of the American Bar*
> *Association and a Committee of Publishers*

McGraw-Hill books are available at special quantity discounts to use as premiums and sales promotions, or for use in corporate training programs. To contact a representative, please visit the Contact Us pages at www.mhprofessional.com.

This book is printed on acid-free paper.

For Terilyn,
Forever

CONTENTS

PREFACE

Investment is most intelligent when it is most businesslike.
                                        —*Benjamin Graham*[1]

Berkshire Hathaway chairman and CEO Warren Buffett described this quote as "the nine most important words ever written about investing,"[2] which is significant given his level of success as both an investor and businessman. Buffett both studied under and worked for the late Benjamin Graham, the founder of what has come to be known as *value investing*.[3] Value investing is a method of analysis that has spawned a large number of highly successful investors since it was first introduced in the 1930s. It has also been the subject of a number of popular books, including Graham's own works, such as

- The seminal *Security Analysis*, which he coauthored with David Dodd in 1934 and updated in subsequent editions, the most recent of which was published in 2008 and edited by noted value investor Seth Klarman
- The popular *Intelligent Investor*, which was first published in 1949 and also updated in subsequent editions, the most recent of which was edited in 2003 by financial author Jason Zweig

The books that followed Graham's essentially have presented different interpretations of value investing, broadly defined, and are generally introductory in nature. This book takes a different approach; rather than introducing a new variation on the value investing theme, it adopts the modern Graham and Dodd approach and applies it in a variety of unique and practical ways. Specifically, the modern Graham and Dodd approach is applied to a number of practical case-based valuations that

- Demonstrate how the Graham and Dodd approach could be used in a mergers and acquisitions (M&A) context. This could be significant, for while Graham and Dodd–based valuation has been highly influential in the investment community (traditional and alternative alike), it has thus far not had the same level of influence on the practice of corporate M&A.
- Explain how macro-related insights can be used in a Graham and Dodd context.
- Show how the basic concepts of Graham and Dodd valuation can be applied to the emerging area of catastrophe-based alternative investments.
- Incorporate the practice of valuation into an integrated business framework that can be used to either assess or manage a *franchise* (which is a firm that is operating with a sustainable competitive advantage).

In short, this book extends the modern Graham and Dodd approach in a number of ways that, it is hoped, will prove useful to current and future practitioners of the discipline. The book is structured with seven chapters and a Conclusion that summarizes an applied value investing approach and clarifies several practical aspects of it for implementation purposes.

The first chapter reviews the basic concepts of net asset valuation and earnings power valuation, the first two levels of Graham and Dodd–based valuation, and it introduces the *base-case value* profile via a case study of an actual equity investment.

The second chapter builds on the foundation of the first by applying base-case valuation to M&A by way of Edward Lampert's 2004 acquisition of Sears. This case is the first of four relatively high-profile valuation case studies, and thus it is important to note that I have no special information on any of those valuations other than what is publicly available.[4] Furthermore, the case studies are not meant to imply that either Edward Lampert or Warren Buffett approaches valuation in the manner presented here. Rather, the cases are presented to demonstrate the practical utility (and research viability) of the modern Graham and Dodd approach via actual investments made by two of the approach's most successful disciples.

In Chapter 3, the concept of a growth-based margin of safety is discussed in the context of Warren Buffett's highly successful acquisition of GEICO in 1995. While growth-based margin of safety acquisitions can be incredibly successful, as the GEICO case fairly dramatically demonstrates, the intangible nature of growth carries with it substantial risk. This risk is illustrated in Chapter 4 through another Buffett acquisition, this one being the 1998 acquisition of the General Reinsurance Corporation (Gen Re).

The fifth chapter pertains to a topic that is not frequently addressed from a Graham and Dodd perspective: macro-based analysis. Relatively few people would disagree with the statement that two of the most successful investors of the late twentieth century were Warren

Buffett and George Soros. Despite the long-term investment success that both of these men have in common, the approaches they use are vastly different: Buffett uses a bottom-up approach that is rooted in the Graham and Dodd tradition, whereas Soros uses a seemingly eclectic top-down or macro-based approach.[5] Just how different these approaches are was illustrated, for example, several years ago at an investment conference that I attended.

During a question-and-answer session at the conference, I asked a presenter about integrating macro-based analysis and value investing. He replied that it would probably be easier to unify gravity and quantum mechanics—the celebrated "theory of everything" that Albert Einstein tried to derive in the final decades of his life, and that current theoretical physicists are diligently working on—than it would be to integrate macro-based analysis and value investing. That reply was obviously said in jest, but it did highlight the fundamental differences between the two approaches. Those differences, however, need not be considered insurmountable. Furthermore, there is much that practitioners (and researchers) of each approach could learn from the other. Toward that end, Chapter 5 presents a method of analysis that can be used to assess and evaluate business cycles from a Graham and Dodd–based perspective, and applies this method to a case study of the recent "new economy" boom and bust, and its aftermath.

Chapter 6 changes gears somewhat by addressing catastrophe-based alternative investments, which are relatively new instruments that have grown in popularity in recent years. This chapter extends the basic concepts of Graham and Dodd to the field of super catastrophe valuation by way of the Pepsi Play for a Billion sweepstakes case. This case study pertains to the pricing of a super catastrophe–based, insurance policy–like alternative investment that was underwritten by a Berkshire

Hathaway subsidiary in 2003. The chapter ends with overview commentary on the somewhat related field of catastrophe bond valuation.

Chapter 7 is the capstone of the book and has its roots in the famous quote of Benjamin Graham that is found at the beginning of this Preface, namely, "Investment is most intelligent when it is most businesslike." Despite the inherent and long-standing logic of this quote, many investors currently do not think like businesspeople. Furthermore, many businesspeople do not think like investors. This divergence even applies to academia in that finance, management, and strategy professors tend to approach their subjects (and their research) very differently, often with very little overlap across disciplines.[6] Chapter 7 provides one approach for integrating these disciplines into a holistic and practical business framework that can be used to either assess or manage a franchise over time.

Finally, in the Conclusion, I highlight some of the key lessons of the book, and I also provide some practical suggestions for implementing an applied value investing approach. The Conclusion is followed by a description of additional information sources that could be referred to by those interested in exploring the Graham and Dodd approach further.

In addition to the subject matter, this book differs from many that precede it in that all of the chapters are based on material that has been published academically, specifically, in the *Journal of Alternative Investments*, *Strategy & Leadership*, the *Quarterly Journal of Austrian Economics*, the *Business Strategy Series*, and *Measuring Business Excellence*. I am grateful to the editors of each of these publications for allowing me to develop and expand the research that they published for a broader audience. That said, it is important to point out that the formal foundation of this book's chapters should not be interpreted to mean that the book is not practical. The Graham and Dodd approach to investing is inherently practical, as its track record since it was first introduced vividly illustrates.

Nevertheless, and according to Professor Bruce Greenwald, who teaches value investing at Columbia University, the Graham and Dodd approach is also a "legitimate academic discipline."[7] I, for one, agree with this statement, but I am apparently in the minority. For example, if one were to look for Graham and Dodd–based published research, one would essentially find material that empirically shows that the approach does, in fact, work, along with applied case studies published by me and my coauthors.*

Empirical studies have a place in value-based research programs, but so do formal case studies. Furthermore, using Graham and Dodd concepts in M&A, in conjunction with macro-based analysis, in super catastrophe valuation, and as part of an integrated analytical business framework appear to be viable avenues for future research and study. If this book helps to inspire such research, while at the same time assisting Graham and Dodd–based practitioners, it will have achieved its objectives.

THE EDUCATION OF A LATE-BLOOMING GRAHAM AND DODDER

I started my business career in the insurance industry while I was still in college. Several years later, in 1992, Hurricane Andrew struck

---

* Thanks to Ranga Dasari (my former student) and Scott Lane (my former professor) for collaborating with me on the GEICO valuation, and to Bob Flynn (friend and fellow traveler) for collaborating with me on the Gen Re valuation and the financial strategy paper.

southern Florida, and the devastation that this storm caused convinced me that the insurance industry would soon be undergoing substantial changes. To better understand those changes, I began a relatively intense research program on a variety of economic and financial topics. Therefore, when the first catastrophe bond issue emerged in the mid-nineties, it did not come as a surprise to me; on the contrary, I sensed that this type of vehicle would grow in popularity, so I began studying derivatives. Me being me, after a period of study, I decided to try my hand at trading, and I did very, very well at it, even though trading was not my full-time job: I did all of the analysis and tactical decision making after hours. This obviously took a substantial amount of time, but I am a natural workaholic with a very, *very* understanding spouse, so I was able to manage the work flow rather well.

After four extremely profitable years, my trading fortunes changed in 1997–1998 as a result of the "Asian contagion," which Roger Lowenstein wrote about so well in his 2001 masterpiece that was aptly titled *When Genius Failed.* While I did not blow out as a result of the contagious volatility, my portfolio did experience a substantial decline. More significantly, however, I did not understand why the decline had occurred: according to the models that I was using at the time, such a loss was just not supposed to happen (at least not in my hopefully long lifetime), and yet it did happen, and it happened to me.

After the Asian contagion, I stopped trading so that I could figure out what exactly had happened and why I had missed it so completely. At the time, the "new economy" boom was underway, and, also significantly, I did not understand why that was happening either. I knew that the economy was not new, but I did not know why so many other people thought that it was. Yes, the Internet itself was new, and yes, it had a great deal of potential (for example, were it not for the Internet, it is very doubtful that I would have ever written this book or the papers that preceded it), but the telephone had been new a hundred years before and it had not ushered in a new economy, so why would the Internet?

And then something else happened: Warren Buffett acquired the firm that I was working for at the time, Gen Re. He paid approximately $22 billion for that firm against a book value of approximately $8 billion, which was a hefty premium for the world's foremost value investor. At that time, a number of my friends asked me to explain the rationale for this acquisition to them, but I could not make sense of it either.

Three significant financial economic events had happened (the Asian contagion, the new economy boom, and Buffett's purchase of Gen Re), and I could not explain or make sense of any of them. That simply was not acceptable to me, so I decided to engage in a different kind of research program. For example:

- I bought and studied everything I could find on Benjamin Graham and value investing.
- I downloaded and studied all of Warren Buffett's shareholder letters.
- I began to study Austrian economics, which is a school of economics that is often ignored by mainstream economists. I reasoned that, as mainstream economics (and economists) are frequently wrong—many times spectacularly so—perhaps an alternative school would provide a greater level of practical insight.

In retrospect, that was an incredibly good decision. First, the inherent logic of Benjamin Graham's approach was immediately compelling to me. I also began to find linkages in Graham's writings with some of the business cycle (or boom-bust) work that Austrian economists had published. In this regard, *Security Analysis* was first published in 1934, which was after the "new era" boom of the "roaring twenties" had ended (Graham started teaching value investing at Columbia in 1928, during the new era boom). And yet, Graham's description of the new era seemed eerily similar to some of the things that I was then witnessing during the new economy of the 1990s.[8] My findings are covered in Chapter 5 of this book.

I also found Warren Buffett's shareholder letters very compelling, as so many others appropriately have. The letters are very candid documents, and they give great advice on what to do, but they do not tell you how to do it. This is consistent with the structure of many books on investing in general, meaning that they give great advice on what to do, but they really do not explain how, exactly, to do it. Therefore, to get a better understanding of the nuts and bolts of the Graham and Dodd approach, I decided to attend the executive version of the value investing course that is offered at Columbia University every year. The firm that I was working for at the time would not pay the tuition for the course, so I paid for it myself and attended the sessions on my vacation (again, I have a very understanding spouse). Fortunately, my monetary and time commitments were very much a "value investment," because from the very first session with Professor Bruce Greenwald, the Graham and Dodd approach became extremely clear to me.

I began to apply the approach immediately, and the first case I analyzed was the Gen Re acquisition. I showed the valuation that

I came up with to people who were familiar with M&A at the time, and they were extremely interested in it. Significantly, I later showed the valuation to others who were familiar with the deal, and they were also impressed with it. That valuation is the subject of Chapter 4 of this book.

I then evaluated Buffett's GEICO acquisition. A number of articles have, appropriately, been published on that acquisition, and it is also the subject of a popular University of Virginia case study. However, no one had ever evaluated GEICO from a Graham and Dodd perspective before, at least not publicly. So I did, and once again the M&A specialists that I showed it to were impressed with the result. That valuation is the subject of Chapter 3.

Around this time, I was approached to teach at the University of Connecticut. The chair of that institution's finance department at the time, Tom O'Brien, had read a number of my papers and inquired whether I would be interested in teaching. After preliminary discussions, it was agreed that I would teach two MBA courses, one of which would be on value investing. As part of the course, I wanted to bring in practicing value investors as guest speakers, and I was very fortunate to secure two of the best: Mario Gabelli, the legendary mutual fund manager, and Robert Wyckoff of Tweedy, Browne Company.

I left regular teaching after a couple of years to take a position in the consulting industry. As luck would have it, my first consulting engagement entailed a substantial valuation, which helped to make the transition to consulting rather seamless for me. Publishing papers can be an important part of a consulting career, so I started to publish the value-based research that I had produced, beginning with my valuation of the Pepsi Play for a Billion case, which you will find as part of Chapter 6. Ironically, that was a case that I had never intended to write.

I got the idea of writing an insurance-based case study while I was preparing to teach a class on insurance pricing theory, which can be a somewhat dry subject (for students and professor alike). I then recalled the insurance policy that one of Warren Buffett's insurance companies had underwritten covering baseball player Alex Rodriguez's massive salary with the Texas Rangers baseball team. I had priced that risk transfer in the past, and the price that I came up with closely tracked with the premium range that was purportedly charged. (I did this, ironically enough, on a bet.) I thought that case would be a great way to spruce up my class, but I could not find either my pricing analysis or the materials that I used to formulate it. That was odd because I normally do not misplace things like that (although I tend to misplace just about everything else). I tried to re-create my valuation, but without the source materials that I had used, I was having considerable trouble doing so. The Pepsi case just happened to be in the news at the time, so I decided to use it instead, and the rest, as they say, is history.

Fortunately, my published papers were very well received, but it did take a while for a number of them to make their way through the academic review process.* During that time, it occurred to me that some of the papers that I was publishing could form the basis for a book. Significantly, no book like it had yet been published, but if someone had published it, I would certainly have bought it. Therefore, I felt (hoped really) that demand for the book would be

---

* At times you can receive valuable input from academic reviews that does help to improve a paper. At other times, though, the process can be torturous.

reasonably good, which is a fairly good reason to pursue a book project. However, I had absolutely no idea how to go about publishing a book, so I pretty much put the project out of my mind for the time being.

Sometime later I was speaking with Robert Randall, who is the editor of the journal *Strategy & Leadership*, and who has published a number of superb books. Robert recommended that I write a book, and he explained exactly how to go about doing so. While I was intrigued by Robert's advice, I have a relatively intense work schedule, so I essentially put a book project out of my mind once again.

About a year or so later, my dad was diagnosed with a severe illness, which hit me particularly hard. A couple of weeks after the diagnosis, I sat down in my home office one Saturday morning, politely asked my wife, Terilyn, to cancel our plans for the day, and put together the proposal for this book following Robert Randall's aforementioned advice. I reasoned that if I were ever going to write a book, I very much wanted my dad to see it, so the time had come to "just do it." I sent my proposal off that Sunday evening, and, as luck would have it, my proposal arrived at McGraw-Hill just as the people there were concluding the editing of the magnificent sixth edition of Graham and Dodd's *Security Analysis* (2008). After several discussions with my outstanding editor at McGraw-Hill, Leah Spiro, I was notified that the firm was going to publish my book. I had two relatively simultaneous reactions to this:

- First, I was extremely happy that my proposal had been found acceptable by the same firm that published Graham and Dodd's seminal work and all of its updates.

● Second, I felt considerable anxiety because I was literally following in Graham and Dodd's footsteps in the publication process.
Needless to say, I very much hope that this book does justice to
the tradition those two giants founded.

In closing this Preface, I hope that you enjoy reading this book as
much as I have enjoyed writing it, and that *Applied Value Investing*
helps you to generate substantial returns at reasonable levels of risk
over time.[9]

ACKNOWLEDGMENTS

The act of writing a book is a solitary exercise, but the process of writing is anything but solitary. I have been helped along the way by many people, the most significant of which is my wife, Terilyn. Without the love, support, and encouragement of this remarkable woman, neither this book nor any of the papers that preceded it would have been possible. Next to Terilyn, no one has encouraged, supported, and motivated me more than our daughter, Alyse, who has shown more grace and courage in her young life than many people demonstrate over an entire lifetime.

My parents, Joseph Sr. and Sharon Calandro; my in-laws, Lawrence and Dolores Vecchione; my grandparents, John Sr. and Theresa Corsano; and my favorite aunt, Janet Maloney, provided continuous encouragement and support, even when I opted to work through family dinners, functions, and holidays. This is both significant and incredibly remarkable, as anyone who understands the dynamics of modern Italian American family life will surely attest to.

A special word of thanks to Dan and Ellen DeMagistris, Mark Gardner, Esq., Bill McDonough, and Sgt. Major Joseph A. Porto, Jr. (USAR, Ret.): I would not be where I am today without the help of each of these people, and thus I will never be able to adequately thank them.

Thanks also to Scott Lane of Quinnipiac University, who very patiently taught me the academic publishing process.

Robert Randall, the editor of *Strategy & Leadership*, and Raj Gupta, the associate editor of the *Journal of Alternative Investments*, both supported and published my work, some of which is contained in the pages you are about to read. Their input and advice—most especially Mr. Randall's—was extremely valuable, and I am very thankful for it.

Special thanks to my editor at McGraw-Hill, Leah Spiro. As noted in the Preface, I could not have hoped for a better editor and sponsor for this book. Thanks also to my fabulous editing manager at McGraw-Hill, Jane Palmieri.

I would also like to thank Sheree Bykofsky (my agent) for her insight, counsel, and guidance throughout the publication process.

Paul B. Carroll, Mario J. Gabelli, Dr. Bruce Greenwald, Mitchell R. Julis, Seth A. Klarman, Dr. Thomas J. O'Brien, Robert M. Randall, Dr. John J. Sviokla, and Patrick Terrion reviewed my manuscript prior to its publication. To say that I am honored to have endorsements from each of these men would be a gross understatement.

In consulting, I had the pleasure of working with and for some truly exceptional people, such as Ian Brodie and Rosemarie Sansone, both of whom supported and encouraged both me and my work.

I must also extend thanks to John and Linda Batten, Saul Berman, Paul Blasé, Robert Blumen, Dr. Mike Bourne of Cranfield University, Mark Brockmeier, Mike Buckmire, David E. Burs, Ron Carr, Dr. Vincent Carrafiello of the University of Connecticut, Peter D. Clark, Esq., Peter Corbett, Michael Corsano, John Corsano, Jr., Ranga Dasari, Greg Derderian, Armel Desir, Jeff Donaldson,

Hal Eskenazi, Michael Farrell, Jr., Bob Flynn, Dr. William Freed, Dr. Richard Freedman ("the Warren Buffett of pediatrics"), Bill Fuessler, Jo Ann Griggs, Yousef Hashimi, Dr. Jeffrey Herbener of Grove City College, Lew and Jill Hutchinson, Cpt. Lynn Kerwin (BPD), Silvia Jelenz-King, Paul King, Barry Knott, Esq., Dave Landry, Rob Lingle, Heidi Mack, Cyd Malone, Christopher J. Maloney, the Mayhew family (Jim, Carol, Reed, and Ben), Jack Mossa (of Giovanni's Deli in Stamford, Connecticut), Brian Neligan, David Notestein, Don Opatrny, Al Paulin, Andrew Peel, Peter Pescatore, Carl Pratt, Mark Purowitz, Claudio Ronzitti, Jr., Esq., Laura Russo, Jeff Scott, Sandeep Samal, Geri Saracino, Tony Scafidi, Dan Severn, Rob Shah, Kit Smith of the University of Connecticut, Bob and Trish Thompson, the late Michael Vecchione (my uncle), Jason Ward, Ken Wessels, Clay and Kathy Yeager, and Jamie Yoder for encouragement, friendship, or support along the way.

The material presented in this book was inspired, first and foremost, by the seminal writings of the late, great Benjamin Graham. It was also inspired by the more current writings and teachings of Bruce Greenwald of Columbia University and Robert S. Kaplan (cofounder of activity-based costing and the Balanced Scorecard) of Harvard Business School. Needless to say, any shortcomings in this book are not in any way attributable to the work of either of these superb scholars.

It is important to note that if any error or omission is found in this book, the responsibility for it is mine. Similarly, the opinions expressed in this book are mine and mine alone, and are not to be attributed to any organization that I am, or have been, affiliated with. Disclaimers now out of the way, it is important to note that I have taken extreme care in writing this book, as I am following in a truly great tradition.

Finally, and to be fair, I must also thank all of the value destroyers and naysayers whom I have encountered along the way, none of whom I will identify for obvious reasons: you have taught me more than you will ever know.

Chapter | 1

THE BASICS AND BASE-CASE VALUE

Every corporate security may best be viewed, in the first instance, as an ownership interest in, or a claim against, a specific business enterprise.

—Benjamin Graham[1]

There should be some advantage to the valuation process in cases where asset values coincide with and reinforce the earnings power value. We may then be able to return to the older, private business approach and to say that in the case of Company X the fair value of the shares is the same as its book value because the earnings, dividends, and prospects support the book value.

—Benjamin Graham and David Dodd[2]

INTRODUCTION

At its core, the Graham and Dodd approach to valuation and investment is a method for identifying and profiting from significant price-to-value gaps. While all long-side investors intend to "buy low

This chapter contains material from the *Journal of Alternative Investments*, © 2005 by Institutional Investor, which is reprinted with permission.

and sell high," Graham and Dodd–based practitioners (who are popularly referred to as "value investors") seek to buy at a level that is appreciably less than an investment's *intrinsic value*, or its inherent worth.[3] The result is a *margin of safety* that "is available for absorbing the effect of miscalculations or worse than average luck."[4] In other words, by investing in "businesses with satisfactory underlying economics at a fraction of the per-share value,"[5] Graham and Dodd practitioners significantly increase the probability that their investments will be successful, or at least not ruinous. The uniqueness of this approach is perhaps best illustrated in a diagram, such as the one presented in Figure 1-1.

The diagram plots price on the *x* axis and value on the *y* axis, inasmuch as value is a function of price,[6] and highlights the difference between a Graham and Dodd–based opportunity and risk. An investment is an *opportunity* if it is offered for less than its intrinsic

Figure 1-1

The Price-Value Paradox

value, and an investment is a *risk* if it is offered at or above its intrinsic value. Risk in this context means that there is no financial buffer, or margin of safety, between the value of an investment and the price at which it is offered. Such an investment is risky because the only way to profit from it is through growth, which is extremely intangible and is influenced by a variety of internal and external factors.

Note that both General Electric (GE) in 1939 and Microsoft are listed as risks in the diagram. Graham and Dodd themselves commented on GE in the second edition of their seminal work *Security Analysis*, which was published in the year 1940:

> We have intentionally, and at the risk of future regret, used an example here of a highly controversial character. Nearly everyone on Wall Street would regard General Electric stock as an "investment issue" irrespective of its market price and, more specifically, would consider the average price [in 1939] of $38 as amply justified from the investment standpoint. But we are convinced that to regard investment quality as something independent of price is a fundamental and dangerous error.[7]

I will have more to say about GE in the coming pages, but comments similar to these could be made about Microsoft today. For example, according to Columbia University Professor Bruce Greenwald and his coauthors, "The ability of even the best analysts in the year 2000 to forecast accurately Microsoft's earnings at 10 years in the future is likely to be limited. Under these circumstances, it is impossible to justify Microsoft as a value investment."[8]

Benjamin Graham originally found investment opportunities in *net-net stocks*, or stocks that were selling for less than their *net-net value*, which is calculated as current assets less total liabilities. Graham referred to this approach as *cigar butt–style* investing because it involved buying troubled companies for what amounted to appreciably less than their liquidation value, which was analogous to picking up spent cigar butts that have a couple of puffs left in them. Cigar butt–style investing has, for the most part, been arbitraged away; for example, the late 1970s was probably the last time it could have been used on any scale in the capital markets of the United States.[9]

To put this into perspective, consider a 1979 article published by *Forbes* magazine titled, "The Return of Benjamin Graham: Think of a Time When Stocks of 191 Important American Corporations Are Selling for Less than Net Working Capital per Share. Are We Talking about 1932? No, 1979" (October 15, 1979, pp. 158–161). Table 1-1 is an excerpt from that article, and it illustrates market conditions that represent near nirvana for traditional Graham and Dodd–based investors.[10]

Capital markets have become substantially more efficient (or, more accurately, proficient) since 1979, and therefore Professor Greenwald and his coauthors updated the traditional or cigar butt style of Graham and Dodd valuation and investment to better reflect the dynamics of modern financial markets. Value is now discerned, and investment opportunities assessed, along a unique continuum such as the one shown in Figure 1-2.

As can be seen from Figure 1-2, the value continuum begins with net asset value, the most tangible level of value, then proceeds to earnings power value and franchise value (or the value of a sustainable competitive advantage) before ending with growth value, the last and least tangible level of value. Not all investments require the utilization

Table 1-1

1979 Net-Net Investment Opportunities

Company	Exchange	Discount from Net Working Capital	Net Working Capital per Share*	Discount from Book Value	Book Value per Share†	Cash per Share	Recent Price	Five-Year Price Range	Latest 12-Month Earnings per Share	P/E Ratio
Cooper Tire & Rubber	NYSE	19%	$15.86	51%	$26.44	$3.66	$12.88	$18.38–$5.25	$3.34	4
Cunningham Drug Stores	NYSE	19%	$14.13	50%	$23.17	$2.40	$11.50	$13.00–$3.63	$1.61	7
Randycrafts	NYSE	19%	$7.08	36%	$8.93	$0.45	$5.75	$6.88–$3.63	$1.66	3
Phillips-Van Heusen	NYSE	17%	$15.70	51%	$26.40	$1.77	$13.00	$18.00–$3.88	$2.35	6
Munsingwear	NYSE	17%	$17.72	50%	$29.54	$0.81	$14.25	$20.98–$11.00	$1.21	12
Fabri-Centers of America	NYSE	17%	$6.15	51%	$10.46	$0.53	$5.13	$12.75–$2.88	$1.13	5
Cannon Mills	NYSE	16%	$23.77	40%	$33.56	$7.09	$20.00	$24.75–$10.25	$3.25	6
Bayuk Cigars	NYSE	15%	$13.58	25%	$15.29	$0.35	$11.50	$12.50–$3.75	$1.83	6
Cluett Peabody	NYSE	14%	$11.62	48%	$19.12	$2.13	$10.00	$14.88–$3.25	$1.68	6
Leslie Fay	NYSE	13%	$8.36	38%	$11.64	$0.59	$7.25	$10.25–$3.00	$1.60	5
Adams Drug	NYSE	11%	$4.75	34%	$6.48	$0.91	$4.50	$6.25–$1.75	$0.69	6
Zale Corp.	NYSE	9%	$24.21	18%	$26.95	$2.77	$22.13	$25.13–$9.75	$3.27	7
Fabergé	NYSE	8%	$10.74	46%	$18.29	$1.08	$9.88	$12.88–$4.50	$1.09	9
Gateway Industries	NYSE	1%	$9.13	33%	$13.37	$6.33	$9.00	$11.38–$1.25	$2.02	4
Springs Mills	NYSE	1%	$18.26	50%	$35.75	$2.42	$18.00	$20.88–$8.63	$3.66	5
Jonathan Logan	NYSE	1%	$13.43	60%	$33.68	$4.27	$13.38	$18.75–$4.25	$1.23	11
General Medical	NYSE	1%	$13.04	25%	$17.40	$0.20	$13.00	$21.50–$6.88	$1.38	9
UDS	ASX	59%	$4.85	62%	$5.28	$0.30	$2.00	$3.75–$0.38	$0.19	11
Damon Creations	ASX	56%	$6.80	69%	$9.61	$0.43	$3.00	$6.00–$1.88	$0.60	5
Splentex	ASX	55%	$11.22	58%	$12.02	$0.17	$5.00	$7.25–$3.63	$0.62	8
Ronco Teleproducts	ASX	55%	$6.08	49%	$5.39	$2.86	$2.75	$5.00–$0.50	$0.81	3
Greenman Brothers	ASX	52%	$5.97	71%	$9.96	$1.34	$2.88	$6.38–$0.63	$0.16	18

* Defined here as current assets minus *total* liabilities.
† Excludes intangibles as of the latest fiscal year-end.
My copy of this article is worn and smudged; therefore, some of these numbers may contain slight errors.

of all four levels along the continuum, however. In fact, the valuation of most firms will probably not proceed to the third level, franchise value, because most firms do not operate with a sustainable competitive advantage. In these valuations, earnings power value will not exceed net asset value, as it does in Figure 1-2, but instead will relatively reconcile to it, as illustrated in Figure 1-3.

I refer to the value profile shown in Figure 1-3 as *base-case value* because the firms that reflect it are for the most part simply fulfilling their fiduciary (or base-case) duty; in other words, the firms are

Figure 1-2

The Modern Graham and Dodd Value Continuum

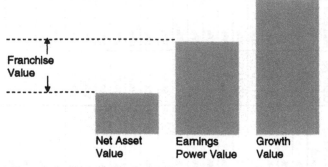

Adapted from Bruce Greenwald, Judd Kahn, Paul Sonkin, and Michael van Biema, *Value Investing: From Graham to Buffett and Beyond* (New York: Wiley, 2001), p. 44.

Figure 1-3

The Value Profile of a Firm That Is Not a Franchise

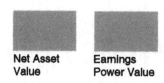

generating profit consistent with the cost of their capital and the reproduction value of the assets under their control—no more, no less. Despite the relatively common occurrence of the base-case value profile, it can present a lucrative investment opportunity if it is offered at a reasonable margin of safety (or discount from estimated value). This is illustrated in the introductory valuation of Delta Apparel, Inc.

BASE-CASE VALUATION

In October of 2002, the equity of Delta Apparel, Inc. (stock symbol DLA), hit one of my screens as a possible investment opportunity. At the time, DLA stock was selling at $14.00 per share, and thus the valuation objective was to determine if that price qualified as a Graham and Dodd–based investment (in other words, to determine if the stock fell within the upper left quadrant of Figure 1-1). To make this determination, I will follow the value continuum shown in Figure 1-2 level by level, beginning with net asset value (NAV).

NAV involves transforming a firm's balance sheet from historical cost to a reproduction-based value so that it more accurately represents economic value. To me, balance sheet analysis sets the tone for every valuation; however, I realize that it is not very popular outside of the value investing community. It is difficult to understand the reasons why this is the case, especially when one considers how successful value investors have been at exploiting balance sheet–driven insights. Indeed, it has been argued that, "The special importance that Graham and Dodd placed on balance sheet valuations remains one of their most important contributions to the idea of what constitutes a 'thorough' analysis of intrinsic value."[11]

Net asset valuation is very much dependent on one's *circle of competence*, as investors must know which balance sheet adjustments they are able to make themselves and which require the services of professional appraisers or independent experts. The efficient and effective use of one's circle of competence (or knowledge base) is critically important in all forms of valuation,[12] but it is absolutely fundamental to the Graham and Dodd approach. Consider Warren Buffett's remarks on the subject:

> Intelligent investing is not complex, though that is far from saying that it is easy. What an investor needs is the ability to correctly evaluate selected businesses. Note that word "selected": You don't have to be an expert on every company, or even many. You only have to be able to evaluate companies within your circle of competence. The size of that circle is not very important; knowing its boundaries, however, is vital.[13]

As noted earlier, one of my investment screens "selected" DLA as a possible investment opportunity, and thus my evaluation of that opportunity began with NAV, as illustrated in Table 1-2.

The exhibit is based on financial data contained within DLA's 2002 Form 10-K (fiscal year ending June 29, 2002). Parenthetical notes in the final column of the exhibit reflect valuation adjustments of mine that are explained in the following narrative. For example, the first asset in Table 1-2 is cash. The 100% reflected in the "Adjustment" column reflects the fact that no adjustment was made to this asset, and therefore the reproduction value of $4,102 equals the 2002 accounting (or book) value of $4,102. Note that all dollar figures are in thousands unless otherwise specified.

Table 1-2

DLA's Net Asset Value

	$000s			
	2002	**Adjustment**	**Value**	**Notes**
Assets				
Cash	$4,102.0	100%	$4,102.0	
Accounts receivable	$22,259.0	$1,512.0	$23,771.0	(1A)
Other receivables	$553.0	100%	$553.0	
Inventories	$35,483.0	100%	$35,483.0	
Prepaid expenses and other current assets	$1,835.0	100%	$1,835.0	
Deferred tax	$1,119.0	89%	$1,001.2	(2A)
Total current assets	*$65,351.0*		*$66,745.2*	
Property, plant, and equipment	$22,992.0		$37,429.5	(3A)
Land, building, and construction	$11,174.0	125%	$13,967.5	(3A-a)
Machinery & equipment	$41,650.0	50%	$20,825.0	(3A-b)
Furniture, fixtures, & IT	$4,283.0	50%	$2,141.5	(3A-c)
Autos	$185.0	50%	$92.5	(3A-d)
Lease Improvements	$806.0	50%	$403.0	(3A-e)
Goodwill/other	$3.0	$11,468.0	$11,471.0	(4A)
Total assets	**$88,346.0**		**$115,645.7**	
Liabilities and equity				
Total current liabilities	*$21,578.0*	100%	*$21,578.0*	
Long-term debt	$3,667.0	100%	$3,667.0	
Deferred tax	$700.0	89%	$626.3	(2A)
Other long-term liabilities	$1,123.0	$10,646.7	$11,769.7	(5A)
Leases		$6,867.0		(5A-a)
Options		$3,779.7		(5A-b)
Total liabilities	**$27,068.0**		**$37,641.0**	
Net Asset Value (NAV)	**$61,278.0**		**$78,004.6**	

All adjustments have been rounded and are the author's.
Data source: DLA Form 10-K, 2002.

The first adjustment, denoted (1A) in Table 1-2, adds the bad debt allowance back to accounts receivable to arrive at an estimate of this line item's economic value. It is necessary to add this allowance back onto the balance sheet in order to reproduce this particular asset adequately. Professor Greenwald and his coauthors explain the reason for this as follows:

> A firm's accounts receivable, as reported in the financial statement, probably contains some allowance built in for bills that will never be collected. A new firm starting out is even more likely to get stuck by customers who for some reason or another do not pay their bills, so the cost of reproducing an existing firm's accounts receivables is probably more than the book amount. Many financial statements will specify how much has been deducted to arrive at this net figure. That amount should be added back.[14]

The second adjustment, (2A), is simply the present value of the deferred tax asset and the deferred tax liability. The adjustment calculations are based on a simple discount factor, which is calculated as follows: $1/(1 + 0.1177)^1 = 89\%$, where 0.1177 is the estimated discount rate for DLA that was used.*

The third adjustment, (3A), pertains to property, plant, and equipment (PPE) and involves analyzing the historical cost of the five given categories of PPE items, gross of depreciation, and then applying adjustment factors to each category to approximate the reproduction value of each item.[15] For example, the historical cost of items (3A-b) to (3A-e) was reduced by 50%, which is a rule-of-thumb-based adjustment, while the category of land, buildings, and construction (3A-a) was increased by 125%, given the generally increasing nature of real

---

* I discuss discount rate estimation in the appendix to Chapter 3.

estate values at the time. Note that these adjustments are rough but informed approximations; according to Graham and Dodd:

> Security analysis does not seek to determine exactly what is the intrinsic value of a given security. It needs only to establish either that the value is *adequate*—e.g., to protect a bond or to justify a stock purchase—or else that the value is considerably higher or considerably lower than the market price. For such purposes an indefinite and approximate measure of the intrinsic value may be sufficient.[16]

In short, the objective of Graham and Dodd–based valuation is not to come up with an exact valuation number; rather, the objective is to be "approximately right rather than precisely wrong" with respect to a valuation.[17] Put another way, it may not be possible to value an asset with 100% accuracy, but it is possible to value it within an acceptable margin of safety.* Doing so is inherently dependent upon one's circle of competence, the importance of which was commented on earlier.

The fourth adjustment [denoted (4A)] pertains to *goodwill.* Goodwill in this context does not refer to the excess paid for an asset over its book value; rather, it refers to the intangible assets that a firm uses to create value, such as its product portfolio, customer relationships, organizational structure, competitive advantage, licenses, and so on. When estimating the value of intangible assets such as these, the modern Graham and Dodd approach "add[s] some multiple of the selling, general, and administrative line, in most cases between one

---

* The Conclusion addresses this in some detail.

and three years' worth, to the reproduction cost of the assets."[18] Therefore, multiplying DLA's 2002 selling, general, and administrative expense of $11,468 by 1, or the low end of the range just described, derived the goodwill adjustment used in my valuation. This is an intentionally conservative estimate, which is a key facet of the Graham and Dodd approach.[19]

Proceeding to the two liability adjustments:

- Note (5A-a) reflects a liability for future lease payments of $6,867, the source of which was Note 8 of DLA's 2002 Form 10-K.
- The Form 10-K was also the source for the option adjustment, note (5A-b), which was found in Note 10 and derived by multiplying the total shares available for future option grants of 959.2 by the weighted-average exercise price of $3.94 (or the simple average of $3.880 and $4.001), which equals an estimated option liability of $3,779.7. Regarding option valuation, there are more mathematically intensive ways to calculate this kind of adjustment, but for practical purposes, the method used here provides a reasonable approximation of the value of DLA's outstanding option liability.[20]

Adding these two adjustments gives the total $10,646.7 adjustment reflected in note (5A).

Processing these adjustments produces an estimated reproduction value–based NAV of $78,004.6, which when divided by the number of shares of DLA's stock that are outstanding gives a per share value of $19.4, which is 27.3% greater than the book value of $61,278 that is listed on the balance sheet. To validate this spread over DLA's book value, I will proceed along the modern Graham and Dodd value continuum to the next level of value, earnings power value (EPV).

EPV adjusts income that a firm has already earned to arrive at an estimate of income that is sustainable in perpetuity. Significantly, it is *not* an objective of earnings power valuation to forecast future earnings and then discount those earnings back to a present value. To illustrate the mechanics of EPV, consider my calculations for DLA, which are presented in Table 1-3.

As with my NAV valuation, a parenthetical note in the table designates an adjustment that is discussed in the following narrative.

The first note, (1E), pertains to DLA's 2002 operating income or earnings before interest and taxes (EBIT). Based on analysis that I conducted at the time, I concluded that this level of operating earnings was, on average, sustainable, and therefore I used it as the foundation for my EPV estimate.

Table 1-3

DLA's Earnings Power Value

	$000s			
	2002	Adjustment	Value	Notes
EBIT	$10,337.0	100%	$10,337.0	(1E)
Option expense		$282.1	$282.1	(2E)
Depreciation adjustment		$3,092.9	$3,092.9	(3E)
Depreciation		$6,390.0		(3E-a)
CAPEX		$5,254.0		(3E-b)
Growth CAPEX		$1,957.0		(3E-c)
Interest earned on cash		$143.6	$143.6	(4E)
Pretax earnings			$13,004.3	(5E)
Tax			$4,291.7	(6E)
Earnings			$8,712.6	(7E)
Earnings Power Value (EPV)			$78,125.9	(8E)

All adjustments have been rounded and are the author's. CAPEX equals capital expenditures.
Data source: DLA Form 10-K, 2002.

The second note, (2E), pertains to the option expense of $282.1, which was derived by multiplying the estimated $0.07 option dilution per share by the number of shares outstanding.[21]

The third note, (3E), involves depreciation, which can be a somewhat challenging adjustment for someone viewing the calculations for the first time. Before I explain the mechanics of this particular adjustment, please review my calculations for it, which are presented in Table 1-4.

In discounted cash flow (DCF) valuation, the noncash adjustment of depreciation is added back dollar for dollar (but netted out by subtracting capital expenditures and changes in net working capital). However, in Graham and Dodd–based valuation, EPV does not encompass growth; therefore, only that portion of depreciation that is needed to "restore a firm's assets at the end of the year to their level at the start of the year" is added back for valuation purposes.[22] This adjustment is consistent with the reproduction-based approach used to derive NAV and can be considered an earnings-based complement to it.

Table 1-4

Depreciation Adjustment Calculations for DLA

Calculation		$000s
(a)	Property, plant, & equipment =	$22,992
(b)	Sales in 2001 ≈	$120,400
(c)	Sales in 2002 =	$131,601
(d) = (c) − (b)	Change in sales =	$11,201
(e)	CAPEX =	$5,254
(f)	Depreciation ≈	$6,390
(g) = (a)/(c) × (d)	Growth CAPEX =	$1,957
(h) = (e) − (g)	Zero-growth CAPEX =	$3,297
(i) = (f) − (h)	**Depreciation adjustment =**	$3,093

All adjustments have been rounded and are the author's.
Data source: DLA Form 10-K, 2002.

Following this introduction, EPV depreciation adjustments become a simple matter of following the calculations. Consider the calculations for DLA in 2002 that are summarized here:

- The $1,957 growth CAPEX = (PPE of $22,992/2002 sales of $131,601) × the $11,201 change in sales.
- The $3,297 zero-growth CAPEX = CAPEX of $5,254 – growth CAPEX of $1,957 (see the previous bullet point).
- The $3,093 depreciation adjustment = depreciation of $6,390 – zero-growth CAPEX of $3,297 (see the previous bullet point).

The fourth note, (4E), pertains to the interest earned on the cash that is reflected on the balance sheet, which I estimated at 3.5% or $143.6.[23]

The fifth note, (5E), is pretax earnings, which equals EBIT minus the options expense plus the depreciation adjustment (see Table 1-4 for details) minus the interest earned on cash, for a total of $13,004.3.

The sixth note, (6E), refers to the tax adjustment, which was derived by multiplying the ratio of the income tax expense to earnings before taxes (EBT) by pretax earnings of $13,004.3, which produces a tax expense of $4,291.7.

Earnings, note (7E), is simply the difference of the tax expense and pretax earnings, which amounts to $8,712.6.

Earnings power value (EPV) is the sum of the cash on the balance sheet ($4,102) plus the capitalized value of earnings, which is calculated as a simple perpetuity: $8,712.6 × (1/discount rate of 11.77%). DLA's estimated EPV is $78,125.9 [note (8E)], which on a per share basis equals $19.4, which is the exact same value as the NAV that was discussed previously.

The relationship of DLA's 2002 NAV, EPV, and price per share (PPS) of $14.0 is presented in Figure 1-4; note the similarity with Figure 1-3 and the margin of safety reflected by the PPS.

Based on this valuation, I purchased DLA stock in October of 2002 for $14.0 per share, and once my order was filled, I put in an order to sell the stock as soon as it hit $19.0 per share. The $5.0 per share spread between the two prices served as the investment's margin of safety.

The margin of safety is, along with the circle of competence that was discussed earlier, absolutely central to Graham and Dodd–based valuation. For example, Warren Buffett stated in the 2002 Berkshire Hathaway Annual Report, "We insist on a margin of safety in our

Figure 1.4

DLA's Base-Case Value Profile

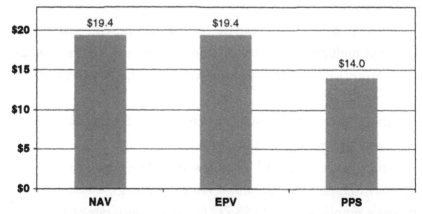

NAV equals net asset value, EPV equals earnings power value, and PPS equals the price per share. All values except PPS are based on the author's calculations.

purchase price. If we calculate the value of a common stock to be only slightly higher than its price, we're not interested in buying. We believe this margin of safety principle, so strongly emphasized by Ben Graham, to be the cornerstone of investment success."[24] I believe the margin of safety is the cornerstone to investment success too, and therefore I cannot overemphasize its importance.

After my sell order was placed, on a "good till canceled" basis, I simply waited for the $5.0 value gap to close over time. Significantly, I was being paid a 1.4% annual dividend yield (= $0.2 dividend per share/$14.0 stock price per share) while I waited for the value gap to close. Frankly, I like being paid while waiting for value gaps to close, and I strongly recommend the practice whenever it is possible.

Dividends have a strong, if somewhat unglorified, place in the history of Graham and Dodd–based investing. For example, noted value investor John Neff, the former manager of the highly successful Windsor Fund, noted in his autobiography that dividends were a powerful contributor to his fund's exceptional total return over time.[25]

A second example is more current: in 2008, Warren Buffett made substantial, distressed-based investments in Goldman Sachs and GE, both of which included 10% dividend yields. For comparison purposes, the 10-year Treasury note was yielding around 4% at the time.[26]

The GE investment, in particular, seems to be a classic Graham and Dodd–based investment. To explain, GE's weakness seemed to be generated from its GE Capital subsidiary.[27] If that proves to be the case, then once this weakness is addressed, GE's stock should be well positioned to rise. If that occurs, and the odds of its occurring seem relatively good given GE's track record of management expertise, then this investment will be another successful one for Buffett.

More importantly, however, it illustrates a central tenet of the Graham and Dodd approach, namely, that the margin of safety is price dependent.[28] In other words, at higher price levels, GE could not be considered a value-based investment, consistent with Figure 1-1 that was presented earlier, but at lower price levels, it could be considered one, as Buffett demonstrated in 2008 with his investment.

CONCLUSION

In January of 2004, my sell order was filled upon closure of the value gap when DLA's stock hit my $19 sell order. In total, this investment realized a gain of $5.25 per share, the extra $0.25 being dividends, for a gain of 37.5% (30% annualized), which represents a fairly typical, successful modern Graham and Dodd–based investment.

The DLA valuation presented in this chapter seemed to be an ideal example with which to introduce the base-case valuation profile because its NAV and EPV came to the exact same amount. Such a "clean" result does not occur often, but it does not have to. The two values (meaning NAV and EPV) will relatively reconcile for any firm that does not operate with a sustainable competitive advantage or is in distress (financial, operational, or strategic), absent valuation errors. The likelihood of such errors declines significantly for valuations that occur within one's circle of competence; however, the likelihood can never be reduced to zero, which is why the margin of safety is so important.

The future is inherently uncertain, so, to quote the noted economist Thomas Sowell, "We never really *know* and the very fact that there are such words in the language as disappointment, regret, etc., is testimony to the pervasiveness and persistence of this feature of the human condition."[29] This is not meant to dissuade investment activities; rather, it is intended to underscore the importance of developing a circle of competence. Doing so will allow you to leverage your specific knowledge base, thereby increasing the likelihood of investment success over time, especially when investments are made at reasonable margins of safety.

The circle of competence and the margin of safety are also important with respect to merger and acquisition (M&A) valuation, as we will see in the next chapter.

Chapter | 2

BASE-CASE VALUE AND THE SEARS ACQUISITION

The purchase of a bargain issue presupposes that the market's current appraisal is wrong, or at least that the buyer's idea of value is more likely to be right than the market's. In this process the investor sets his judgment against that of the market.

—Benjamin Graham[1]

*An investment operation is one that can be justified on **both** qualitative and quantitative grounds.*

—Benjamin Graham and David Dodd[2]

INTRODUCTION

In Chapter 1, I discussed the first two levels of value along the modern Graham and Dodd value continuum, and I introduced the valuation profile that I refer to as *base-case value*. The usefulness of that profile was demonstrated in a case study of an actual stock investment.

This chapter contains material from *Strategy & Leadership*, © 2007 by Emerald Publishing, which is reprinted with permission.

I structured Chapter 1 that way because a large number of Graham and Dodd–based practitioners are stock market investors. The reason for this is fairly obvious: the Graham and Dodd approach works. Less obvious is the reason why, despite the approach's track record, the Graham and Dodd approach has not achieved the same level of acceptance in the practice of corporate mergers and acquisitions (M&A).

It is well known that many corporate M&A deals fail to deliver the value that was expected at the time that the deals were announced. One well-known cause of M&A failure is overpayment.[3] A margin of safety–oriented acquisition strategy controls for overpayment risk, and therefore an argument could be made that the disciplined use of such an approach could lead to greater overall levels of corporate M&A success. This is not merely an opinion of mine; a number of alternative investment firms, such as hedge funds, that use a Graham and Dodd–based approach have been remarkably successful in the field of M&A. Consider, for example, Edward Lampert of ESL Investments.

Lampert acquired both Kmart and Sears, and by so doing became a force in the field of retail sales. In fact, he has been so successful that, according to shareholder value expert Alfred Rappaport, "Former shareholders of Kmart are justifiably asking why the previous management was unable to similarly reinvigorate the company and why they had to liquidate their shares at distressed prices."[4] Rappaport's comment, and others like it, seems to suggest that suboptimal valuation was a factor behind the retrospectively identified "distressed price" sale of Kmart, and possibly Sears. Whatever the factors actually were, it is clear that the former shareholders and management of Kmart did not appreciate the investment opportunity that Lambert identified in the firm.[5]

In this chapter, I will apply the base-case value profile to Lampert's acquisition of Sears and show how it supports his acquisition price of $10.9 billion. More importantly, though, this chapter demonstrates how the modern Graham and Dodd approach can be successfully applied to the field of M&A. In this regard, corporate M&A specialists have access to considerable knowledge-based resources that could be leveraged during both the valuation and the due diligence phases of M&A within the context of the modern Graham and Dodd framework.

Before proceeding with the valuation we will first review the celebrated history of Sears & Roebuck, Inc.

THE RISE AND FALL OF SEARS[6]

An overview history of Sears can essentially be broken down into three stages: birth, growth, and decline. The birth of Sears occurred in 1886 when Richard Sears identified an entrepreneurial opportunity in selling pocket watches to customers that he referred to as "plain folks." Sears' initial operation was an immediate success, and in an effort to grow the business, he moved to Chicago, where he teamed up with watchmaker Alvah Roebuck. Two years later, Sears and Roebuck began to issue the now famous Sears catalog. The strategy behind the Sears and Roebuck catalog was twofold:

- First, offer goods for sale that were not readily available to many of their targeted customers.
- Second, market those goods with a certain degree of showmanship.

Sears and Roebuck's customers responded to their catalog strategy so favorably that in less than 10 years the firm had grown to such an extent that Richard Sears was no longer able to run it by himself (Alvah Roebuck had sold his shares in the firm in the year 1895). He subsequently hired Julius Rosenwald to manage Sears, and Rosenwald managed the firm so well that Sears soon grew into "a catalog empire."

Sears remained a *franchise*, or a firm operating with a sustainable competitive advantage, for many years. However, over time, the retail-customer landscape started to change; in other words, Sears' customer base began migrating away from traditional rural (or, in Sears' vernacular, "plain folk") areas to more urban ones in search of economic opportunities. During this period of time, Rosenwald transferred control of Sears to Robert Wood,[7] who modified the firm's strategy by converting its mail-order plants into retail stores while maintaining the ever-popular catalog. Following this organizational realignment, Sears was able to grow its franchise successfully for decades more.

A key reason for Sears' long-term success up to this point in time was that Richard Sears, Julius Rosenwald, and Robert Wood had all accurately identified and assessed the preferences of their customers, and aligned the resources under their control to satisfy those preferences efficiently over time. However, after Wood retired, the direction of the firm started to change.

For example, despite Sears' long-standing expertise in retail sales, its executives diversified the firm into financial services by expanding the insurance operation (Allstate) it had founded back in 1931, and by acquiring broker Dean Witter, credit card provider Discover, and real estate broker Coldwell Banker. One rationalization for Sears' diversification was that, given its retail-based core competency, it was well positioned to create value by offering financial services to its loyal customer base. At that time, Sears' slogan was "Where America shops for value," in effect placing no limit (theoretically) on the kinds of things that Sears might offer its customers.

However, in expanding its business portfolio, Sears diverted managerial attention away from retail—its core competency—and toward financial services.[8] This diversion created an opportunity for a more focused and disciplined retailer with a similar value proposition (in other words, selling to "plain folks" with a certain degree of showmanship) that would eventually overtake Sears. That retailer was, of course, Wal-Mart.

To compound Sears' competitive woes, other focused and disciplined retailers, such as Target, engaged it in competition that further eroded its franchise over time. The result of this was that by the year 2004, Sears was no longer a franchise, even though it had long before divested its financial services businesses to refocus its attention on the retail business. This does not mean that Sears was without value; it still had considerable resources under its control that made it a potent competitor. For example, in 2004 Sears began to make the transition away from its traditional shopping-mall store locations to "off mall" or "big box" locations such as those used so successfully by Wal-Mart and Target.[9] While this strategic move was arguably late—by that time, Wal-Mart and other retail competitors had employed the big box model for many years—if Sears had been able to implement it well, it could have led to greater levels of profitability, and hence value creation over time.

VALUING SEARS

Before I present my valuation of Sears, it is important to highlight a point that I raised in the introduction—namely, that this valuation is my work product alone. I do not know Edward Lampert, and I do not know how he values investments. Similarly, I do not know Warren Buffett, and I do not know how he values investments either. In this chapter and the two chapters that follow it, I evaluate the acquisitions of successful Graham and Dodd–based practitioners through the lens of the modern Graham and Dodd framework in an effort to determine if that approach derives a value that supports those acquisitions.

Now that the disclaimer is out of the way, my valuation of Sears will begin with net asset value (NAV), which is consistent with the approach that was presented in the first chapter. Recall that NAV is derived by estimating the reproduction value of a firm's assets and liabilities through the adjustment of accounting (or book) values to make those values more consistent with economic values. The adjustment mechanics are not complicated, but it is important to know which adjustments you have the knowledge to make yourself, and which require the services of professional appraisers or independent experts. I identify areas in the following valuation that could benefit from appraiser or expert input, and note that it is areas such as these that make the Graham and Dodd method seemingly ideal for corporate M&A (and, of course, investment management), as I will explain.

Table 2-1 presents my NAV for Sears; as in Chapter 1, a parenthetical note designates items that are discussed in the following narrative. All dollar figures are in millions unless indicated otherwise.

Note (1A) adds the bad debt allowance back to reported credit card receivables to arrive at an estimate of the reproduction value of those receivables.[10] The rationale for this type of adjustment was discussed in Chapter 1.

Note (2A) adds back the bad debt allowance to the other receivables at the same ratio as that used for credit card receivables. In other

Table 2-1

Sears' NAV

	$000,000s			
	2004	Adjustment	Value	Notes
Assets				
Cash and cash equivalents	$4,165	100%	$4,165	
Credit card receivables, net	$1,239	$36	$1,275	(1A)
Other receivables	$642	103%	$661	(2A)
Merchandise inventories, net	$5,549	$42	$5,591	(3A)
Prepaid expenses, deferred charges, and other current assets	$493	100%	$493	
Deferred income taxes	$475	100%	$475	
Total current assets	$12,563		$12,660	
Property and equipment:				
Land	$402	300%	$1,206	(4A)
Buildings and improvements	$7,542	75%	$5,657	(5A)
Furniture, fixtures, and equipment	$4,979	50%	$2,490	(6A)
Capitalized leases	$618	100%	$618	
Gross property and equipment	$13,541		$9,970	
Less accumulated depreciation	$6,792		N/A	
Total property and equipment	$6,749		$9,970	
Deferred income taxes	$271	0.9052	$245	(7A)
Goodwill	$963	$10,120	$12,368	(8A)
Trade names and other intangible assets	$1,285			
Other assets	$643	100%	$643	
Total assets	$22,474		$35,885	
Liabilities and Equity				
Short-term borrowings	$685	100%	$685	
Current portion of long-term debt and capitalized lease obligations	$330	100%	$330	
Merchandise payables	$2,962	100%	$2,962	
Income taxes payable	$412	100%	$412	
Other liabilities	$3,146	100%	$3,146	
Unearned revenues	$1,081	100%	$1,081	
Other taxes	$581	100%	$581	
Total current liabilities	$9,197		$9,197	
Long-term debt and capitalized lease obligations	$3,473	100%	$3,473	
Pension and postretirement benefits	$1,685	125%	$2,106	(9A)
Minority interest and other liabilities	$2,027	100%	$2,027	
Off-Balance-Sheet Commitments	-	$1,545	$1,545	(10A)
Warranties	-	$131	$131	(11A)
Value of options outstanding	-	$865	$865	(12A)
Total liabilities	$16,382		$19,345	
Net Asset Value (NAV)	$6,092		$16,541	

Dollars are in millions. All adjustments have been rounded and are the author's.
Data source: Sears 10-K, 2005.

words, other receivables were adjusted by 103% = 100% + ($36 bad credit card debt reserve/$1,239 in credit card receivables).[11]

Note (3A) adds back the LIFO reserve of $42 to net merchandise inventory to derive the reproduction value of inventory.[12]

Note (4A) pertains to Sears' land holdings, for which my estimated 300% of historical cost (or book value) is a significant estimate of perceived embedded (or deep) value and thereby requires a rationale. On November 5, 2004, 12 days before Lampert announced his acquisition of Sears, Vornado Realty Trust announced that it had purchased 4.3% of Sears' common stock. Vornado could be described as a value-based real estate investment firm, or a firm known for purchasing margin of safety–rich real estate assets. A commentary on Vornado's purchase noted that Sears' booked $402 in real estate assets was generally believed to be undervalued on the market.[13]

The United States real estate boom was in full swing in 2004, and based on informal surveys of real estate brokers, I learned that, in general, price appreciation levels of two to five times historic (or book) values were not uncommon for some commercial real estate holdings. For my purposes here, I adjusted Sears' book land value by 300%—or the midlevel of book and five times book—to estimate the reproduction value of those holdings. If this were an actual M&A valuation, this adjustment could be validated by an in-depth real estate valuation conducted by licensed real estate appraisers. For my purposes here, a midlevel adjustment of 300% is a reasonable but conservative estimate. As indicated in the previous chapter, conservatism is a key facet of the Graham and Dodd approach.

Note (5A) adjusts Sears' buildings and improvements down to 75% of book value. This reduction in book is also based on a subjective assessment—made after informal consultation with commercial general contractors—that the buildings and improvements in question would probably be able to be reproduced at that level. This is another adjustment that could have been validated by professional appraisers if this were an actual M&A valuation.

Note (6A) reduces furniture, fixtures, and equipment by 50%, which is yet another subjective estimate that could be validated through professional appraisal.

Note (7A) discounts deferred taxes by an estimated 10.5% discount rate for Sears, which is discussed in the later section on earnings power value.

Note (8A) is the largest adjustment in the valuation and pertains to *goodwill*. In a Graham and Dodd context, goodwill refers to the value of a firm's intangible assets, such as its product portfolio, brand names, consumer loyalty, and so on, as explained in the first chapter. The value of intangible assets can decline substantially when a firm suffers an "identity crisis," such as the one suffered by Sears.[14] This terminology refers to Sears' move from its core business into financial services, and then its reversion to retail. Despite the firm's identity crisis, the value of Sears' goodwill in 2004 could still be considered relatively significant for two key reasons:

- First, the Sears brand name had the power of more than 100 years—many of them very successful—of large-scale retail operations behind it. Granted, some of that power had eroded over the recent past, but the overall Sears brand was certainly not without value.
- Second, Sears distributed many high-quality products with powerful brand names, such as Kenmore, DieHard, and Craftsman, that had become linked to the firm. Such a linkage

can involve aspects of customer captivity and positive customer relationships[15] that obviously have value even though
they are intangible.

When estimating the worth of intangible assets such as these, and
as noted in Chapter 1, the modern Graham and Dodd methodology
"add[s] some multiple of the selling, general, and administrative line,
in most cases between one and three year's worth, to the reproduction
cost of the assets."[16] Consistent with this guideline, my valuation of
Sears' intangible assets was derived by multiplying Sears' 2004 selling
and administrative expense of $8,245 by 1.5, or one-half of the range
just described.[17] In practice, this is another area of perceived embedded (or deep) value that could be validated through professional
appraisal—possibly by a marketing or consulting firm.

Note (9A) reflects a subjective 125% adjustment to estimate the
reproduction value of Sears' pension and postretirement benefits. In
practice, pension actuaries could be retained to assess this liability
more accurately.

Notes (10A) through (12A) add back various off-balance-sheet
liabilities that for purposes of M&A should be factored into the
valuation. Adjustments such as these could also be subjected to
audit and/or professional appraisal for validation. To summarize the
adjustments:

● Note (10A) is an adjustment made up of off-balance-sheet
  commitments totaling $1,545: $1,039 in securitized borrow-
  ings + $198 in import letters of credit + $100 in secondary
  lease obligations + $151 in standby letters of credit + a $57
  guarantee.[18]

- Note (11A) refers to the product warranty liability of $131.[19]
- Note (12A) is an $865 options adjustment, which was derived by multiplying a weighted-average exercise price of $38.2 per share by the end-of-year balance of Sears' options of 22.657.[20]

Subtracting the reproduction value of the liabilities of $19.35 billion from the reproduction value of the assets of $35.89 billion gives a NAV of approximately $16.54 billion, which is 171.5% greater than Sears' reported book value of $6.09 billion.[21] To validate this premium over book, I will proceed along the modern Graham and Dodd value continuum to the next level of value, earnings power value (EPV).

As explained in Chapter 1, EPV adjusts the income already earned by a firm to arrive at an estimate of income that is sustainable in perpetuity. To illustrate, consider my EPV calculations for Sears in 2004, which are presented in Table 2-2.

As with my NAV exhibit, parenthetical notes designate calculations that are discussed in the following narrative.

Note (1E) pertains to expected sustainable operating income, which was derived by taking the average of Sears' operating income for the most recent three years (2004, 2003, and 2002). Estimating expected sustainable earnings in this manner—as a simple average— goes back to the seminal work of Benjamin Graham and David Dodd in 1934,[22] but this estimate is more than just a simple average: it is an estimate of the income that Sears' operations should be able to earn in perpetuity based on a sustainable level of operating efficiency.

Note (2E) adds back the depreciation and amortization charge of $989 dollar for dollar. As Sears' sales declined to $35.72 billion in

Table 2-2

Sears' EPV

	$000,000s	Notes
Expected sustainable operating income	$1,255	(1E)
Depreciation and amortization	$989	(2E)
Interest earned on cash	$125	(3E)
Options expense	$123	(4E)
Pretax earnings	**$1,996**	**(5E) = (1E) + (2E) – (3E) – (4E)**
Effective tax rate	34.3%	(6E)
Expected taxes	$685	(7E) = (5E) × (6E)
Earnings	**$1,312**	**(8E) = (5E) - (7E)**
Discount rate	10.5%	(9E)
Earnings multiple	9.5	(10E) = 1/(9E)
Earnings power	$12,522	(11E) = (8E) × (10E)
Cash	$4,165	(12E)
Earnings Power Value (EPV)	**$16,687**	**(13E) = (11E) + (12E)**

Dollars are in millions. All adjustments have been rounded and are the author's.
Data source: Sears 10-K, 2005.

2004 from $36.37 billion in 2003, there was no need to adjust depreciation.[23]

Next, note (3E) assumed a 3% interest rate on Sears' $4.16 billion in cash and cash equivalents, which was subtracted from operating income. As the capitalized value of interest earned on cash is the amount stated on the balance sheet, that figure will be added back to capitalized earnings to arrive at the EPV, as will be shown later.[24]

Note (4E) subtracts the options expense of $123 that was reflected in Sears 2004 Form 10-K (p. F-15).

Note (5E) starts with expected sustainable operating income of $1.26 billion and adds depreciation and amortization of $989, subtracts cash interest of $125, and subtracts the $123 options expense, giving a pretax earnings estimate for Sears of approximately $2 billion.

Note (6E) is the expected effective tax rate, which, to be consistent with the expected sustainable operating income estimate, was derived by taking the average of the effective rates for the most recent three years (2004, 2003, and 2002).

Note (7E) is the estimated tax expense, which is the product of the estimated pretax earnings of approximately $2 billion and the 34.3% effective rate.

Earnings [note (8E)] was derived by subtracting the estimated tax expense from pretax earnings.

The discount rate that I used in my valuation was estimated at 10.5% [note (9E)], or 2½ times the November 2004 10-year Treasury note yield of 4.19%,[25] which when divided into 1 gives a price/earnings multiple of 9.5 [note (10E)]. This multiple is significant because it is less than the well-known Graham and Dodd earnings multiple threshold of 16,[26] which means that it is relatively conservative.

Earnings power [note (11E)] is calculated by simply multiplying earnings of $1.31 billion by 9.5.

Finally, the cash on the balance sheet [note (12E)] is added to earnings power to derive the EPV of approximately $16.69 billion [note (13E)]. Note that my estimate of Sears' EPV is essentially equal to my estimate of Sears' NAV of $16.54 billion, and as such this valuation reflects the base-case value profile that was introduced in Chapter 1. As explained in the previous chapter, this profile is not uncommon: most valuations will reflect it because most firms are not operating with a sustainable competitive advantage.*

---

* An exception is firms in distress, which exhibit a different value profile. Distress-based investing is outside the scope of this book. For a superb introduction, see J. Ezra Merkin, "Blood and Judgement," in Benjamin Graham and David Dodd, *Security Analysis*, 6th ed. (New York: McGraw-Hill, 2008 [1934]), pp. 265–288.

If Sears was operating with a sustainable competitive advantage, its EPV would have been much greater than its NAV, necessitating a valuation of the franchise, which is the third level of value along the continuum. Similarly, growth—the fourth and final level of value—is considered in Graham and Dodd–based valuation only if the firm being valued is a franchise (which again is not the case here, but it is important to underscore the importance of this at this point in the chapter).

Despite the common occurrence of base-case value, it can present a lucrative M&A opportunity so long as it is accompanied by a reasonable margin of safety. In Graham and Dodd–based valuation, a typical margin of safety is one-third, which can be applied to the Sears acquisition by discounting NAV—the lesser of my two values—as follows: $16.54 billion × (1 − 0.3334) = $11.03 billion, which is a price that is very close to the actual price of this acquisition, as shown in Figure 2-1.

Upon review of that figure, a question similar to the one that was raised at the beginning of this chapter could arise, namely, why would Sears' shareholders sell their stock at an apparently "distressed" price? One possible answer to this question could involve the methodology that the shareholders used to value Sears at the time. For example, at a price of $10.9 billion, this acquisition was 1.8 times Sears' book value of $6.09 billion. A book multiple of 1.8 could be considered significant for a firm facing the kinds of competitive and operational issues that Sears was facing at the time. However, a Graham and Dodd–based valuation would probably have provided substantial insight into many of the elements of Sears' value—transparent and embedded (or deep) alike—and by so doing could have revealed that a price of 1.8 times book contained a reasonable margin of safety, as indeed my valuation did.

Figure 2-1

Sears' Base-Case Value Profile

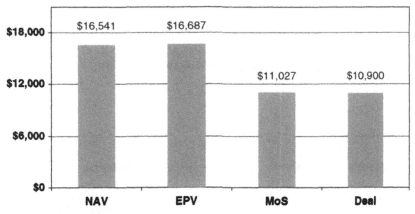

Dollar values are in millions where "NAV" equals net asset value, "EPV" equals earnings power value, "MoS" equals the margin of safety–adjusted price, and "Deal" equals the actual price that Lampert paid for Sears in 2004. All figures with the exception of the deal price are the author's.

To help put valuations such as this into context for strategic decision-making purposes, M&A buyers and sellers alike could identify key value drivers for further analysis. This process could begin, for example, with the construction of a *value drivers diagram* such as the one that I prepared for Sears, which is presented in Figure 2-2.

As the figure illustrates, assets and earnings drivers flow directly from my valuation, while franchise and growth drivers were omitted from the diagram, as they did not apply to Sears.* Examples of how the value that is embedded in these drivers could possibly be leveraged to create (or realize) value include

● Discerning the economic value of Sears' real estate portfolio through professional appraisals, and then formulating a plan to communicate that value to the capital markets effectively.

---

* Franchise value and growth value are covered in Chapters 3 and 4 of this book.

Figure 2-2

Sears' Value Drivers Diagram

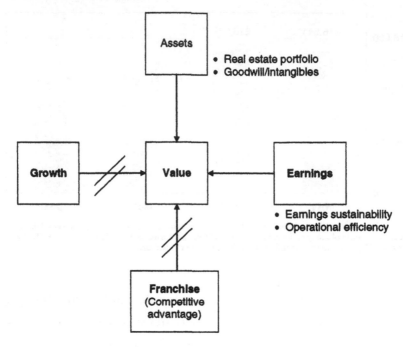

- Determining the economic value of Sears' goodwill (or intangible assets), possibly through a detailed private-market-value-based analysis,[27] and leveraging that value strategically.
- Evaluating expected sustainable earnings and the level of operational efficiency required to generate it over time.

Real estate and goodwill adjustments were particularly significant in my valuation, and therefore if this were a live M&A valuation, those adjustments would be singled out for scrutiny during the due diligence process. Also, there is a natural link between goodwill and earnings that could (and should) be explored during due diligence.* This is particularly significant for corporate M&A specialists because they have significant knowledge-based resources that could be leveraged in due diligence activities such as this. For example, Lampert obviously leveraged the knowledge he gained in the Kmart acquisition in his valuation of Sears, which is an approach that any other retailer seemingly could also have used. Significantly, this observation is not retail-specific; it could apply to any industry.

The information obtained during due diligence could then be used to formulate an M&A negotiating strategy, a comprehensive shareholder value communication plan, and a performance improvement plan. In short, the information could be used by acquirers to negotiate the most economic deal possible *and* by sellers to ensure that value is not uneconomically transferred (or to ensure that a firm is not sold at what might later appear to be a "distressed price").

POSTACQUISITION PERFORMANCE

Sears Holdings' stock price has experienced volatility since Lampert's acquisition; for example, the stock reached a high of $193 per share in 2007 before declining to $86.02 per share in early 2008 (note the chart of Sears' stock prices that is presented in Figure 2-3). To help put this volatility into context, consider the following: on Friday, January 25, 2008, Sears' market capitalization was approximately $14 billion, which is 28% above the $10.9 billion purchase price (recall that this acquisition occurred in 2004). This figure reflects value created by the acquisition, as Lampert himself has observed,[28]

* The Conclusion presents a process for accomplishing these types of activities.

Figure 2-3

Sears' Weekly Stock Prices

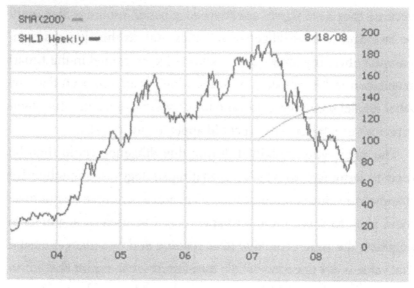

SHLD equals Sears Holdings Corp. and SMA (200) equals the simple 200-week moving average.
Source: www.wsj.com.

and it is relatively equal to the Graham and Dodd margin of safety threshold of approximately one-third.

The source of Sears' volatility seems to involve three areas: real estate, earnings, and stock market speculation. With respect to real estate volatility, newspaper articles in early 2008 estimated the value of Sears' real estate at between $4.7 and $10 billion,[29] a range that is substantially higher than my conservative $1.2 billion estimate, which was presented in Table 2-1. The spread between these estimates seems to be influenced, at least in part, by the speculative excesses experienced during the U.S. real estate boom. For example, real estate–based prices soared during the boom, which began after the "new economy" bust in 2001,* only to plunge during the subsequent bust. As real estate in general is relatively illiquid, equity prices tended to fall in tandem with real estate prices for firms with significant real estate holdings, such as Sears.

This raises an interesting value-based question: if the market placed such a high premium on Sears' real estate, did it also undervalue the firm's goodwill or intangible assets? This is an interesting question — and one that I do not currently have an answer for — that provides a convenient segue to the second potential source of Sears' stock volatility, earnings.

Sears Holdings' earnings in 2007 were $2.49 billion, but 2008 earnings were expected to decline to $1.94 billion. Both of these figures were apparently driven by intense cost-cutting initiatives. However, this level of earnings seems to have come at a cost: it has been claimed that Sears cut expenses too deeply and increased prices by too much, thereby alienating some of its customers.[30] Anecdotally, I confirmed that this may indeed have occurred: several members of my family who shopped at Sears told me that they were not at all satisfied, for both customer experience and pricing reasons, and that as a result they would no longer patronize the retailer. If this observation applies more widely, then Sears could seek to implement operational changes and initiatives to improve its performance; however, such changes and initiatives require a certain amount of time to implement and become effective. Nevertheless, Sears appears to have the brand power required to undertake initiatives like this.

For example, one potential initiative could involve leveraging the synergies within the combined firm, meaning Sears and Kmart.

---

* See Chapter 5 for more information on the "new economy" boom and bust.

Revenue enhancements for Kmart and Sears could arise because the combined firm has a level of critical mass or scale that could be leveraged from a marketing perspective through the firm's various brands, such as Kmart's Martha Stewart home-goods line and Sears' Craftsman line. This could be a significant option because a key dynamic of the Graham and Dodd approach is that the pricing of each deal must stand on its own; in other words, synergistic effects are usually not considered in a valuation, and indeed they were not considered in my valuation. As a result, any synergistic benefit could be a pure economic gain for Lampert and the investors in his fund. However, it is not clear that Sears has the operational skill required to realize this benefit over time.[31]

A third possible reason for the volatility of Sears' stock price could be stock market–based speculation, driven by the perception that, given Lampert's past success with Kmart, Sears would be transformed after its acquisition into a franchise (which, once again, is a firm operating with a sustainable competitive advantage) that could be grown. Such a perception would have resulted in a higher valuation and hence a higher stock price. However, as discussed in this chapter, Sears was not (and, indeed, is not) a franchise; if it were, its valuation pattern would reflect a much different value profile. That particular value profile is the subject of the next two chapters.

Chapter | 3

FRANCHISE VALUE AND THE GEICO ACQUISITION

The stock of a growing company, if purchasable at a suitable price, is obviously preferable to others.

—*Benjamin Graham*[1]

The investor who can successfully identify such "growth companies" when their shares are available at reasonable prices is certain to do superlatively well with his capital. Nor can it be denied that there have been investors capable of making such selections with a high degree of accuracy and that they have benefited hugely from their foresight and good judgment.

—*Benjamin Graham and David Dodd*[2]

This chapter contains material from *Strategy & Leadership,* © 2007 by Emerald Publishing, which is reprinted with permission.

INTRODUCTION

In the first two chapters, we concentrated on the first two levels of value along the modern Graham and Dodd value continuum, net asset value and earnings power value, and the resulting base-case value profile. In this chapter, I will add the last two levels of value along the continuum to my valuation: franchise value and growth value. To illustrate how all four levels can be used in a modern value investment, I will apply them to a valuation of Warren Buffett's appropriately celebrated 1995 acquisition of GEICO.

Buffett's track record as an investor correctly receives a great deal of attention; however, his merger and acquisition (M&A) track record receives far less attention, even though it is as good as, if not better than, his investment track record. To put this observation into context, consider the following comment that was made by Arthur Levitt, Jr., former chairman of the Securities and Exchange Commission: "From 1982 to 2003, Warren Buffett's Berkshire Hathaway has acquired companies worth $45 billion, a fact that many investors don't think about. Is he a great investor, or an even greater M&A specialist?"[3]

There could be many reasons for Buffett's M&A success, but a key one is probably his effective approach to valuation and pricing; in other words, Buffett generally does not overpay for acquisitions, as so many others seem to. To illustrate this in a Graham and Dodd context, I will value the GEICO acquisition, which is arguably Buffett's most successful acquisition, in this chapter.

Buffett frequently uses a painting metaphor to describe his portfolio of companies; for example, he has referred to Berkshire Hathaway as a "canvas" that can be viewed and examined by anyone, like a work of art. It may, however, be more helpful to think of Berkshire Hathaway as an art gallery rather than as a canvas, and at the center of that gallery is its version of da Vinci's *Mona Lisa*: GEICO. While some skeptics may snicker at this analogy, I make it in good faith: out of all the investments and acquisitions that I have studied—and I have studied many—I have never seen one as effective as GEICO. An analysis of the GEICO acquisition, therefore, is indeed something to be both studied and enjoyed, like a work of art.

To help put my valuation into context, I begin this chapter with an overview of GEICO's history in a manner similar to the way I opened the discussion of the Sears valuation in Chapter 2.

GEICO

In 1936, Leo and Lillian Goodwin founded the Government Employees Insurance Company (GEICO). From the outset, GEICO differentiated itself from other insurance companies by selling direct to its targeted customers, rather than through the traditional insurance agent distribution channel. GEICO's customers were relatively "safe" drivers such as federal employees and noncommissioned military officers. GEICO thrived using this strategy; for example, in 1972 its stock price reached a high of $61 per share. However, its performance started to decline in 1973, and by 1975 its stock had declined to $7 per share. In 1976, the firm announced a loss of $126 million and was on the verge of bankruptcy.

The cause of GEICO's poor performance was primarily the firm's deviation from its strategy, which was profiled in the previous paragraph; in other words, in the pursuit of revenue or premium growth, GEICO insured drivers who were less than safe. In 1976, the firm took steps to reverse its fortunes by appointing noted turnaround expert John J. Byrne as chief executive officer (CEO). Simply put,

Byrne's brilliant managerial initiatives both saved GEICO and returned it to profitability.[4]

After the turnaround was complete, Byrne left GEICO to pursue other opportunities, so in 1985, the firm appointed William B. Snyder as CEO. Snyder diversified GEICO into other lines of insurance, and once again the firm's move beyond its core was not profitable, causing its stock price to decline. GEICO replaced Snyder with Olza "Tony" Nicely in 1993, and in 1995 the firm completely returned to its core—selling automobile insurance to safe drivers—when it sold its homeowners' book of insurance business to Aetna Casualty & Surety.[5] By this time, GEICO's definition of a safe driver had evolved beyond government employees to people with safe driving records. "Safe" in this context very generally means a person whose driving record is without either moving violations or accidents over a period of time.

On August 25, 1995, it was announced that Berkshire Hathaway was acquiring the 49.6% of GEICO that it did not then own for $70 per share, which amounted to a total of $2.3 billion. That price represented a 25.6% premium over the $55.75 stock market price per share at the time, which is an interesting statistic for the world's foremost value-based investor (or someone who is known for buying bargain assets). Therefore, the objectives of my valuation are to determine if the modern Graham and Dodd approach

- Supports Buffett's $70 per share acquisition price.
- Reflects a reasonable margin of safety.
- Provides insight into GEICO's intrinsic value at the time of its acquisition.

VALUING GEICO

GEICO is a fairly dramatic example of the *circle of competence*, which was discussed in the first chapter and can be defined as a personal area of expertise that allows an investor or analyst "to identify and understand the sources of a company's franchise and the nature of its competitive advantages."[6] A circle of competence can be industry-specific, company-specific, or both industry- and company-specific, as GEICO was for Warren Buffett.

Buffett first became interested in GEICO while studying under Benjamin Graham at Columbia University. At the time, Graham was also the chairman of GEICO. This piqued Buffett's interest, so he took a train to GEICO headquarters one Saturday in January 1951, where he met Lorimar Davidson, a GEICO executive and its future CEO. Davidson spent four hours talking to Buffett about the insurance business in general and GEICO in particular, and from that point on Buffett was clearly "hooked" on the firm. For example, when he started his career as a stockbroker after graduating (in 1951 with a Master of Science in Economics), he admitted to focusing almost entirely on GEICO stock. For instance, on December 1, 1951, Buffett published an article about GEICO in the *Commercial and Financial Chronicle* titled, "The Security I Like Best," which was reprinted in the 2005 Berkshire Hathaway Annual Report.[7] More significantly, he accumulated a total position at a cost of $10,282, which equates to $79,502 in 2007 dollars assuming that the investment occurred in 1952, before selling it for $15,259 (a 48% gain).[8]

After selling off his position, Buffett continued following GEICO, especially when it fell upon hard times in 1976. According to biographer Roger Lowenstein,

[Buffett] harbored a secret desire to revisit the company in a big way. . . . For someone so rational, Buffett was sentimental about his past (though not so misty-eyed as to invest in GEICO when the stock was dear). But now GEICO was cheap. What's more, it was in deep trouble. And Ben Graham . . . still had his savings in it. Helping to salvage the company would be a sort of double fantasy: following in Graham's footsteps and rescuing his company.[9]

Therefore, by 1995 Buffett's deep familiarity with both the insurance industry and GEICO allowed him to confidently and accurately make the adjustments and estimates necessary to value the firm.

Regarding my valuation of GEICO, it is important to reiterate that it is my work product: I do not know Warren Buffett, and I do not know how he values investments. This chapter is based on my application of the modern Graham and Dodd valuation approach to the GEICO acquisition. I seem to be the first person who has publicly evaluated Buffett's purchases from a Graham and Dodd perspective, as far as I can tell. I do not know the reason for this, and I hope to show the insight that can be gained from evaluating high-profile acquisitions in this manner.

I begin the valuation with net asset value (NAV), which once again is derived by reconstructing the balance sheet on a reproduction basis. Table 3-1 is my NAV for GEICO, and as in the prior chapters, a parenthetical note designates adjustments that are explained in the following narrative. Note that I list liabilities before assets in the table, which is contrary to the traditional structure of balance sheets. I did this to underscore the fact that for insurance companies, the liability side of the balance sheet represents the goods and services sold

Table 3-1

GEICO's NAV

	$000s			
	1994	**Adjustment**	**Value**	**Notes**
Liabilities				
Policy liabilities:				
P&C loss reserve — Note G	$1,704,718	$100,400	$1,805,118	(1A)
Loss adjustment expense reserve — Note G	$307,606	105%	$322,986	(2A)
Unearned premiums	$747,342	100%	$747,342	
Life benefit reserves & policyholders' funds	$101,298	105%	$106,363	(2A)
	$2,860,964		$2,981,809	
Debt — Note I				
Corp. and other	$340,378	100%	$340,378	
Finance company	$51,000	100%	$51,000	
	$391,378		$391,378	
Amounts payable on purchase of securities	$8,408	105%	$8,828	(3A)
Other liabilities	$291,413	105%	$305,984	(3A)
Total liabilities	**$3,552,163**		**$3,687,999**	
Assets and Equity				
Investments	$4,102,866	100%	$4,102,866	
Cash	$27,580	100%	$27,580	
Loans receivable, net — Note E	$59,448	$1,500	$60,948	(4A)
Accrued investment income	$67,255	100%	$67,255	
Premiums receivable	$238,653	100%	$238,653	
Reinsurance receivable	$127,189	100%	$127,189	
Prepaid reinsurance premiums	$10,361	100%	$10,361	
Amounts receivable from sales of securities	$2,022	100%	$2,022	
Deferred policy acquisition costs — Note F	$72,359	100%	$72,359	
Federal income taxes — Note J	$98,975	0.8992	$88,996	(5A)
Property and equipment	$141,741	$85,209	$226,950	(6A)
Other assets	$49,656	100%	$49,656	
Goodwill	$0	$100,022	$100,022	(7A)
Total assets	**$4,998,105**		**$5,174,857**	
Net Asset Value (NAV)	**$1,445,942**		**$1,486,858**	(8A)

All adjustments have been rounded and are the author's.
Data source: GEICO Form 10-K, 1994.

(namely, the assumption of risk), and therefore it, rather than the asset side, is of primary importance. Insurance company assets essentially represent the management of the company's liabilities.

It is once again important to note that if this were a live M&A valuation, professional appraisers could be retained to validate certain adjustments. This is particularly significant with respect to insurance company valuation, as insurance companies can generally be difficult to value because of the time lag or *tail* between when insurance is sold and when insurance-related claims may manifest and be resolved.

Note (1A) pertains to a property and casualty (P&C) loss reserve adjustment composed of two parts:

- First, $85,400 (all dollars are in thousands unless otherwise specified) in anticipated salvage and subrogation recoveries was added back to the reserves to reflect the reproduction value.[10]
- Second, a subjective 15% adjustment was levied on GEICO's $100 million of commercial umbrella reserves. According to the firm's 1994 Form 10-K:

The ultimate development of losses related to the significant risks of this long-tail business, which includes environmental and product liability risks, is uncertain. Losses for GEICO's commercial umbrella business cannot be projected using traditional actuarial methods. The reserve for this business represents management's estimate of the ultimate liability which will emerge from a small number of potentially large claims. (Note G)

In practice, this subjective adjustment could be based on on-site claims audits and actuarial appraisals.[11]

Notes (2A) and (3A) pertain to subjective (and minor) 5% adjustments to the loss adjustment expense reserve, life benefit reserve, amounts payable on the purchase of securities, and other liabilities. In practice, these adjustments could also be based on on-site claims audits and actuarial appraisals.

Note (4A) adds the bad debt reserve back to loans receivable in order to derive an estimate of the reproduction value of this line item.

Note (5A) discounts the deferred tax asset by my estimated discount for GEICO of 11.2%, the calculation of which is discussed in this chapter's appendix.

Next, the reproduction cost of property and equipment is estimated by subjectively adding 75% of the total depreciation claimed in GEICO's financials to the listed book value [note (6A)]. If this were a live valuation, this adjustment could be based on, or validated by, a professional appraisal.

The final adjustment, note (7A), pertains to *goodwill*, which, as explained in prior chapters, refers to the intangible assets that a firm uses to create value, such as its product portfolio, customer relationships, organizational structure, competitive advantage, licenses, and so on. In this chapter, the key intangible asset that I valued was GEICO's existing customer base, which generates repeating premiums and underwriting profit from safe (or low-claim-generating) drivers, and the organizational structure the firm designed to service and retain that customer base. When valuing intangible assets such as these, the modern Graham and Dodd approach adds "some multiple of the selling, general, and administrative (SG&A) line, in most cases between one and three year's worth, to the reproduction cost of the assets."[12] However, insurance companies generally do not have an SG&A line on their income statements; rather, they record this type of expense under the acquisition costs line entry. In 1994, GEICO claimed $200,044 in acquisition costs.[13] As GEICO's goodwill was essentially operational in nature and contained no demand advantages—for example, search costs and switching costs for personal lines automobile insurance were (and are) generally low—I estimated its value at 50% of acquisition costs, or $100,022. This adjustment is also one that could be validated by a professional appraisal if this were a live M&A valuation, possibly from a marketing or consulting firm.

Subtracting the reproduction value of GEICO's liabilities of $3,687,999 from the reproduction value of its assets of $5,174,741 generates a NAV of $1,486,742, or $44.15 per share.[14] As this figure is a long way from Buffett's $70 per share acquisition price, I will proceed along the modern Graham and Dodd value continuum to the next level of value, earnings power.

Earnings power value (EPV) adjusts the income that a firm has already earned to arrive at an estimate of income that is sustainable in perpetuity. By ignoring growth, the analytical focus can be directed toward core earnings power, which, in turn, can be reconciled with NAV. This dynamic is a key strength of the Graham and Dodd approach.

My EPV calculations for GEICO are presented in Table 3-2, and consistent with the convention that I have used thus far, a parenthetical note designates calculations that are explained in the following narrative.

Note (1E) refers to my estimate of GEICO's expected sustainable operating income, which was derived by taking the average earnings

Table 3-2

GEICO's EPV

	$000s	Notes
Expected sustainable EBT	$298,761	(1E)
Depreciation and amortization adjustment*	$11,979	(2E)
Interest on cash	$1,023	(3E)
Pretax earnings	**$309,717**	(4E)
Tax rate	16.9%	(5E)
Taxes	$52,252	(6E)
Earnings	$257,465	(7E)
Earnings power	$2,296,104	(8E)
Cash	$27,580	(9E)
Earnings Power Value (EPV)	**$2,323,684**	(10E)

All calculations have been rounded and are the author's.
* Calculations are illustrated in Table 3-3.
Data source: GEICO Form 10-K, 1994.

before tax (EBT) margin of the three most recent years and then multiplying that figure by the firm's most recent revenue: $298,761 = 11% average EBT margin × 1994 revenue of $2,716,009.

Note (2E) pertains to my depreciation and amortization adjustment, the calculations of which are presented in Table 3-3. An explanation of the mechanics of this adjustment was provided in the first chapter.

Next, the interest earned on cash is deducted [note (3E)]. As the capitalized value of interest earned on cash is the amount stated on the balance sheet, this figure will be added back to capitalized earnings to arrive at an EPV, as will be shown later.

In the next step, note (4E), the depreciation and amortization adjustment is added to average operating income and the interest earned on cash subtracted from it to derive pretax earnings.

I then calculated the expected tax liability by using GEICO's 1994 *effective tax rate*, note (5E), which was derived by dividing paid

Table 3-3

GEICO's Depreciation and Amortization Adjustment

Calculation		$000s
(a)	Property & equipment	$141,741
(b)	1994 revenue	$2,716,009
(c)	1993 revenue	$2,638,300
(d)	Amortization	$13,687
(e)	Depreciation	$22,434
(f)	CAPEX	$28,197
(g) = [(a)/(b)] × [(b) − (c)]	Growth CAPEX	$4,055
(h) = (f) − (g)	Zero-growth CAPEX	$24,142
(i) = (d) + (e) − (h)	Depreciation and amortization adjustment	$11,979

All calculations have been rounded and are the author's.
Data source: GEICO Form 10-K, 1994.

and deferred taxes by EBT, resulting in 16.9% = [$58,056 + ($15,677)]/$251,194.[15]

Multiplying the effective tax rate by pretax earnings of $309,717 gives a tax expense of $52,252 [note (6E)].

Earnings, note (7E), are calculated simply by subtracting the tax expense from pretax earnings, giving $257,465.

Note (8E) pertains to capitalizing earnings as a nongrowth perpetuity. To accomplish this, I first divided 1 by GEICO's estimated discount rate of 11.2% (see the appendix for the calculations that derive this rate), which gives a multiple of 8.9. This multiple is roughly half of the Graham and Dodd multiple threshold of 16,[16] which means that it is a relatively conservative estimate. The product of the multiple and GEICO's earnings is the capitalized value of the earnings.

Next, I added the amount of cash on GEICO's balance sheet [note (9E)] to the earnings power of $2,296,104 to estimate GEICO's EPV [note (10E)]. On a per share basis, this equals $69, which is approximately equal to Berkshire's $70 per share acquisition price. However, as the EPV is substantially greater than GEICO's $44.15 per share NAV, the value of the firm's franchise must be validated.

A *franchise* is a firm operating with a sustainable competitive advantage that generates economic profit (or income in excess of the opportunity cost of capital) in perpetuity. This profit is reflected in the valuation by a substantial spread between EPV and NAV, which in my GEICO valuation equals $24.85 per share = $69 per share EPV – $44.15 per share NAV.

Competitive advantages drive a franchise, and they are rare. Competitive advantages are also, as Professors Bruce Greenwald and Judd Kahn have observed, generally local in nature, meaning that they are found in discrete regions or market segments.[17] GEICO's focus on insuring safe drivers can be considered an example of this.

GEICO's strategy for protecting its niche, and the economic profit that niche generates, is to be the insurance industry's low-cost provider of personal lines automobile insurance so that it can profitably compete on price at levels at which its competitors probably cannot.[18] This combination of a niche market focus and industry-leading cost control is a potent combination that generates a substantial competitive advantage, or "moat," to use a term that I believe was introduced by Warren Buffett. He explained the use of this term in, for example, the 1993 Berkshire Hathaway Annual Report:

> The might of their [Coke's and Gillette's] brand names, the attributes of their products, and the strength of their distribution systems give them an enormous competitive advantage, setting up a protective moat around their economic castles. The average company, in contrast, does battle daily without any such means of protection. As Peter Lynch says, stocks of

companies selling commodity-like products should come with a warning label: "Competition may prove hazardous to human wealth."[19]

In short, a "protective moat" sustains the profitability that generates an EPV-to-NAV spread and the value resulting from it. Therefore, identifying and assessing the strength of moats is a key objective of franchise valuation. I have already identified GEICO's competitive advantage, so the next step in the assessment process is to determine if this advantage is sustainable over time.

A key consideration when assessing the sustainability of a franchise is the quality of the firm's management and its intention to exercise discipline in defending *and* perpetuating its advantage over time. As GEICO's history reflects, its executives had a somewhat spotty record when it came to sustaining the company's franchise. However, as Buffett was acquiring the firm (in 1995), it could be reasonably assumed that he would focus on its advantage to ensure the integrity of the franchise. Additionally, I assumed that GEICO's CEO, Tony Nicely, was committed to first protecting and then perpetuating his firm's advantage; in other words, he had no intention of trying to grow GEICO beyond its extremely profitable niche (put another way, he had no intention of growing outside of his firm's circle of competence).

Having now validated that GEICO was indeed a sustainable franchise in 1995, I will turn to the final level of value along the modern Graham and Dodd continuum, growth value.

Growth is the final and most intangible level of value, but it can nevertheless be an important variable to consider in the valuation process. This may come as a surprise to those who feel that Graham and Dodd–based investing and growth-based investing are polar opposites, but Warren Buffett himself has characterized the two approaches as "joined at the hip."[20] This is significant because thus far my valuation has not yet identified a margin of safety for this acquisition, and therefore it must lie within growth, as this is the final level of value.

Financial theory is clear that growth creates value only when it is economically profitable, or when growth-generated profitability exceeds the opportunity cost of capital. One way in which the modern Graham and Dodd approach estimates growth value is through the practical utilization of select NAV and EPV variables. To explain, the first step in this process is to divide a firm's earnings by its net asset value to calculate the return on net asset value (or RNAV). Next, RNAV is divided by the discount rate to derive a growth multiple. If this multiple is greater than 1, growth will create value, and therefore multiplying it by the EPV will derive a growth value (GV). Conversely, if the growth multiple is less than 1, growth will destroy value, so it obviously should not be undertaken. To illustrate this approach, consider my calculations for GEICO, which are presented in Table 3-4.

My $3,588,388 GV for GEICO equates to $106.55 on a per share basis. Therefore, with this final level of value in place, a complete value continuum for GEICO can be constructed as shown in Figure 3-1 (note the similarity to the theoretical profile illustrated in Figure 1-2 of Chapter 1).

GEICO was acquired for $1 more than my EPV of $69 per share; therefore, if this acquisition's margin of safety was based on a GV of $106.55 per share, in percentage terms it equals 52.5% = ($106.55/$70) – 100%.[21] As this margin of safety is greater than the Graham and

Table 3-4

GEICO's Growth Value

Calculation		$000s	Source
(a)	Earnings	$257,465	Table 3-2
(b)	Net asset value	$1,486,858	Table 3-1
(c) = (a)/(b)	Return on net asset value	17.3%	
(d)	Cost of equity	11.2%	Table 3-5
(e) = (c)/(d)	Growth multiple	1.5	
(f)	Earnings power value	$2,323,684	Table 3-2
(g) = (e) × (f)	Growth Value (GV)	$3,588,388	

All calculations are the author's and have been rounded. Calculations assume all earnings are invested at the above return on net asset value.

Figure 3-1

GEICO's Value Continuum

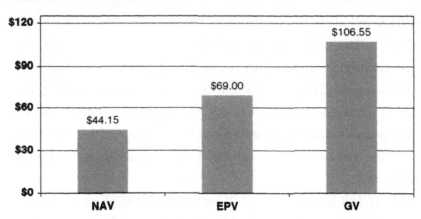

NAV equals net asset value, EPV equals earnings power value, and GV equals growth value (franchise value, or the positive difference between EPV and NAV, is not expressly illustrated). All calculations are the author's.

Dodd margin of safety range of approximately 30 to 33%, it suggests that the GEICO acquisition at $70 per share was a significant value-based acquisition, despite the 25.6% premium over the stock price at the time.

POSTACQUISITION PERFORMANCE

Writing the year following this acquisition in Berkshire Hathaway's annual report, Buffett indicated that GEICO management had "pushed underwriting and loss adjustment expenses down further to 23.6% of premiums, nearly one percentage point below 1994's ratio."[22] To put this performance into context, consider the following:

- A 1% insurance improvement equates to $20,585,029 (in absolute dollars) after taxes = $2,476,276,000 in 1994 premium × 1% × (1 − the 1994 effective tax rate of 16.9%).[23]
- If we assume that this performance is sustainable, we can capitalize it at a multiple of 8.9 (see the EPV section of this chapter), which gives a value of $183,579,878, or $5.45 per share. On a percentage basis, this per share amount represents roughly 8% of the $70 per share purchase price.

Needless to say, performance such as this is a significant accomplishment, but more importantly, from a value perspective, it was not a factor in my valuation. Thus, this roughly 8% benefit could have been a pure economic gain for Berkshire Hathaway. Furthermore, subsequent to its acquisition, GEICO launched what is in all likelihood the most innovative and successful marketing campaign in the history of the insurance industry.[24] Television commercials featuring an animated gecko lizard, which is the firm's mascot, a psychologically challenged caveman, and celebrity spoof skits have generated substantial business for GEICO—so much so, in fact, that GEICO's value at the present time (the year 2009) probably far exceeds my GV of $106.55 per share. In other words, GEICO's growth has probably created value far in excess of the acquisition's margin of safety.

One reason for GEICO's incredible success is that its growth initiatives flow logically from its strategy of being the low-cost provider of automobile insurance to safe drivers, to the quantitative depictions of that strategy in the value continuum, to the firm's highly innovative marketing campaign. This logic can be illustrated in a value drivers diagram such as the one presented in Figure 3-2.

Note the common cost theme that runs from earnings to franchise to growth. Theme commonality such as this is a powerful indicator that growth-based initiatives rest on a logical foundation and thus have a higher probability of success. The lesson here is that if such logic

Figure 3-2

GEICO's Value Drivers Diagram

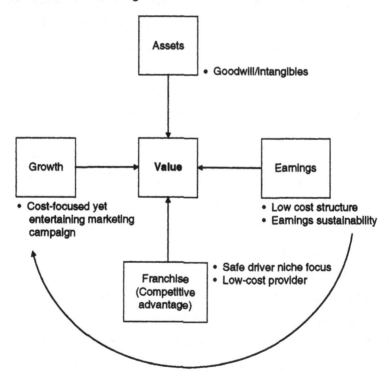

can be discerned and validated before the buyout—during due diligence—managers can have greater confidence in both their valuations and their subsequent growth initiatives.

Of course, GEICO's growth initiatives also leverage three very powerful brands that contributed to the success of its initiatives:

- The GEICO name itself, which is virtually synonymous with low-cost automobile insurance
- The firm's readily recognizable gecko lizard and psychologically challenged cavemen characters, which sell GEICO products in a highly entertaining manner
- The Berkshire Hathaway brand of unparalleled capital strength and responsible corporate governance

Leveraging brands effectively is obviously important in growth-based initiatives, but it must be remembered that brands and growth are intangible, which means that they can be inordinately difficult to analyze and value. As a result, both intangible assets and growth contain fairly high levels of risk. This holds true even for modernity's most successful investor, as we shall see in the next chapter.

APPENDIX: ESTIMATING GEICO'S DISCOUNT RATE

In current mathematical approaches to investment decisions, it has become standard practice to define "risk" in terms of average price variations or "volatility." . . . We find this use of the word "risk" more harmful than useful for sound investment decisions—because it places too much emphasis on market fluctuations.

—Benjamin Graham[25]

Techniques for estimating investment and M&A discount rates tend to generate friction between Graham and Dodd practitioners and financial economists (especially academic financial economists),* which is a reason why I have not addressed this subject to any extent up to this point in the book.

In this appendix, I will highlight some of the reasons behind the discount rate estimation–related friction in the context of the GEICO valuation. But before I do, a determination must be made as to whether GEICO should be evaluated from an equity perspective or from an enterprise perspective.

Several finance scholars have indicated that "since the net present value of writing new [insurance] policies is usually positive, reserves are a liability that create value for shareholders. For this reason, it makes sense to use an equity rather than an enterprise approach for valuing insurance companies."[26] Following this logic, I will use GEICO's cost of equity as the discount rate in this valuation rather than its weighted-average cost of capital (or WACC).

The most popular economic model for estimating the cost of equity is the Capital Asset Pricing Model (CAPM). The CAPM essentially holds that an equity-based discount rate is a function of the risk-free rate of return plus an equity risk premium. The equity risk premium is estimated by multiplying a relative volatility factor, which is formally known as beta,[27] by the difference between the expected equity market return and the risk-free rate of interest. Applying these

---

* Another point of friction pertains to market behavior. Graham and Dodd practitioners universally reject the efficient market theory of financial economics. I comment on this further in Chapter 5.

variables on an equity basis gives the following CAPM-based cost of equity equation:

$$\text{Cost of equity} = \text{risk-free rate} + (\text{equity beta} \times \text{equity risk premium}) \qquad (3\text{-}1)$$

University of Virginia finance professor Robert Bruner, in his dividend discount model–based case study of the GEICO acquisition, provided the following CAPM-related inputs for GEICO at the time Buffett took it private:

- A risk-free rate of 6.86% based on the yield of the 30-year U.S. Treasury bond
- An equity beta of 0.75
- An equity risk premium of 5.5%[28]

Plugging these inputs into equation (3-1) yields a cost of equity for GEICO of 11% = 6.86% + (0.75 × 5.5%).

Value investors in general reject the use of beta-based models such as the CAPM. In addition to the quote from Benjamin Graham that introduced this appendix, consider Warren Buffett's thoughts:

Academics, however, like to define investment "risk" differently, averring that it is the relative volatility of a stock or portfolio of stocks—that is, their volatility as compared to that of a large universe of stocks. Employing data bases and statistical skills, these academics compute with precision the "beta" of a stock—its relative volatility in the past—and then build arcane investment and capital-allocation theories around this calculation. In their hunger for a single statistic to measure risk, however, they forget a fundamental principle: It is better to be approximately right than precisely wrong.[29]

Understandably, many Graham and Dodd–based practitioners hold similar views. For example, Mario Gabelli presented similar views in a presentation to my value investing class at the University of Connecticut (Stamford branch) on March 4, 2004.[30] Seth Klarman also presents similar views in his superb book titled *Margin of Safety*, which identifies a key practical failing of the model, namely, that "beta views risk solely from the perspective of [past] market prices, failing to take into consideration specific business fundamentals or economic developments."[31]

To estimate GEICO's cost of equity for use in my valuation, I simply rearranged the popular dividend discount model to produce a dividend growth model–based cost of equity. The equation for this approach is as follows:

$$\text{Cost of equity} = (\text{expected dividend/stock price}) + \text{expected growth} \qquad (3\text{-}2)$$

The expected growth variable in equation (3-2) can be estimated through the popular DuPont method by multiplying a firm's return on equity (ROE) by the difference between 100% and the firm's payout ratio, which is basically the ratio of dividends to net income [in other words, expected growth = return on equity × (1 − payout ratio)].

I apply equation (3-2) in Table 3-5 to estimate GEICO's cost of equity in 1995. As you can see from that table, my 11.2% DGM-based cost of equity relatively reconciles with the CAPM-based cost of equity of 11% that was discussed earlier, as financial theory suggests that it should. However, this level of reconciliation does not always occur, especially in non-dividend-paying firms.[32]

Table 3-5

GEICO's DGM-based Cost of Equity

Calculation			Note
(a)	Dividend per share	$1.00	Per share
(b)	Price per share	$55.75	Per share
(c) = (a)/(b)	Dividend yield	1.8%	
(d)	1994 net income	$207,764	In 000s
(e)	1994 book equity	$1,445,942	In 000s
(f)	1993 book equity	$1,534,579	In 000s
(g) = [(e) + (f)] / 2	Average equity	$1,490,261	In 000s
(h) = (d)/(g)	Return on equity	13.9%	
(i)	Dividends	$69,864	In 000s
(j) = (i)/(d)	Payout ratio (p)	33.6%	
(k) = 1 − (j)	1 − p	66.4%	
(l) = (h) × (k)	Expected growth	9.3%	
(m) = {(a)×[1+(l)]/(b)} + (l)	Cost of equity	11.2%	

All calculations are the author's.
Data sources: Price per share is from Robert Bruner, *Warren E. Buffett, 1995,* Darden School of Business Case Services, #UVA-F-1160, 1998 [1996]. Dividend per share is from GEICO Form 10-K, 1994. Net income, book equity, and dividends (not per share dividends) are also from GEICO Form 10-K, 1994. I assume that the inputs are current for valuation purposes.

In closing this discussion, I note that whether you like them or not, asset pricing models such as the CAPM remain a staple of modern finance, and therefore they are heavily used in modern valuations.[33] This, perhaps, is a reason behind a comment made by one of my former alternative investment clients: "We use the CAPM, like most others do, I suppose, but we hold our noses when we do." Perhaps one day a Graham and Dodd–oriented researcher will develop a more practical and acceptable approach.

Chapter | 4

THE GEN RE
ACQUISITION AND
FRANCHISE RISK

Confusion may be avoided if we apply the concept of risk solely to a loss of value which either is realized through actual sale, or is caused by a significant deterioration in the company's position—or, more frequently perhaps, is the result of the payment of an excessive price in relation to the intrinsic worth of the security.
—Benjamin Graham[1]

It is natural and proper to prefer a business which is large and well managed, has a good record, and is expected to show increased earnings in the future. But these expectations, though seemingly well-founded, often fail to be realized. Many of the leading enterprises of yesterday are today far back in the ranks. Tomorrow is likely to tell a similar story.
—Benjamin Graham and David Dodd[2]

This chapter and its appendix contain material from the *Journal of Alternative Investments*, © 2005 by Institutional Investor, and from *Strategy & Leadership* and *Measuring Business Excellence*, © 2008 by Emerald Publishing, which is reprinted with permission.

INTRODUCTION

Following the GEICO acquisition, which was a phenomenal success, as described in the previous chapter, Warren Buffett acquired the General Reinsurance Corporation (Gen Re) in 1998. As I did with GEICO, I will value Gen Re using the modern Graham and Dodd approach and demonstrate how that approach highlights the key drivers and risks of that acquisition, especially with respect to the intangible aspects of franchises and growth. First, however, some background to help put this deal into context.

On June 19, 1998, Berkshire Hathaway announced the purchase of Gen Re for "approximately $22 billion." At this figure, Gen Re was Buffett's largest acquisition. In the press release announcing the acquisition, Buffett noted possible synergies resulting from it, and concluded by stating that the deal "virtually assures both Berkshire and General Re shareholders that they will have a better future than if the two companies operated separately."[3] However, Gen Re's results turned down almost immediately after its acquisition, as profiled here:

- In 1999, Gen Re sustained an operating loss of $1.18 billion.
- In 2000, it sustained a loss of $1.25 billion.
- In 2001, which was the year of the tragic September 11 terrorist attacks, it lost $3.67 billion.
- In 2002, the loss was $1.39 billion, for a total operating loss of $7.5 billion.[4]

Significantly, these losses do not take into account the lost value of Gen Re's franchise, which Buffett paid so much for: Gen Re's book value in 1997 was $8.16 billion;[5] therefore, a substantial portion of the approximate $22 billion purchase price was for the intangible assets of a franchise that did not exist.

How did such a loss occur? And how can the scope of it be reconciled from a value investing, margin of safety–based perspective? Before either addressing these questions or presenting my valuation, I will briefly discuss Gen Re's product, *reinsurance*, and provide an overview of the firm's history.

GEN RE AND THE BUSINESS OF REINSURANCE

Reinsurance is "a contract that one insurer makes with another to protect the first insurer from a risk he has already assumed."[6] In short, reinsurance can be described as insurance for insurance companies. Insurance companies purchase reinsurance for the same reason that individuals purchase insurance: to transfer unwanted risk. Significantly, as the reinsurance transaction is between a reinsurance company and an insurance company, no individual policyholder is a party to it; therefore, state insurance departments do not regulate reinsurance, which substantially lowers its costs.

Insurance in general is a commodity product, and thus it is reasonable to infer that reinsurance is equally a commodity, if not more so. After all, insurance companies are sophisticated bearers of risk, so what value could a reinsurer possibly bring to an insurancelike transaction, other than a willingness to assume risk? At an early stage in Gen Re's development, its executives recognized that the firm's operations could not generate *economic profit* (or income greater than the opportunity cost of capital) if they did not successfully address this strategic question.[7] Building a brand, increasing market share, and establishing a sustainable franchise depend on the formulation of a competitive advantage–based business model, and early Gen Re executives designed a highly innovative one.

First, the executives decided to sell reinsurance directly to insurance companies rather than through traditional reinsurance brokerage channels. Second, they bundled consultinglike and relationship-based services into the basic reinsurance product offering. For example, if an insurance company was considering underwriting a risk that it did not have expertise in, or if it received a claim that it did not have the expertise to handle, the insurance company could call a Gen Re underwriter or claims representative for technical consultation, advice, and assistance. Such expert-based services satisfied Gen Re's customers' needs and filled a market void, especially for smaller midwestern and southern mutual insurance companies. Significantly, both aspects of the strategy were mutually reinforcing: direct selling and technical consultation brought and kept Gen Re personnel close to the firm's clients. As a result, Gen Re's operations generated significant economic profit for decades.

Gen Re leveraged its "customer intimate" strategy with highly effective marketing and goodwill initiatives.[8] One illustrative story that has rightly become legendary occurred after a particularly severe hurricane. Apparently, a midsized insurance company had not purchased adequate catastrophe reinsurance, and as a result it was essentially insolvent because of the claims related to the hurricane. The president of that firm called a Gen Re executive at the time, John Etling, to essentially say goodbye before his firm was taken over by local insurance regulators. Rather than saying goodbye, Etling reportedly advised the insurance executive that—because of the long-standing relationship between the two companies—Gen Re was going to provide the insurance company with all the catastrophe coverage it needed to stay in business. While this gesture undoubtedly cost Gen Re millions in the short term, the goodwill it earned the firm over the long term most likely significantly exceeded that amount. Indeed, it was through acts like this, in conjunction with the firm's highly innovative strategy, discussed earlier, that turned Gen Re into a powerful franchise.

In the early 1980s, Gen Re's board of directors appointed as CEO Ronald Ferguson, a well-regarded actuary who invented a reserving methodology that bears his name, the Bornhuetter Ferguson Method.[9] At the time of Ferguson's appointment, Gen Re could be described as a customer-intimate/marketing-oriented firm, and thus Ferguson's appointment could be interpreted as a move to instill actuarial (or mathematical) rigor into the franchise so that it could be refined and grown. And from the mid-1980s to the mid-1990s, that strategy seemed to work. For example, and as Figure 4-1 illustrates, from 1987 to 1997, Gen Re's return on equity (ROE) averaged 20.1% and the firm consistently bought back shares, thereby increasing its earnings per share (EPS).

VALUING GEN RE

Modern Graham and Dodd practitioners characterize a firm displaying a profitability profile like Gen Re's as a *franchise*, which, as explained previously, is a firm operating with a sustainable competitive advantage. To determine whether Gen Re was, in fact, a franchise, I will evaluate it along the modern Graham and Dodd value continuum. Table 4-1 presents my calculation of the net asset value (NAV) of Gen Re using data from the firm's 1997 annual report.

Figure 4-1

Gen Re Performance from 1987 to 1997

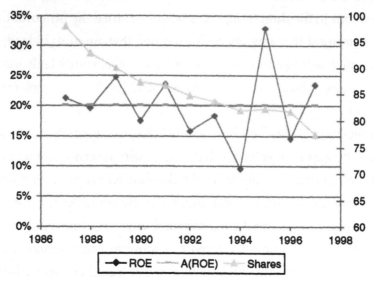

Shares are in millions where "ROE" equals Return on Equity and "A(ROE)" equals Average Return on Equity.
Data source: General Re Corporation 1997 Annual Report, p. 32–33.

A parenthetical note once again designates adjustments that are explained in the narrative.

As I did in my GEICO valuation, I list liabilities before assets in the exhibit. For reinsurance companies as for insurance companies, the liability side of the balance sheet represents the goods and services sold—in other words, the assumption of risk—and therefore I placed it first in my valuation.

Note (1A) pertains to loss reserve adjustments. Loss reserves are amounts of money set aside for future claim payments, and therefore this entry is arguably the most significant item on an insurance or reinsurance company's balance sheet. While it is now well known that the insurance industry in general was significantly underreserved in

Table 4-1

Gen Re's NAV

	$000,000s			
	Book	**Adjustment**	**Value**	**Notes**
Claims and expenses	$15,797	105%	$16,587	(1A)
Policy benefits for life/health contracts	$907	105%	$952	(1A)
Unearned premium	$1,874	100%	$1,874	
Other reinsurance balances	$2,948	100%	$2,948	
Notes payable	$285	100%	$285	
Income taxes	$1,104	0.9323	$1,029	(2A)
Leases	$0	$297	$297	(3A)
Other liabilities	$997	100%	$997	
Minority interest	$1,032	100%	$1,032	
Financial services liabilities	$8,351	110%	$9,186	(4A)
ESOP related	$3	100%	$3	
Total liabilities	**$33,298**		**$35,191**	(5A)
Investments	$24,576	100%	$24,576	
Cash	$193	100%	$193	
Accrued investment income	$358	100%	$358	
Accounts receivable	$1,858	$60	$1,918	(6A)
Funds held by reinsured companies.	$488	105%	$512	(7A)
Reinsurance recoverable	$2,706	$60	$2,766	(6A)
Deferred acquisition costs	$476	100%	$476	
Goodwill	$968	338%	$4,242	(8A)
Other assets	$962	100%	$962	
Financial services assets	$8,874	100%	$8,874	
Total assets	**$41,459**		**$44,876**	
Net Asset Value (NAV)	**$8,161**		**$9,686**	(9A)

All adjustments are the author's, and have been rounded.
Data source: General Re Corporation Annual Report,1997, p. 36.

1997–1998, that fact was not widely known at the time of the Gen Re acquisition.[10] Furthermore, and as indicated earlier, Gen Re's CEO was a well-regarded reserving actuary, and the firm was AAA rated. In light of these factors, I subjectively increased Gen Re's reserves by only 5%. Were this adjustment to occur today, it could be based on on-site claims and actuarial audits, which would quantify the adequacy of the firm's reserving practices.[11]

Note (2A) refers to the tax liability being discounted by Gen Re's discount rate, the estimation of which is discussed later.

Note (3A) adds the lease liability onto the balance sheet.[12]

Note (4A) is a subjective estimate of future financial services liabilities, which is a batch entry that is composed of

- Securities sold under agreements to repurchase at contract value
- Securities sold but not yet purchased at market value
- Trading account liabilities
- Commercial paper
- Notes payable
- Other liabilities

Given the dynamics of these liabilities, a subjective 10% volatility-based adjustment was made for analytical convenience in this valuation. Were this adjustment to occur today, each group classification could be carefully scrutinized, possibly with the aid of professional appraisers or financial consultants.

With respect to the final liability note, (5A), it signifies that I made no pension liability adjustment in the valuation. Gen Re executives estimated this liability on a relatively conservative basis at the time: at a discount rate of 7.0% and an expected long-term rate of return of 8.5%.[13] Subsequent events revealed inadequacies in pension valuations across all industries, and thus this is another adjustment that, if it were made today, could be based on a professional appraisal conducted by a pension actuary.[14]

Turning to Gen Re's assets, note (6A) pertains to the bad debt allowance that was added back into accounts receivable and *reinsurance recoverable*, which represents money owed to Gen Re by its reinsurers.[15] As with accounts receivable, it is necessary to add back any bad debt allowance onto the balance sheet in order to adequately reproduce the assets. According to Gen Re's 1997 Annual Report (p. 41), the total bad debt allowance was $119 (all dollars are in millions unless otherwise specified), so that figure was split evenly between accounts receivable and reinsurance recoverable to derive a basic reproduction estimate for valuation purposes.

Note (7A) pertains to *funds held by reinsured companies*, which is premiums that are due to Gen Re but are held by the insurance companies that purchased reinsurance as allowed by contract. As Gen Re earned interest on this money, I subjectively adjusted it for reproduction purposes. This is another area where the input of professional appraisers or actuarial consultants could possibly be used.

My final balance sheet adjustment, note (8A), pertains to *goodwill*. Once again, goodwill in a modern Graham and Dodd context does not pertain to the excess paid for an asset over its book value; rather, it pertains to the key intangible assets that a firm uses to create value. In this case, the key intangible asset that I valued was Gen Re's niche, "customer intimate" strategy, which had two mutually reinforcing elements:

- A direct distribution channel (similar to the distribution channel used by GEICO)
- Consultinglike services built into the commodity reinsurance offering

Graham and Dodd practitioners typically value this line item by adding "some multiple of the selling, general, and administrative (SG&A) line, in most cases between one and three year's worth, to the reproduction cost of the assets."[16] Reinsurance companies, like insurance companies such as GEICO, generally do not have an SG&A line on their income statements; instead, they also record this type of expense under the acquisition costs line entry. In 1997, Gen Re claimed $1,414 in acquisition costs,[17] and given the historical strength of its strategy—as commented on earlier—I valued this intangible at three times that amount, or $4,242. Such a high multiple reflects the difficulty of copying the effects of years of goodwill-based initiatives such as the late John Etling's, which was mentioned earlier.

Subtracting the estimated reproduction value of the assets of $44,876 from the estimated reproduction cost of the liabilities of $35,191 gives a NAV of $9,686, which is 19% greater than Gen Re's reported book value of $8,161. Nevertheless, it is a long way from the "approximately $22 billion" purchase price. Therefore, I will proceed along the value continuum to the next level of value, earnings power.

My earnings power value (EPV) calculations for Gen Re are presented in Table 4-2, and once again a parenthetical note designates calculations that are discussed in the following narrative.

The first two entries in the table are taken directly from Gen Re's income statement, so my adjustments begin with the third entry, note (1E). This is a significant—and subjectively derived—adjustment to earnings that I define as *unused underwriting power*, which is the value of expected sustainable earnings improvement generated from underwriting operations. In this case, in the press release on the acquisition,

Table 4-2

Gen Re's EPV

	$000,000s	Notes
Earnings before tax	$1,327	
Goodwill amortization	$29	
Unused underwriting power*	$665	(1E)
Interest on cash	$6	(2E)
Pretax earnings	$2,016	(3E)
Taxes	$459	(4E)
Earnings	$1,557	(5E)
Cost of equity	7.3%	(6E)
Multiple	14	(7E)
Earnings Power Value (EPV)	$21,631	(8E)

All calculations are the author's and have been rounded.
* Calculations are illustrated in Table 4-3.
Data source: General Re Corporation Annual Report, 1997, p. 35.

Warren Buffett listed Gen Re's "ability to write more business" as a reason justifying "the premium price that Berkshire is paying."[18] Therefore, the objective of this adjustment is to estimate the value of this "ability" in the context of Gen Re's current earnings. The mechanics of my adjustment are presented in Table 4-3.

Here is my explanation of the adjustment on a calculation-by-calculation basis:

- Calculations (a) and (b) were taken from Gen Re's 1997 Annual Report (p. 35).
- Calculation (c) is the ratio of claims paid to premiums.
- Calculation (d) is simply the average of the three yearly ratios (from 1995 to 1997).
- Calculation (e) is my subjectively derived estimate of Gen Re's "ability to write more business." It is based on the

Table 4-3

Gen Re's Estimated Unused Underwriting Power

Calculation		$000,000s		
		1997	1996	1995
(a)	Claims paid	$3,788	$3,984	$3,680
(b)	Written	$6,545	$6,661	$6,102
(c) = (a)/(b)	Claims paid/written	57.9%	59.8%	60.3%
(d) = A(c)	Average claims paid/written	59.3%		
(e)	Sustainable improvement(%)*	25.0%		
(f) = (e) × (b)	Sustainable improvement($)	$1,636		
(g) = (f) × (d)	Expected claims on improvement	$971		
(h) = (f) − (g)	Unused underwriting power	$665		

* This estimate was derived subjectively. The accuracy of estimates like this is greatly enhanced if it is formed within one's circle of competence. Additionally, according to Graham and Dodd, *Security Analysis*, 3rd ed. (New York: McGraw Hill, 1951 [1934]), p. 493: "The object is not to determine exactly what earnings may be realized as of some specific date in the future, but rather to arrive at a level of earnings, with a certain margin of give and take, that may reasonably be looked forward to as achievable within a future period of time." According to Seth Klarman, *Margin of Safety: Risk Averse Investment Strategies for the Thoughtful Investor* (New York: HarperBusiness, 1991), p. 90: "It would be a serious mistake to think that all the facts that describe a particular investment are or could be known. Not only may questions remain unanswered; all the right questions many not even be asked. Even if the present could somehow be perfectly understood, most investment investments are dependent on outcomes that cannot be accurately foreseen."

All calculations are the author's and have been rounded.
Data source : General Re Corporation Annual Report,1997, p 35.

expected potential of leveraging the synergy of the firm's 1996 purchase of National Re and its 1994 merger with Cologne Re backed by Berkshire Hathaway's powerful capital base.

● Calculation (f) is simply the monetary value of the expected premium improvement.

● Calculation (g) is an estimate of the amount of claims the additional premium will generate.

● Finally, subtracting (g) from (f) gives my estimated *unused underwriting power* adjustment [calculation (h)].

To sum up my earnings power valuation thus far (see Table 4-2), the first two entries, earnings before tax (EBT) and goodwill amortization, were taken directly from Gen Re's income statement, while the third entry, unused underwriting power, was estimated as shown in Table 4-3. I next deducted the interest earned on cash [note (2E)]. As the interest rate for that adjustment was not readily assessable, I assumed 3% for valuation purposes.

The next step, note (3E), pertains to pretax earnings, which were calculated by adding EBT, goodwill amortization, and unused underwriting power, and then subtracting interest earned on cash. I then calculate expected taxes by using Gen Re's *effective tax rate*, which was calculated by dividing paid and deferred taxes by EBT: 22.8% = ($254 + $48)/ $1,327.[19]

Multiplying pretax earnings of $2,016 by the effective tax rate gives a tax expense of $459, note (4E).

Earnings, note (5E), are calculated by subtracting the tax expense from pretax earnings, giving $1,557.

The next step involves capitalizing earnings as a nongrowth perpetuity. To accomplish this, I used Gen Re's estimated cost of equity as the discount rate, which I estimated at 1.25 times the December 1997 10-year Treasury note yield of 5.81%,[20] which equals 7.3% [note (6E)]. Given the level and stability of Gen Re's performance at the time (see, for example, Figure 4-1) and its AAA credit rating, a discount rate at this level, at the time of the firm's acquisition, seems warranted.

To capitalize earnings as a simple, nongrowth perpetuity, I first divided 1 by the cost of equity, which equals 14 [note (7E)]. Note that this multiple is less than 16, which, as noted in prior chapters, is a key Graham and Dodd earnings multiple threshold.[21] However, also note that this multiple is significantly higher than the multiple of 8.9 that was used in Chapter 3's GEICO valuation. Multiplying 14 by Gen Re's estimated earnings of $1,557, and then adding the amount of cash on the balance sheet, $193,[22] provides an EPV of $21,631 = ($1,557 × 14) + $193, note (8E),[23] which is "approximately $22 billion," or the amount that Buffett paid for Gen Re.

However, as Gen Re's EPV is substantially greater than its NAV of $9,686, the value of its franchise must be validated. Therefore, I will proceed along the value continuum to the next level of value, franchise value.

To recap franchise value, absent a competitive advantage, a firm is not a franchise, and therefore its NAV will approximately equal its EPV, as we saw in Chapters 1 and 2. When a firm's EPV significantly exceeds its NAV, it could be a franchise, but it must always be remembered that sustainable competitive advantages are rare, especially in commodity-like industries such as reinsurance and insurance. However, franchises do exist in these industries; GEICO is a case in point, as we saw in Chapter 3.

GEICO and Gen Re share a strategic similarity in that they both use a direct distribution channel. Gen Re's use of that model resulted in close contact and interaction with its customers as reinsurance information (such as risk, loss, and premium payment information) flowed back and forth between the firm and its clients. Such contact and interaction enabled Gen Re's underwriters and claims personnel to get very close to their clients over time, which allowed them to better serve their clients' needs. This type of dynamic is what can make a customer-intimate-based strategy so valuable, meaning that it can generate deep levels of customer satisfaction and thus substantial switching costs.

As indicated earlier, the successful execution of this strategy generated a great deal of economic profit for Gen Re over time. For example, as illustrated in Figure 4-1, Gen Re's average ROE was 20.1% over a 10-year period, which is an incredible number for any firm, let alone one in a commodity industry. Additionally, and aside from the 1994–1995 swing, those returns were relatively nonvolatile, which is another sign of a potential franchise.

In light of this information, it could be reasonably argued that at the time of this acquisition, Gen Re was indeed a franchise. Therefore, the next step in the valuation is to determine if that franchise was sustainable. A franchise is sustainable only when its management is committed to both protecting *and* perpetuating it over time. Frankly, it is difficult in retrospect to comment objectively on the sustainability of Gen Re's franchise in 1998. Fortunately, its CEO at the time provided his thoughts in Berkshire Hathaway's aforementioned press release:

> I am very enthusiastic about our merger with Berkshire. The combined entity is a unique and extraordinary business model that provides us with the long-term commitment, the financial resources and the optimal platform to serve our clients and, thus, grow our franchise. General Re's future has never been brighter.[24]

Having validated Gen Re's franchise status for now—I revisit it later—I will proceed along the Graham and Dodd value continuum to the fourth and final level of value, growth. As my valuation thus far has not yet identified a margin of safety for this acquisition, it must lie within growth, as that is the final level of value.

Table 4-4

Gen Re's Growth Value

Calculation		$000,000s	Source
(a)	Earnings	$1,557	Table 4-2
(b)	Net asset value	$9,686	Table 4-1
(c) = (a)/(b)	Return on net asset value	16.1%	
(d)	Cost of equity	7.3%	Table 4-2
(e) = (c)/(d)	Growth multiple	2.2	
(f)	Earnings power value	$21,631	Table 4-2
(g) = (e)×(f)	Growth Value (GV)	$47,876	

All calculations are the author's and have been rounded.

My calculations for Gen Re's growth value (GV) are presented in Table 4-4. As noted in Chapter 3, growth has value only when it is profitable, and a measure of profitability is the ratio of the return on net asset value (RNAV) to the cost of equity. If this ratio is greater than 1, growth will create value, so multiplying it by the EPV will derive Gen Re's growth value.

Dividing Gen Re's earnings of $1,557 into its NAV of $9,686 gives a RNAV of 16.1%, which when divided by the 7.3% cost of equity equals a growth multiple of 2.2. Multiplying this figure by the EPV of $21,631 equals a GV of $47,876.

With this final level of value in place, Gen Re's value continuum can be illustrated as shown in Figure 4-2.

If we assume a purchase price at the EPV of $21,631, which is "approximately $22 billion," and compute the margin of safety off the GV, it equals 121% = ($47,876/$21,631) – 100%, which is a significant amount by any standard. Therefore, it can be argued that, based on a valuation like the one presented in this chapter, Gen Re in 1998 appeared to be a value-based acquisition.

Figure 4-2

Gen Re's Value Continuum (1997–1998)

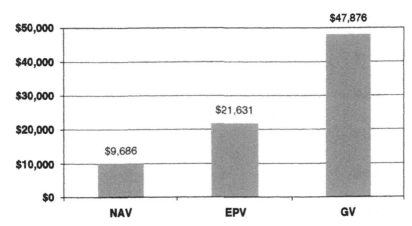

Dollars are in millions, calculations are the author's.

POSTACQUISITION PERFORMANCE

As noted previously, Gen Re sustained tremendous losses right after Buffett acquired it. Those losses are presented in graphical form in Figure 4-3.

Viewing that figure immediately raises questions, such as:

● What, exactly, happened here?
● How could the franchise-based Gen Re acquisition have gone so wrong while the seemingly similar franchise-based GEICO acquisition turned out so well?

To help put questions such as these into context, consider the value drivers diagram that I prepared for Gen Re, which is presented in Figure 4-4.

Figure 4-3

Gen Re's Earnings Post Acquisition from 1998 to 2007

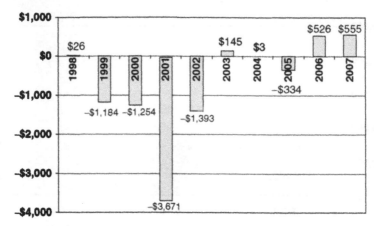

Dollars are in millions. The results appropriately exclude investment income as that income was generated by Buffett, not by Gen Re. *Data sources*: Berkshire Hathaway Annual Reports, 1998 to 2007.

Figure 4-4

Gen Re's Value Drivers Diagram

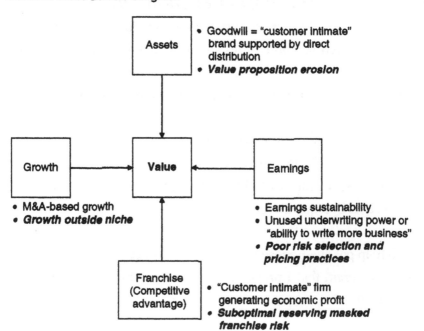

This diagram takes the same form as those in the prior chapters, with the modification that selected risks have been identified along with value drivers (risks are presented in **bold italic** font). I discuss the risks here.

With respect to Gen Re's asset risks, it seems clear that the value of its goodwill had significantly eroded prior to Buffett's acquiring it. This erosion could have occurred for a variety of reasons. For example:

- First, consider Gen Re's direction from the early 1980s to its acquisition in 1998. Recall that in the early 1980s, an actuary was appointed Gen Re's CEO. At the time, Gen Re's customer-intimate strategy was supported by a marketing-based organizational structure. An actuarial science (or mathematical) driven approach to reinsurance operations was bound to change that structure; exactly what effect the changes would have—positive or negative—remained to be seen, but the important point is that there were going to be changes.
- A second reason began to emerge in the 1980s. As Gen Re's customers became more technically sophisticated, the demand for underwriting and claims-related consulting and relationship-based services declined. This happened gradually over time, but it did happen, thereby eroding the value of Gen Re's franchise.
- A third reason pertains to Gen Re's acquisition strategy. According to the firm's 1997 annual report (pages 42 and 43), it purchased Cologne Re on December 28, 1994, and National Re on October 3, 1996. However, neither of these acquisitions was part of Gen Re's core franchise: National Re used a brokerage distribution channel, and Cologne Re

was based in Germany. Gen Re used direct distribution and underwrote the vast majority of its business in the United States. Therefore, in the vernacular of value investing, Gen Re grew through acquisition outside its circle of competence, thereby increasing the risks of its franchise (this is reflected in the diagram under the growth caption) without seemingly receiving any scale advantages.

Moving on to the risk of Gen Re's earnings, the key earnings drivers in my valuation were the estimated sustainable earnings level, the estimated unused underwriting power, and the relatively high earnings multiple of 14 (see the EPV section of this chapter). Central to each of these value drivers is premium pricing, which was assumed to be driven by Gen Re's strategy, resulting in the EPV-to-NAV spread of a franchise. Thus, pricing power sustainability equates to franchise sustainability; however, and as Warren Buffet noted, "Gen Re's culture and practices had substantially changed and unbeknownst to management—and to me—the company was grossly mispricing its current business."[25]

This statement is somewhat difficult to reconcile (for example, how could a firm's culture and practices change without not only its management's knowledge but also its support?); however, a challenge of the insurance/reinsurance business is that the costs of assuming risk may not be manifested right away (or shortly after insurance/reinsurance policies have been underwritten). In fact, the time lag or *tail* between when insurance is sold (and the premium is collected) and when claims are paid out can amount to many years. As a result, the consequences of poor pricing practices may not be readily apparent if the loss reserves that have been established to pay the claims do not accurately reflect the risk of the claims. This seems to have occurred at Gen Re; for example, as Buffett observed: "One obvious cause for its [Gen Re's] failure is that it did not reserve correctly and therefore severely miscalculated the cost of the product it was selling. Not knowing your costs will cause problems in any business. In long-tail reinsurance, where years of unawareness will promote and prolong severe underpricing, ignorance of true costs is dynamite."[26]

As indicated earlier, Gen Re's CEO was a celebrated reserve actuary, so a reasonable assumption, especially considering the firm's performance displayed in Figure 4-1, absent intensive due diligence, was that the firm was adequately reserving its risks. It is important to note that underreserving does not necessarily imply nefarious behavior: the entire insurance industry has been substantially underreserved at times.[27] One reason for systemic underreserving is that the process of forming loss reserves is a subjective one—much like valuation in general—and as such it is inherently prone to error.

While these reasons could have contributed to the erosion of Gen Re's franchise, it is doubtful that they alone could have generated the types of losses the firm sustained. Two other reasons probably combined with them to form a perfect stormlike set of circumstances that devastated the firm following Buffett's purchase of it:

● The first was the reinsurance price war of the 1990s. As Gen Re's product offering increasingly became a commodity, the firm was forced to compete on price during a particularly vicious price war. Significantly, the effects of a reinsurance price war are usually not felt right away because of the tail of the products, which possibly contributed to a misjudgment of the price war's eventual impact.

● The second factor was the substantial impact of the tragic September 11 terrorist attacks. As Buffett himself indicated, "Had Gen Re remained independent, the World Trade Center attack alone would have threatened the company's existence."[28]

CONCLUSION

The Gen Re case illustrates that M&A deals involving franchises (or firms operating with a sustainable competitive advantage) can be particularly difficult to value. This difficulty can be magnified for reinsurance/insurance companies, where numerous factors combine to obfuscate valuation efforts. For example, consider the following factors:

● The time lag or tail of loss events and claims payments
● Cyclical price competition
● Catastrophic events
● The universal challenge of valuing intangible assets

These are only some of the challenges that must be overcome in insurance company valuation, which proved costly to even the world's most successful investor. In 1998, he paid approximately $22 billion for Gen Re, a firm with a book value of just over $8 billion. Unfortunately, the franchise he paid for no longer existed, perhaps for some of the reasons just identified.

This is not to suggest that mega-insurance deals are not advisable; after all, Buffett's acquisition of GEICO was a tremendous success.

Rather, it demonstrates that extensive strategic and operational due diligence should be carefully conducted before any such deal is consummated. Such activities in the Gen Re case, for example, could have revealed the nature and extent of the firm's operational changes, and the potential consequences of its growing outside of its circle of competence.

Gen Re returned to marginal profitability in 2003, but that profitability was driven by Berkshire Hathaway's financial strength, not necessarily Gen Re's operations. In fact, Berkshire Hathaway's financial support enabled Gen Re to maintain its AAA rating, and as a result Gen Re is now the only AAA-rated reinsurer.[29] Obviously, this rating can be a significant advantage, but it can be leveraged only by addressing the operational and marketplace factors that are affecting Gen Re's operations.

For example, in addition to mispricing, legal and regulatory factors have also affected Gen Re's performance, and threatened Berkshire Hathaway's franchise as well, 10 years after the firm's acquisition. For instance, Gen Re came under substantial scrutiny when the Australian firm HIH Insurance Group collapsed. This collapse was Australia's largest corporate failure,[30] which essentially means that it was the Australian version of WorldCom. Additionally, Gen Re was investigated by the Securities and Exchange Commission (SEC) and had been sued by insurance regulators in Virginia and Tennessee for loss-mitigation insurance policies. The theory behind this litigation was essentially that the policies were intended to smooth earnings rather than transfer risk.[31] Furthermore, Gen Re came under substantial investigation with respect to a $500 million *finite reinsurance* transaction with insurer AIG that went incredibly wrong.

According to the National Association of Insurance Commissioners (NAIC):

> Finite Reinsurance is a type of reinsurance that transfers only a finite or limited amount of risk to the reinsurer. Risk is reduced through accounting or financial methods, along with the actual transfer of economic risk. By transferring less risk to the reinsurer, the insurer receives coverage on its potential claims at a lower cost than traditional reinsurance. Due to the highly complex structure of these risk instruments, there can be abuses where no risk is transferred and the insurer's income is improved.[32]

The issue with this type of product is that in the absence of risk transfer, a finite reinsurance product resembles a loan, and, obviously, the accounting for a loan is different from the accounting for reinsurance. In the Gen Re–AIG transaction, it was alleged in a criminal complaint that the finite reinsurance sold by Gen Re to AIG did not involve risk transfer, but that AIG nevertheless accounted for the transaction as reinsurance—instead of as a loan—in order to defraud investors. It was further alleged that Gen Re executives knew of AIG's accounting intentions beforehand and thereby facilitated the fraud. The case went to trial, and the defendants—who included Gen Re's former CEO, Ronald Ferguson, and its former CFO as well as AIG's former reinsurance chief—were all found guilty.

Shortly after the verdict Warren Buffett dismissed Gen Re's then CEO, Joseph Brandon, seemingly under pressure from federal authorities to do so.[33]

In addition to the reputational costs that actions like these generate, they also generate substantial direct costs, such as attorney's fees, employee time responding to inquiries, and so on, which Berkshire Hathaway was responsible for. Significantly, from a valuation perspective, these costs were not considered in my valuation, and as a result they could represent a net loss to Berkshire Hathaway.

Since Gen Re's troubles emerged, Buffett has been asked if he regretted buying the firm; however, in my opinion, the more appropriate question to be asked is, should Gen Re have been valued at approximately $22 billion? Considering what happened after the buyout, the answer to that question is clearly no. In fact, the risks to the Gen Re franchise at the time that Buffett purchased it were so great that had he waited just one quarter, he would probably have been able to purchase it for considerably less than $22 billion.[34]

Some may argue that the Gen Re buyout was desirable irrespective of the price paid because it gave Buffett access to Gen Re's reserves for investment purposes, which was clearly to his competitive advantage. However, Buffett had (and has) plenty of capital to invest pre-Gen Re, and he even commented that he was having trouble finding adequate investments for it all;[35] therefore, that argument seems untenable to me.

While the final chapter of the Gen Re acquisition remains to be written, a key lesson of it seems clear: the intangible aspects of franchises and growth can be a tremendous source of value, as we saw, for example, with GEICO, but the volatility of intangible assets makes them inherently difficult to value, thus requiring even the most successful investors and M&A specialists to advance cautiously.

One final comment on the Gen Re acquisition: Buffett used Berkshire Hathaway stock to finance it, which was a popular acquisition tactic during the "new economy" boom of the 1990s. Therefore, an argument can be made that Buffett purposely paid a premium for

Gen Re and that he used overvalued Berkshire Hathaway stock to finance it in order to mitigate any potential loss.[36] While this is certainly possible, it would have been uncharacteristic of Buffett to approach an investment in this manner—in other words, paying more for an acquisition because the market valued his stock too highly. However, the linkage between this acquisition and the new economy boom is a curious one. In the next chapter, I discuss the new economy boom and bust, and attempt to address it from a Graham and Dodd–oriented perspective.

APPENDIX: ASSESSING THE RISK OF M&A

The safety sought in investment is not absolute or complete; the word means, rather, protection against loss under all normal or reasonably likely conditions or variations.
                        —*Benjamin Graham and David Dodd*[37]

Introduction

A question that I am often asked is, "Can the risk of acquisition failures like Gen Re be reasonably assessed beforehand, and if so, how?" I believe that to some extent this type of risk can be assessed prospectively. One risk assessment approach that I have found useful is the real disaster–based framework that was presented by Robert Bruner,[38] a finance professor who specializes in M&A at the University of Virginia's Darden School of Business.

A *real disaster* is an incident involving substantial levels of bodily injury or property damage. Real disasters may cause financial disaster, as, for example, when an insurance company fails in the aftermath of a natural catastrophe, but the two kinds of disasters are inherently different. What Bruner did was study the causes of a number of real disasters (see the first sidebar for information on the specific disasters) and develop a risk assessment framework from the results of that study. Bruner's framework is composed of six factors that can be used proactively to assess M&A risk. The factors are:

1. *Complexity.* Something in the target's business and/or in the deal itself makes it difficult to understand and value.
2. *Tight coupling.* There is limited to no flexibility available to absorb "the effect of miscalculations or worse than average luck," to borrow a phrase from Benjamin Graham.[39] From a Graham and Dodd perspective, tight coupling is caused by speculating (or investing without a margin of safety) and/or preparing a valuation in a less than conservative manner.
3. *Unusual business environment.* Turbulence in the business environment can produce or contribute to valuation error(s).
4. *Cognitive biases.* These include such things as overoptimism and arrogance.
5. *Adverse management choices.* Unintended consequences can increase the risk of a deal.
6. *Operational team flaws.* These arise from cultural differences, lack of candor, political infighting, and aberrant leadership.[40]

Significantly, Bruner observed that none of these factors alone is likely to result in a financial disaster (although from a Graham and Dodd perspective, tight coupling is clearly a risk to be avoided), but that the risk of disaster will increase if most or all of these factors are present. According to Bruner, "The convergence of disaster causes is, I think, the most important foundation required of the thoughtful practitioner for understanding M&A failures, or for that matter, all business failures."[41]

To demonstrate how this framework could be used in M&A, Bruner applied each of these factors to a number of insightful case studies, such as Sony's 1989 acquisition of Columbia Pictures, AT&T's 1991 acquisition of NCR, and AOL's 2001 merger with Time Warner. He closes the case section of his book by contrasting Tyco's relatively unsuccessful M&A program under former CEO L. Dennis Kozlowski with the generally successful M&A program of Berkshire Hathaway Chairman and CEO Warren Buffett.[42]

BRUNER'S SAMPLE "REAL DISASTERS"

In his study, Professor Bruner observed, "The catalogue of disasters is quite long and entails virtually all institutions of society." To illustrate this point, Bruner listed a number of classic governmental disasters, such as

- War and its destruction over the centuries; for example, Napoleon's famously disastrous invasion of Russia that destroyed an army of 500,000. Obviously, and unfortunately, this is not the only example that could be given under this category. For further information, see, for instance, Eliot Cohen and John Gooch, *Military Misfortunes: The Anatomy of Failure in War* (New York: Free Press, 1990).
- Bruner also listed disasters based on governmental economic mismanagement, such as China's disastrous Great Leap Forward in 1969, which "induced deaths by famine for 30 million." Governmental economic mismanagement can

be a somewhat contentious topic that I will leave for another day, as it is (way) beyond the scope of this book.

● Governmental technological disasters, such as the $1.5 billion snafu that occurred with the Hubble Space Telescope. Technological disaster is one of the topics covered by Robert Mittelstaedt in his extremely thought-provoking book *Will Your Next Mistake Be Fatal? Avoiding the Chain of Mistakes That Can Destroy Your Organization* (Upper Saddle River, N.J.: Wharton, 2005).

● Governmental disasters were not chosen for Bruner's study, however; rather, the following five disasters were chosen "for the diversity of issues they raise with the aim of finding common elements that might be extended to the world of M&A":

● The collapse of the walkway at the Kansas City Hyatt Regency Hotel in July 1981
● Chernobyl in April 1986
● Bhopal in December 1984
● The Ocean Ranger in February 1982
● The Mount Everest expedition in May 1996[43]

For further information, see Robert Bruner, *Deals from Hell: M&A Lessons That Rise Above the Ashes* (New York: Wiley, 2005).

However, as we saw earlier in this chapter, Buffett has not been immune to the occasional "deal from hell," borrowing from the title of Bruner's superb book. In this appendix I will apply Bruner's framework to the Gen Re case to discover whether it helps in assessing the relative risk of failure of that acquisition. Note that there will be some level of overlap between this appendix and the material covered in the chapter itself, which is inevitable given the subject matter. I will endeavor to keep the overlap to a minimum and to present the material in a different manner to the extent that I can.

Assessing the Risk of the Gen Re Acquisition

To recap, Gen Re's business is reinsurance, which essentially is insurance for insurance companies. For example, many insurance companies insure homes against a variety of perils, such as rain, wind, fire, and flood. As the volume of homes insured increases, insurance companies are at risk of a catastrophic loss resulting from a single hurricane, tornado, or other natural disaster. To manage this risk, some insurance companies routinely contract with reinsurance companies to transfer part of such a loss.

1. Complexity

In many ways, reinsurance is inherently complex. For example, consider the time lag (or tail) between when insurance events occur and when the claims resulting from those events are reported to a reinsurance company. The tail of a hurricane, for example, is relatively short because homeowners tend to file hurricane-related claims very quickly and, in turn, insurance companies report such claims to their reinsurers quickly. Conversely, the tail for certain casualty-related claims can be very lengthy. Consider asbestos claims, which in some cases are first reported to insurance companies, and hence to reinsurance companies, decades after exposure to asbestos. Claims reporting is delayed because the injury caused by asbestos may not immediately manifest itself. While asbestos liability is an extreme example, it does convey the complexity inherent in reinsurance company valuation.

2. Tight Coupling

As noted previously, one cause of tight coupling is paying too much for an acquisition. High prices reduce the flexibility that an acquirer has to absorb the effects of "worse than average luck" that may arise. One measure of paying too much in a deal is the price/book ratio (P/B): generally, lower P/B deals provide greater flexibility, while higher P/B deals could reflect tight coupling. Applying this measure to the Gen Re acquisition, I note that Buffett purchased the firm for $22 billion, which was nearly three times Gen Re's book value of $8 billion. This premium over book does not in and of itself reflect overpayment, but it was probably based on significant and relatively aggressive asset, earnings, franchise, and growth assumptions, which means that it was risky (or prone to loss). As it turned out, that risk did manifest itself as Gen Re's losses (profiled in Figure 4-3) accumulated.

The significant loss that Gen Re sustained in 2001 (see Figure 4-3) was caused, in part, by the tragic September 11 terrorist attacks, which, as noted previously, would have threatened Gen Re's ability to remain a going concern had it not been acquired. While such a loss could not have been foreseen, the relatively nonconservative valuation assumptions and high P/B of this deal afforded no flexibility to absorb "the effect of miscalculations or worse than average luck." In short, this deal was tightly coupled.

3. Unusual Business Environment

Bruner's third risk factor is that business is not as usual, and in the insurance business, the September 11 attacks on the World Trade Center are an obvious example. For the Gen Re acquisition, however, business was unusual in 1998 for other reasons, including the new economy boom. As discussed in Chapter 5, the speculative buying that characterized the new economy was far broader than the technology sector, and I would argue that it was to some extent a factor in the Gen Re acquisition. For example, that deal was structured as a stock exchange: Gen Re shareholders had the option of accepting either 0.0035 Class A Berkshire Hathaway share or 0.105 Class B Berkshire Hathaway share for each of their shares.[44] This structure is interesting, as the majority of Buffett's acquisitions have been made with cash, not stock. However, in the late 1990s, stock-based acquisitions were extremely popular as a result of new economy–generated momentum.

One approach to identifying unusual potential performance issues that I have found useful is to risk-adjust selected performance measures. This approach essentially uses a coefficient of variation-like construct to risk-adjust (or, more accurately, volatility-adjust) selected performance measures, and takes the form:

$$\text{Risk-adjusted performance} = (\text{metric} - \text{target})/S_{DP} \qquad (4.1)$$

where:

S_{DP} = sample standard deviation of differential performance, or the difference *metric – Target*

To demonstrate how this approach could be used in practice, Scott Lane, Ranga Dasari, and I created a measure that we call *RaM*, which is short for risk-adjusted margin.[45] We chose to risk-adjust margin given its linkage with the ROE measure (and by extension RNAV) as explained in the sidebar "Margin and Practical Risk Adjustment." RaM is calculated very simply as follows:

$$RaM = [(\text{net income/revenue}) - \text{target margin}]/S_{DM} \qquad (4.2)$$

where:

S_{DM} = sample standard deviation of the differential margin, or the difference *margin – target*

In our study Scott, Ranga, and I calculated the historic RaM for Gen Re using the data and approach presented in Table 4-5.

The output from this exercise includes a RaM profile for Gen Re that is illustrated in Figure 4-5, which clearly shows a significantly reduced risk-adjusted margin over time. That result seemed unusual given Gen Re's profitable track record as illustrated, for example, in Figure 4-1, and as such it could have been used as the rationale for a round of intensive senior management performance-oriented questions and targeted due diligence activities designed to identify the drivers of the volatility. Once the drivers and any other issues were identified, a determination could be made whether to revise the valuation or whether to revisit the rationale for the deal.

While measures such as the one presented here can at times be very useful, I cannot emphasize too strongly that there is a *significant* difference between risk adjustment (which, as noted earlier, is really volatility adjustment) and the risk of loss. Standard deviation–based constructs like this one assume a normal distribution, and thus should be used with extreme caution, as life simply does not follow a bell curve.[46] The use of sample standard deviation in the model should help to forestall the

Table 4-5

Gen Re's Risk-Adjusted Margin (RaM)

Year (1)	Total Revenue (2)	Net Income (3)	Margin (4) = (3)/(2)	Target Margin* (5)	Differential Margin (6) = (4) - (5)	Sample Standard Deviation† (7) = s(6)5 Years	RaM (8) = (6)/(7)
1997	$8,215	$968	11.8%	10%	1.8%	4.1%	0.4
1996	$8,296	$894	10.8%	10%	0.8%	4.4%	0.2
1995	$7,210	$825	11.4%	10%	1.4%	3.7%	0.4
1994	$3,837	$665	17.3%	10%	7.3%	1.4%	5.3
1993	$3,560	$711	20.0%	10%	10.0%	0.9%	10.8
1992	$3,387	$657	19.4%	10%	9.4%	1.6%	5.9
1991	$3,207	$657	20.5%	10%	10.5%	2.3%	4.6
1990	$2,954	$614	20.8%	10%	10.8%		
1989	$2,742	$599	21.8%	10%	11.8%		
1988	$2,719	$480	17.7%	10%	7.7%		
1987	$3,115	$511	16.4%	10%	6.4%		

* A target margin of 10% was subjectively selected by the author for analytical convenience.
† The sample standard deviation [denoted s in column (7) and in equations 4-1 and 4-2] used in the calculation occurred over a period (or volatility horizon) of five years. The small data size is the reason why sample standard deviation is used in the calculation and not population standard deviation. For information on the differences between sample and population standard deviation, refer to any introductory statistics textbook.
Dollars are in millions, and all calculations are the author's and have been rounded.
Data source: General Re Corporation Annual Report, 1997, pp. 32–33.

Figure 4-5

Gen Re's Risk-Adjusted Margin (RaM)

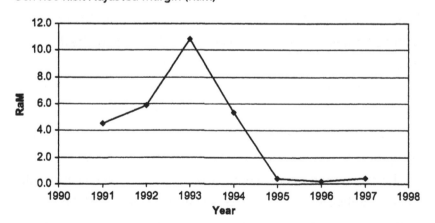

Created from the data contained in column (8) of Table 4-5.

levels of overconfidence that sometimes accompany the use of models in general: for example, in the use of "portfolio insurance" in 1987, in the collapse of the hedge fund Long-Term Capital Management in 1997–1998, and recently during the subprime/credit contagion of 2007–2008. Additionally, and as I explain in this book, the best way to manage risk is through the circle of competence, margin of safety, and conservative valuation. To the extent that measures like risk-adjusted performance and RaM contribute to conservative valuation, they should be used, but they should be used only in a support capacity, as statistics are *not* a substitute for a properly formulated valuation.

4. Cognitive Biases

Bruner's fourth factor, identifying and analyzing cognitive biases such as overconfidence, can be extremely difficult to accomplish in practice.[47] To help demonstrate cognitive bias in M&A, Bruner constructed a table that listed (1) CEOs' words about their respective deals at announcement, (2) the financial loss incurred in the deals, and (3) CEOs' words when the M&A failure had been acknowledged (denoted "at the end"). I prepared a similar table in Table 4-6 for the Gen Re acquisition without reference to the financial loss (which is illustrated in Figure 4-3).

In addition, the 1998 Gen Re acquisition followed the very successful 1995 GEICO acquisition, which occurred at a premium of 25.6% over GEICO's stock price at the time. Subsequent events with GEICO dramatically demonstrated the value that could be created in an insurance franchise–based acquisition,[48] which probably served to support the logic of and increase confidence in the Gen Re deal. In short, it could be argued that without GEICO and its monumental success,

Table 4-6

Warren Buffett's Comments on the Gen Re Acquisition

At the Announcement (1998)	At the End (2007)
"But the main attraction of the merger is synergy,* a word that heretofore has never been used in listing the reasons for a Berkshire acquisition. In this transaction, however, there are at least four areas of powerful synergy, which . . . justify the premium price that Berkshire is paying.	"For decades, General Re was the Tiffany of reinsurers, admired by all for its underwriting skills and discipline. This reputation, unfortunately, outlived its factual underpinnings, a flaw that I completely missed when I made the decision in 1998 to merge with General Re. The General Re of 1998 was not operated as the General Re of 1968 or 1978."
"First, this transaction removes constraints on earnings volatility that have caused General Re, in the past, to decline certain attractive business and, in other cases, to lay off substantial amounts of the business that it does write. Because of both its status as a public company and its desire to maintain its AAA credit rating, General Re has, understandably, been unable to operate in a manner that could produce large swings in reported earnings. As part of Berkshire, this constraint will disappear, which will enhance both General Re's long-term profitability and its ability to write more business. . . .	
"Second, General Re has substantial opportunities to develop its global reinsurance franchise. As part of Berkshire, General Re will be able to make investments to grow its international business as quickly as it sees fit.	
"Additionally, General Re will gain tax flexibility as a result of the merger. . . .	
"Finally, Berkshire's insurance subsidiaries *never* need to worry about having abundant capital. . . .	
"These synergies will be coupled with General Re's pristine worldwide reputation, long-standing client relationships and powerful underwriting, risk management and distribution capabilities. This combination virtually assures both Berkshire and General Re shareholders that they will have a better future than if the two companies operated separately."	
Source: www.berkshirehathaway.com/news/jun 998.html.	*Source:* www.berkshirehathaway.com/letters/2007ltr.pdf.

* Note that synergy has been identified as one of the seven strategies that seem to consistently generate strategic failures. This does not mean that synergy-based strategies never create value; only that such strategies frequently fail to do so. For more information see Paul Carroll and Chunka Mui, *Billion Dollar Lessons: What You Can Learn from the Most Inexcusable Business Failures of the Last 25 Years* (New York: Portfolio, 2008).

the Gen Re acquisition would not have occurred, or if it had occurred, the price would have been far lower than approximately $22 billion.

5. Adverse Management Choices

In the Gen Re acquisition, perhaps the most significant of Bruner's risk factors was adverse management choices. As Gen Re's performance deteriorated, Buffett appropriately replaced the Gen Re CEO, Ronald Ferguson. Clearly, given the results illustrated in Figure 4-3, a management change was warranted. However, Buffett replaced Ferguson with Gen Re's then CFO, Joseph Brandon, who had worked closely with Ferguson and who was widely considered to be Ferguson's heir apparent. Additionally, Ferguson was retained by Gen Re as a consultant after his dismissal as CEO. These management decisions generated an incredible series of unintended consequences.

In 2000, Ferguson, in his capacity as a consultant with Gen Re, facilitated a $500 million "finite risk" reinsurance deal with insurer AIG that went incredibly wrong. Finite risk is an inherently complex reinsurance product. I defined this product earlier, and I present a more detailed definition here:

> While this custom-tailored contract [finite risk] can take many forms, it commonly involves a limited period and a very large premium. An insurer, such as reinsurer General Re, writes a finite policy for a corporate client or another insurance company that covers potential claims up to a set limit. Over a given period, such as three years, the client pays premiums that altogether come close to the maximum coverage. If there has been no claim by the end of this period, the insurer returns all or most of the premium to the client.

The insurer receives a fee and, since the premiums are so large, does not risk severe loss. By paying such large premiums, the client effectively bears nearly all the cost of a catastrophic event by itself. But by spreading the premiums over several years, the client avoids taking the hit all at once. Hence, finite insurance can be used to smooth out the client's financial results.[49]

As financial history has shown time and again, financial products designed to manage financial results must be treated with extreme care. With respect to the Gen Re–AIG finite risk contract, government investigators alleged that its motivation was to artificially inflate AIG's reserves by $500 million to satisfy financial analysts' concerns about a possible reserve shortfall of that amount. They also alleged that the Gen Re–AIG finite contract did not involve risk transfer; in short, it was a loan, but it was accounted for as reinsurance and therefore constituted fraud.[50]

Criminal charges were brought against Ferguson, as well as against Gen Re's former CFO (Elizabeth Monrad) and former associate general counsel and AIG's former reinsurance chief. After a lengthy trial, all of the defendants were found guilty of the charges brought against them.[51] Shortly after the verdict, Gen Re CEO Brandon resigned. According to a newspaper account of the resignation, "Federal prosecutors have been pressing Berkshire to replace Mr. Brandon following fraud convictions of four former General Re executives earlier this year. . . . His removal was seen as part of an effort to conclude the government's investigation into General Re."[52] While Brandon was not charged criminally, he was the recipient of a "Wells notice" (which is a letter from the SEC to those it is planning to bring an enforcement action against) and thus was considered a likely target of future legal action.[53]

Needless to say, all the legal activity arising out of this finite risk contract generated legal fees, which were probably substantial and which may not be reflected in the financial loss data presented in Figure 4-3. If they are not, the total financial loss from this acquisition would have to be increased by those costs. It would also have to be increased by the value of the time spent on this matter at the expense of other, potentially more value-creating matters (economists refer to this value as "opportunity cost"). This cost is also likely to be substantial, especially with respect to Warren Buffett's time. All because a former CEO (Ferguson) and CFO (Brandon) were not terminated when they arguably should have been, following substantial postacquisition performance issues.

6. Operational Team Flaws

The final factor in Bruner's framework pertains to operational team flaws, of which culture is arguably the most significant. Berkshire Hathaway's superb results over time accurately reflect its performance-driven culture. The results that Gen Re produced after its acquisition (see Figure 4-3) do not reflect a performance-driven culture and seem symptomatic of operational team problems.

One way to assess operational team–related risk is by comparing a target's operational structure with the acquirer's. An approach for accomplishing this is presented in Table 4-7.

This approach to operational team assessment starts with a vigorous analysis that is summarized in a narrative that thoughtfully considers each element. As a final step, each cell in Table 4-7 could contain either a numerical rating (such as, for example, 1 for low risk to 5 for unacceptably high risk) or a short summary of the risk assessment findings (high risk, moderate risk, or low risk). Either approach can

Table 4-7

Operational Team Assessment*

Dimension	People	Process	Technology	Measures
Executive management				
Customer services				
Internal operations				
Knowledge management				

* This framework is based on the popular Balanced Scorecard concept. For more information, see Robert Kaplan and David Norton, *The Execution Premium: Linking Strategy to Operations for Competitive Advantage* (Boston: HBS Press, 2008), and Robert Kaplan and David Norton, *Alignment: Using the Balanced Scorecard to Create Corporate Synergies* (Boston: HBS Press, 2006).

work so long as the risk assessment process is a vigorous one that produces a narrative that thoughtfully considers each element.

For example, consider the application of this approach to the "executive management" dimension of a target. Such an assessment could involve the following:

- *People.* Formally profiling each of the target's key executives to assess personality fit
- *Process.* Evaluating the processes through which the executives implement their strategy
- *Technology.* Assessing the technology used to generate executive information (and determining whether that technology is compatible with the acquirer's)
- *Measures.* Determining whether executive-level performance and risk measures are appropriate, and whether they reconcile with the acquirer's

Such analysis provides a reasonable diagnostic with which to assess operational team–related risk, as long as it includes both a well-researched narrative and a numerical score or word summary to highlight areas in need of targeted senior managerial attention during the integration process.

Avoiding Future M&A Disasters

Used prospectively as a risk assessment tool, Bruner's real disaster–based framework seemingly identified four outright risks in this acquisition, and another two potential risks:

- *Factor 1 (risk)*. The Gen Re deal involved a *complex* business (reinsurance) and a complex valuation.
- *Factor 2 (risk)*. The deal was *tightly coupled* in that it had a relatively high price/book ratio that was seemingly based on several less-than-conservative valuation assumptions.
- *Factor 3 (risk)*. The *business environment was unusual* given the new economy boom and Gen Re's drastically reduced risk-adjusted margin.
- *Factor 4 (risk)*. The Gen Re acquisition seemed to involve *cognitive bias* (see, for example, the first column in Table 4-6).
- *Factor 5 (potential risk)*. There does not seem to have been a formal process in place for addressing *adverse management choices*.
- *Factor 6 (potential risk)*. There seemed to be significant *operational team–related risk* with this acquisition.

These factors help to explain how a skilled acquirer like Warren Buffett could suffer loss as a result of M&A risk. Frankly, if Warren Buffett could suffer this kind of loss, anyone can; therefore, using frameworks like this one prospectively, as a risk assessment tool, could prove beneficial. For example, corporate leaders could treat each of Bruner's risk factors as a question (or series of questions) to be addressed prior to going to contract. Consider the example presented in Table 4-8.

This table shows one practical way of applying Bruner's framework to assess M&A risk.[54] However, it must be remembered that the predominant way to control risk in a Graham and Dodd context is through the margin of safety as applied through a well-defined circle of competence and conservative valuation. Risk-specific frameworks like the one presented in this appendix are meant to augment margin

Table 4-8

M&A Risk Assessment

	Risk Factor	Risk Inquiry
1.	Complexity	• Is either the target's business or the deal itself complicated (broadly defined)?
		• If so, what steps are being taken to mitigate the complexity?
2.	Tight coupling	• Is a premium being paid for the target?
		• If so, have the assumptions supporting that premium been validated to the extent possible?
		• Was the valuation prepared conservatively or somewhat aggressively?
		• If aggressively, why?
3.	Business not as usual	• Is the business or its environment unusual in some way?
		• If so, what mechanism is being used to control (or mitigate) the effects of those events?
4.	Cognitive biases	• Are deal-specific risk management devices (such as earn-outs, collars, etc.*) being used?
		• Have contingency plans been established to deal with unexpected developments that may arise postacquisition?
5.	Adverse management choices	• What are the processes to identify and address in a timely manner deal and postdeal issues that may arise?
6.	Operational team flaws	• How is operational team–related risk assessed and managed?

* See Robert Bruner, *Deals from Hell: M & A Lessons That Rise above the Ashes* (Hoboken, N.J.: Wiley, 2005), p. 34, for further information.

of safety–based analysis, not replace it. Furthermore, the use of statistical models (such as risk-adjusted performance measures like RaM) should be used sparingly and only as circumstances warrant to illuminate a valuation and to test the strength of its margin of safety. In short, statistics can serve as a useful method of analysis to augment fundamental analysis; they are *not* a substitute for such analysis.

MARGIN AND PRACTICAL RISK ADJUSTMENT

In my Gen Re valuation, I used the return on net asset value (RNAV) measure, which was calculated as earnings/net asset value. That measure is analogous to the popular return on equity (ROE) measure, which is calculated as net income/ equity. The popular DuPont method decomposes ROE into its component parts in a variety of ways, the simplest of which is presented here:

$$ROE = \text{margin} \times \text{turnover} \times \text{debt-to-equity} \qquad (4.3a)$$

or

$$ROE = (\text{net income/Revenue}) \times (\text{revenue/assets})$$
$$\times (\text{assets/equity}) \qquad (4.3b)$$

Evaluating performance can be incredibly complicated in practice;[55] therefore, to simplify matters, I try to link performance and risk assessment within the context of a valuation whenever I can. In this case, given the historic strength of Gen Re's ROE over time (see, for example, Figure 4-1), I decided to evaluate a key ROE driver—margin—on a

(Continued)

risk-adjusted basis to assess the strength of the ROE. The declining RaM (see Figure 4-5) reflects both a falling margin and increased volatility over the calculated volatility horizon used in the calculation, which meant that Gen Re's historically impressive ROE and any valuation based on that performance were at risk. The choice of risk-adjusted margin in this case therefore facilitated an internally consistent analysis within the context of the valuation, and it augmented the valuation. However, and as noted earlier, while statistics can at times be a useful supplement to fundamental analysis, they are *not* a substitute for fundamental analysis, no matter how rigorous they may appear to be.

Chapter | 5

MACROANALYSIS, OPPORTUNITY SCREENING, AND VALUE INVESTING

Buy during periods of pessimism and low prices; sell during periods of optimism and high prices.

—Benjamin Graham[1]

Abnormally good or abnormally bad conditions do not last forever. This is true not only of general business but of particular industries as well. Corrective forces are often set in motion which tend to restore profits where they have disappeared, or to reduce them where they are excessive in relation to capital.

—Benjamin Graham and David Dodd[2]

This chapter contains material that was previously published in the *Quarterly Journal of Austrian Economics,* which is reprinted with the editor's permission.

INTRODUCTION

Benjamin Graham popularized his cigar butt–style investment approach after the bust of the "new era" boom, which occurred during the "roaring 1920s." Despite this historical linkage with a significant macroeconomic event, modern value investing is usually approached from a market-neutral perspective; in other words, each value investment stands on its own, irrespective of market conditions, aside from some general rules (such as the one represented by the first quote that introduces this chapter). A specialty discipline has arisen that focuses on identifying investment opportunities from macroeconomic events: macroinvesting.

As the Graham and Dodd approach is a bottom-up investment approach, there has not been a great deal of convergence between value investing and macroinvesting. Nevertheless, I believe there is a great deal that practitioners of each approach can learn from the other; for example, it could be easier to "buy during periods of pessimism and low prices" if you understand the macroeconomic reasons behind the pessimism. Additionally, macro-based insights could also be used in a Graham and Dodd context to screen for potential investment opportunities.

Nonetheless, it is important to point out that I am *not* advocating that value investors become quasi macroinvestors; I am well aware of Benjamin Graham's feelings on macroinvesting.[3] However, I note that even he used macroanalysis from time to time, such as in a 1960 article for the *California Management Review*.[4] My objective in this chapter is to show how macro-based insights can be used in a modern Graham and Dodd context, most especially with respect to investment opportunity screening.*

---

* The Conclusion addresses the subject of the investment opportunity screening process.

A first step in macro-based analysis is adopting a theory of market behavior to work with. Modern financial theory holds that markets are *efficient,* which means that market prices reflect publicly available information instantaneously. There are three forms of market efficiency:

- *Weak-form efficiency,* in which market prices reflect "the information contained in the record of past prices"
- *Semi-strong-form efficiency,* in which market prices reflect "not just past prices but all other published information, such as you might get from reading the financial press"
- *Strong-form efficiency,* where market prices reflect "all the information that can be acquired by painstaking analysis of [a] company and the economy"[5]

In strong-form market efficiency, which is the most academically popular of the three forms, it is not possible to earn a return greater than the general market return over time. According to a popular finance textbook, the academic evidence in support of strong-form efficiency "has proved to be sufficiently convincing that many professionally managed funds have given up the pursuit of superior performance. They simply, 'buy the index.'"[6]

Graham and Dodd practitioners strenuously disagree with financial economists on this theory. For example, Warren Buffett noted in the 1988 Berkshire Hathaway Annual Report that the investing track record that he, Benjamin Graham, and other value investors had achieved is proof that the market is not always efficient. He went on to say:

The disservice done students and gullible investment professionals who have swallowed EMT [efficient market theory] has been an extraordinary service to us and other followers of [value investing founder Benjamin] Graham. In any sort of a contest—financial, mental, or physical—it's an enormous advantage to have opponents who have been taught that it's useless to even try. From a selfish point of view, Grahamites should probably endow chairs to ensure the perpetual teaching of EMT.[7]

Other investors have also taken exception to EMT. For example, consider noted macroinvestor George Soros's following comments:

The [efficient market] theory is manifestly false—I have disproved it by consistently outperforming the averages over a period of twelve years. Institutions may be well advised to invest in index funds rather than making specific investment decisions, but the reason is to be found in their substandard performance, not in the impossibility of outperforming averages.[8]

Soros goes beyond merely criticizing the EMT by propounding a market theory of his own, which he calls *reflexivity*. The theory of reflexivity holds that market pricing is not a one-way phenomenon: it does not just proceed from information to market price. Rather, it proceeds via an interactive, two-way feedback loop between information and market pricing.[9] In Soros's theory, market behavior is not limited to strictly discounting fundamental information; it is also value determinative, meaning that the investment decisions of market participants influence firms' fundamental decisions (sales, purchases, capital, and so on), and as a result their future performance. The reflexive influence in shaping the fundamentals distorts the valuation process because the process seeks to value, in part, the performance of the very people who are doing the valuing.

Interactive feedback ensures that market behavior relatively reflects the fundamentals, and vice versa, as the future unfolds. However, there are times when the reflexive feedback loop can close, thereby widening a gap between market pricing and the fundamentals. If such a situation is allowed to continue, it will exacerbate boom-bust behavior, thereby generating large price discrepancies,[10] which are of particular interest to most investors in general and to Graham and Dodd practitioners in particular.[11]

BUSINESS/BOOM-BUST CYCLES

George Soros observed business/boom-bust cycle market behavior to such an extent during his long and successful investment career that he formulated a graphical model of it, which is reproduced in Figure 5-1.

Figure 5-1

Soros's Boom-Bust Model

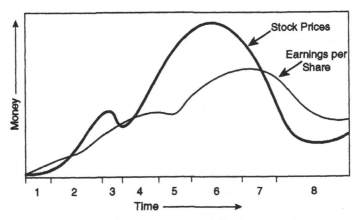

Source: George Soros, *The Crisis of Global Capitalism* (NY: PublicAffairs, 1998), p. 52.

That figure illustrates a typical boom-bust cycle through the use of two variables: earnings per share (EPS), which represent the fundamentals, and stock prices, which represent market behavior. The boom wave of a business cycle is characterized by an explosive price uptrend *and* dramatic price/earnings expansion, and the subsequent bust wave is characterized by a powerful price downtrend *and* price/earnings contraction.[12]

Soros describes the individual phases of a boom-bust cycle only generally.[13] He also does not specify the cause of boom-bust cycles, but he has commented that the business cycles that he speculates on "always [have] a political element."[14] Governmental economic intervention as the cause of business cycles has been written about extensively by the Austrian School of economics, which Roger Garrison cogently summarizes as follows:

> In the broadest terms the Austrian [business cycle] theory is a recognition that an extra-market force (the central bank) can initiate an artificial, or unsustainable, economic boom. The money-induced boom contains the seeds of its own undoing: the upturn must, by the logic of the market forces set in motion, be followed by a downturn [or bust].[15]

By synthesizing Soros's boom-bust model, Austrian business cycle theory (ABCT), and behavioral characteristics, I developed specific criteria, which are presented here, for each of the eight stages of a business cycle that are illustrated in Figure 5-1. I also comment on the nature and extent of postcycle recovery. Significant insight into business cycle behavior can be gained by using these criteria, as I will show in an analysis of the recent "new economy" boom and bust.

THE EIGHT STAGES OF A BUSINESS CYCLE

Stage 1 of a business cycle presents a classic political economic dilemma: the fundamentals (as illustrated in Soros's model by EPS) are much stronger than the market's valuation of them (as reflected by the stock price), and therefore it could be perceived that the market process is not performing optimally. Politicians can interpret this situation as a threat to their elected positions, and if so, they will strive to rectify it before it becomes a political issue at election time. A popular method of stimulating economic activity is expansion of the money supply.

ABCT postulates that central banks stimulate market behavior by expanding the money supply to lower interest rates below the market-determined (or natural) rate of interest. Artificially low interest rates lead to overconsumption and artificially low discount rate calculations, which in turn lead to artificially high valuations or *valuation inflation*, and *malinvestment* or investment along the wrong lines.[16]

During *Stage 2* of a business cycle, the powerful marginal buying and ever-strengthening fundamentals—driven predominantly by revenue growth—reflect favorably on the governmental intervention in the first stage. Stage 2 is characterized by powerful price appreciation, which has the obvious effect of pleasing both market participants and the politicians who claim credit for it.

In *Stage 3*, the market forms a short-term price top as the inevitable *correction* of the prior stage's powerful price appreciation occurs. A correction in this context means a temporary price reversal to a level that more closely reflects the fundamentals. The short-term price top made during this stage is a critically important graphical, or technical, benchmark to monitor throughout the business cycle, as I explain later.

Up to this point in the cycle, and despite expansionist monetary policies, market behavior has been fairly typical: arguably depressed prices had a run-up that ended in a correction. However, during *Stage 4*, market behavior begins to change. Given the apparently strong fundamentals generated from the expansion of the money supply—driven predominantly by revenue growth—the probability of the market price recovering from the Stage 3 correction is relatively strong. Therefore, intense focus is directed to that stage's short-term top; if market behavior pushes the market price above that top with significant momentum, it will signal to technically oriented traders that a powerful trend has begun, causing them to buy aggressively.[17]

Toward the middle of *Stage 5*, the fundamentals begin to weaken, and as a result the boom is in danger of not only ending, but also reversing. To prevent this from occurring, market participants can close the reflexive feedback loop.[18] Yale economist Robert Shiller describes this type of phenomenon as follows:

> The essence of a speculative bubble is a *sort of feedback*, from price increases, to increased investor enthusiasm, to increased demand, and hence further price increases. The high demand for the asset is generated by the public memory of high past returns, and the optimism those high returns generate for the future. The feedback can amplify positive forces affecting the market, making the market reach higher levels than it would if it were responding only directly to these positive forces.[19] (Emphasis added.)

The most common way in which the reflexive feedback loop is closed is through the widespread use of *fundamental substitutes*,[20] such as

- Performance measures that rely on creative accounting methods[21]
- The exaggerated use of alternative profit measures and pro forma statements at the expense of traditional balance sheet, earnings, and cash flow analysis
- The use of highly theoretical and/or overly complicated valuation techniques

Fundamental substitutes are used to justify and perpetuate a boom that is the result of a politically motivated expansion of the money supply that market participants misinterpret as the "wealth effect" of some new economic condition,[22] and that they understandably want to have continue.[23] Therefore, as fundamental data will no longer support the boom during this stage, market participants replace fundamental analysis with fundamental substitute analysis that will support the boom.[24] Significantly, the fundamental substitutes that are adopted are consistent with the perceived "new" economic condition driving the perceived wealth effect.[25]

The boom's powerful price appreciation resumes, which in turn stimulates further valuation inflation and malinvestment. Such stimulation quickly causes the actual fundamentals to recover—predominantly as a result of revenue growth—as the boom proceeds, but it does so in an environment in which the fundamentals and market behavior no longer reflect each other. This is vividly illustrated in Soros's technical model by the ever-widening price/earnings expansion; in other words, by the growing divergence between stock prices and EPS.[26] The duration of the boom is now limited because a market cannot continue indefinitely without fundamental feedback; the reflexive feedback loop must eventually reopen or the market will crash.

With the closure of the reflexive feedback loop, the momentum of marginal buying increases dramatically, which generates positive news reports that, in turn, generate even more buying,[27] a phenomenon that has been popularly referred to as *irrational exuberance.*[28] Irrespective of the popularity of former Fed Chairman Greenspan's coined term, irrational exuberance is not a new phenomenon. For example, in 1852, Charles Mackay wrote the following in the preface to that year's edition of his popular book, *Extraordinary Popular Delusions and the Madness of Crowds*:

> We find that whole communities suddenly fix their minds upon one object, and go mad in its pursuit; that millions of people become simultaneously impressed with one delusion, and run after it. . . . Money, again, has often been a cause of the delusion of multitudes. Sober nations have all at once become desperate gamblers, and risked almost their existence upon the turn of a piece of paper.[29]

Closing the reflexive feedback loop during this stage of a business cycle reignites the boom's momentum, and this significantly increases the value of every portfolio that is aligned with it. Momentum is a value multiplier that has made those who have exploited it extremely wealthy; therefore, the desire of market participants to exploit a boom's momentum for as long as possible is neither mad nor irrational. However, momentum is a short- to intermediate-term phenomenon because the valuation inflation and malinvestment that generate it cannot last forever. Unfortunately, market participants usually do not make this distinction during a boom because they have come to believe that the boom is the result of the wealth effect of some new economic condition that will last forever. That misconception results in a widespread failure of market participants to formulate investment exit strategies, which *is* irrational and ensures that deep portfolio losses will be incurred in the coming bust.

This temporal disconnect is a by-product of the money supply expansion that appears to generate wealth-producing economic growth when in fact it is politically leveraged growth, which has all of the short-term pluses and long-term minuses of debt.[30] I therefore refer to this phenomenon as the boom's *leverage effect,* and readily acknowledge that the momentum it generates over the short to intermediate term will yield abnormally high portfolio returns. However, as those returns are being realized, market participants would do well to keep the following *trader's riddle* in mind:

Question: What's the difference between bull markets and smart money managers?
Answer: Bull markets make money managers look smart; smart money managers know this.[31]

George Soros refers to the business cycle's next stage, *Stage 6*, as the "twilight period."[32] Given marketwide exuberance, as well as the sheer power and duration of the boom, the last remaining marginal investors finally buy in. Such buying powerfully fuels the market price to even greater heights, but this is the boom's final hurrah. As the added money fueling the boom makes its way through the economy, overconsumption causes prices to rise,[33] which the politicians who initiated the boom must deal with in order to divert a market crash. Such a response will most likely be the reversal of the interference that caused the boom, and "whenever the central bank reverses its monetary stance, a stock market bust is set in motion."[34] The rise in interest rates slows the pace of consumption and increases discount rates, which causes valuations to decline, thus halting further malinvestment. And with no new buying and malinvestment to fuel further price appreciation, the market hits an *inflection point* and starts to decline. An inflection point is a technical change in trend from boom to bust that occurs as a result of the reversal of the market intervention that caused the boom.[35]

In *Stage 7*, the actual fundamentals begin to decline as a result of the lack of buying, which in conjunction with the rising interest rates causes the fundamental substitutes to deteriorate, which in turn generates increasingly intensive investment liquidation and marginal short selling. This market behavior feeds off itself, thus perpetuating a *bust*, or the dynamic reversal of a boom. As the bust proceeds, its market behavior generates an *irrational despondency*, which results in mass selling. Just as the euphoria of a boom exacerbates investors' preference for making abnormally large returns, a bust exacerbates the despondency of suffering deep portfolio losses.

Spurred on by the gloom of growing portfolio losses, investors undertake a so-called flight to quality that involves liquidating perceived risky investments in favor of government securities or precious metals to preserve the balance of their portfolios. This type of behavior will preserve what is left of their portfolios; however, fundamentally sound investments are often liquidated along with unprofitable ones, thus creating a price discrepancy, or *value gap*,[36] that astute investors in general, and Graham and Dodd practitioners in particular, can profit from.

The undeniable emergence of value gaps, and the equally undeniable results of those who exploit them, reflects the fact that they can be a source of substantial profit. Therefore, as excessive selling creates value gaps, the opportunity costs of engaging in such selling are substantial.[37] Unfortunately, this distinction is usually not made during a bust, which is the primary reason why the despondency of market participants during this stage is irrational. Such market behavior will eventually take the market price below the significant short-term price top formed in Stage 3, thus giving the business cycle its distinctive and unmistakable *bubble* shape. For the sake of clarification, a bubble is the shape that a market takes over the course of its boom-bust cycle; as such, a market bubble does not "pop" during a bust.

During *Stage 8*, the market is in a full-blown *reversal* as both market prices and the fundamentals decline below prebubble levels. The complete market reversal comes as a shock to most market participants, and that shock can in time reopen the reflexive feedback loop. Once the loop reopens, malinvestment liquidation begins in earnest, thus enabling the market to recover from the business cycle's volatility.[38]

RECOVERY

In general, before recovery from a business cycle can be achieved, all malinvestment must be purged from the economy. That purging will once again reconcile the fundamentals (revenues, costs, capital, and so forth) with market behavior (buying and selling), thus creating an environment that is conducive to economic growth. Unfortunately, this process usually entails delinquencies, defaults, bankruptcies, layoffs, and the inevitable scandal or two as the market recovers from all the malinvestment of the boom. Recovering from these effects, and from the pervasive scope of malinvestment liquidation, generally will not occur quickly.[39]

Given the turmoil inherent in business cycle recoveries, politicians are understandably anxious to conclude them quickly. However, efforts other than tax cuts and budgetary discipline to jump-start a recovery only exacerbate the turmoil. Markets need time to recover from the intervention that causes business cycles, not further interference; in fact, further interference in the market process is not only counterproductive but also dangerous to long-term economic vitality.[40]

In the following section, I apply the framework just presented to the recent "new economy" boom and bust.

THE "NEW ECONOMY" BUSINESS CYCLE

The "new economy" was unique in the sense that many new economy firms had weak fundamentals, meaning that they were not profitable. This could be a reason why I found EPS data for the Nasdaq index difficult to obtain at the time this chapter was initially written. In order to create a graphical comparison of the new economy boom and bust with Soros's model, I needed a reasonable proxy for EPS, which had to both be a reasonable barometer of value and trend consistently with the Nasdaq, as the new economy business cycle will be illustrated, in part, by the divergence between the Nasdaq and the proxy. The proxy chosen was the market value of blue chip stocks as reflected in the Dow Jones Industrial Average (DJIA).* A chart of the Nasdaq overlaid with the DJIA from 1991 to 2002 is presented in Figure 5-2.

The bottom panel of that chart contains a 12-period momentum measurement, which is a common technical indicator.[41] The use of

---

* The reasons for using the DJIA are discussed in appendix 2 to this chapter.

Figure 5-2

The New Economy Business Cycle, 1991 to 2002

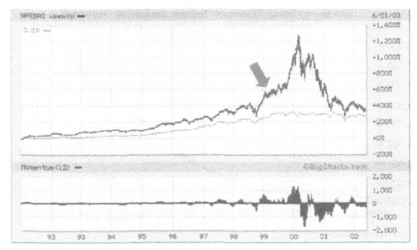

Source: BigCharts.com.

this indicator will be secondary to the analysis that follows, and will be used only to amplify it.

Stage 1 began, according to Bob Woodward's biography of Alan Greenspan, in early 1994, when Greenspan's Fed adopted the *soft landing doctrine*, which involved making a preemptive monetary policy strike against expected price inflation.[42] The rationale behind the policy was to "take the top off the coming boom, moderate and stabilize the economy and prevent inflation—and recession." Woodward reported that this was accomplished with President Bill Clinton's blessing after Greenspan predicted economic problems in 1996, a presidential election year.[43] Therefore, between early 1994 and mid-1995, the fed funds rate was increased by nearly 100%.[44]

As can be seen in Figure 5-2, Nasdaq market behavior during that period of time was essentially flat. But as Figure 5-3 illustrates, the Fed

Figure 5-3

M3 Growth, 1990 to 2003

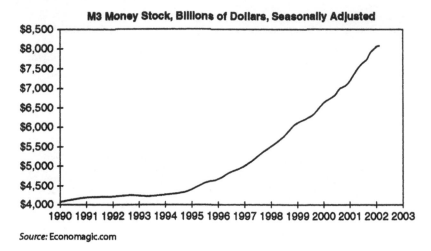

Source: Economagic.com

reversed its monetary policy in late 1995 by dramatically expanding the money supply to decrease interest rates. Shortly thereafter, consumer spending began to increase significantly through a new distribution channel, the Internet. For example, the purchase of collectibles from eBay.com, books from Amazon.com, and travel accommodations and other such things from Priceline.com would soon become all the rage. The boom that came to be known as the new economy had begun.

Powerful price appreciation followed the Fed's credit expansion, which pleased both politicians and market participants on Wall Street. For example, on August 9, 1995, Netscape, a firm that manufactured and *gave away* Web browsers, which were used to navigate the then-nascent Internet, issued stock through an initial public offering (IPO). The market behavior of that IPO drove the price of the then-budding

Web browser manufacturer up from $28 per share to $75 per share before closing at $58¹/4 per share. Entrepreneurs took note and started forming a variety of technology or *dot-com* firms, which were willingly funded by venture capitalists and capital market participants. According to Woodward's biography, "Greenspan knew he had helped hand Clinton what he called 'a pro-incumbent type economy'"[45]— Stage 2.

In Stage 3, which occurred in mid-1998, the market formed a significant short-term price top, which is identified in Figure 5-2 by the down arrow. This top was significant for the following reasons:

- It occurred around the psychologically significant price level of 2,000.[46]
- The upswing preceding the top occurred on low momentum, which suggested that it was not sustainable.
- The correction or downswing immediately following the top occurred on strong momentum, which suggested that it was sustainable.
- The correction significantly narrowed the spread between the Nasdaq and the DJIA.
- The correction retraced more than 25% of the Nasdaq (the short-term top occurred at slightly higher than 2,000, while the correction took the market down to slightly less than 1,500), and was therefore technically significant.

The fundamentals at this time were perceived to be quite strong even though many dot-com firms did not have earnings. That misconception was based on strong revenue growth in the supposed new economy.[47] Therefore, the market's powerful price appreciation resumed after the correction bottomed out in late 1998, and its record high momentum at the time carried the Nasdaq strongly above the prior stage's short-term price top. Technically oriented traders took note and started buying aggressively: Stage 4.

While the fundamentals did not weaken during this time as the technical model suggests (recall the general lack of earnings for new economy firms), it can be estimated that the market's entry into Stage 5 occurred in mid-1999 for the following reasons:

● During that period of time, the divergence between the Nasdaq and the DJIA started to grow historically large.

● It is the time period just prior to the Nasdaq's final, most powerful run.

● It is about the time that two popular fundamental substitutes emerged: *eyeballs* and *real option* valuation.

Eyeballs is a term that was used to describe the number of times that an Internet Web site was "hit" or visited by an individual Internet user. In eyeball valuation, each of these hits was assigned a monetary value, the sum of which purported to be the value of the new economy firm. This technique is analogous to assigning a monetary value to every window-shopper at a traditional brick-and-mortar store, and then using the sum of those values to determine the store's value. As silly as it no doubt sounds now, this approach was relatively well received at the time.

The second fundamental substitute was *real options valuation*. Options are equity derivatives that are used predominantly for risk management and compensation. In the early 1970s, Professor Stewart Myers of MIT developed real options theory, or options on real assets, as a capital budgeting tool, and it has proved useful as such.[48] Indeed, both traditional options pricing and real options pricing can be valuable financial tools (when they are used properly). However, by comparing a direct investment, instead of a derivative investment, in a going concern with the purchase of a call option and using real options theory to justify that investment, market participants abused real options theory.

Options are by definition a *wasting asset*, for if they are not *in the money* by maturity, they are worthless. This is significant to all investors inasmuch as option speculation can be an extremely risky endeavor: time erosion and the lack of intrinsic value generally make option speculating unprofitable for all but the most skilled investors. But more importantly, firms are supposed to be going concerns and thus have no maturity. Also, real options theory was never intended to replace, nor is it capable of replacing, fundamental equity valuation such as Graham and Dodd–based valuation.

Arguments in favor of using real options theory in the valuation of dot-com firms centered on the volatility and flexibility of certain intangible value drivers such as technological patents, different business models, and other such factors.[49] However, similar arguments have been made and addressed in prior business cycles, for example:

> The "new era" doctrine—that "good" stocks (or "blue chips") were sound investments regardless of how high the price paid for them—was at bottom only a means of rationalizing under the title of "investment" the well nigh universal capitulation to the gambling fever. We suggest that this psychological phenomenon is closely related to the dominant importance assumed in recent years by intangible factors of value, *viz.*,

goodwill, management, expected earning power, etc. Such value factors, while undoubtedly real, are not susceptible to mathematical calculation; hence the standards by which they are measured are to a great extent arbitrary and can suffer the widest variations in accordance with the prevalent psychology. The investing class was the more easily led to ascribe reality to purely speculative valuations of these intangibles because it was dealing in good part with surplus wealth, to which it was not impelled by force of necessity to apply the old established acid test that the principal value be justified by the income.[50]

This was written by Benjamin Graham and David Dodd in 1934 in the first edition of their seminal work, *Security Analysis*, about the market behavior exhibited during the boom of the 1920s. And yet, if you substitute "new economy" for "new era" and "tech stocks" for "blue chips," you have a remarkably similar description of the market behavior exhibited during the new economy boom of the 1990s. Interestingly, the key fundamental substitute of the new era boom was the projected trend of earnings, which can be a valid and useful methodology when used properly. However, as the 1920s progressed, market participants abused that theory to justify and perpetuate the new era boom,[51] which is analogous to the abuse of real options theory during the new economy boom of the 1990s; the focus of both methods was expected future earnings rather than present sustainable earnings.[52]

Thus, the new economy boom adopted two significant fundamental substitutes. The first, eyeballs, was somewhat silly, but the second, real options, was a valid theory that was simply abused. The new economy also embraced pro forma–based performance measures and, as everyone now knows, some accounting chicanery, all of which carried the boom substantially higher. The following quote from a *Knowledge@Wharton* article describes the market behavior at the time: "As more and more IPOs came to market, a steady valuation inflation took hold as each new IPO was valued by the most recent. 'The second wave was valued off the first wave and it fed off itself,' he [Chris Hastings of Bear Stearns & Co.] added."[53] This quote closely tracks with Professor Shiller's earlier quote and is indicative of Stage 5 behavior. Nevertheless, not all market participants were "irrationally exuberant" at this point in time. Specifically, one very distinguished investment mind saw problems with the new economy, and he carefully outlined his reasons why in a popular business magazine.

In November of 1999, Warren Buffett wrote an article in *Fortune* magazine that stated in part, "The inescapable fact is that the value of an asset, whatever its character, cannot over the long-term grow faster than its earnings do."[54] In other words, growth creates value if, and only if, a firm earns more than its cost of capital over time.[55] However, market participants in general considered neither the article nor, incredibly, even the man who wrote it. A metaphor of the market's reaction at the time was a *Money* magazine article published roughly two months after Buffett's article. It was titled "Buffett Hits a Bumpy Road," and had the following subtitle: "The Technophobe Sees His Stock Tumble."[56] Thus, not even the most successful and influential investor of modern times could temper the new economy boom, the power of which was nothing short of incredible.

As Figure 5-2 illustrates, the divergence between the Nasdaq and the DJIA grew to be inordinately large. Additionally, the market's momentum reading was consistently positive, reflecting powerful marginal buying, from late 1998 to early 2000. Given the momentum fueling this boom, it was only a matter of time before prices started to rise, which the Fed would be forced to respond to in order to avert a market crash. And as Figure 5-4 illustrates, that is exactly what occurred in mid-1999. The Fed identified price inflation and promptly reversed its monetary policy by increasing the fed funds rate:[57] Stage 6.

Predictably, the credit tightening slowed the pace of buying and malinvestment; therefore, an inflection point was imminent, and it occurred in March 2000 after the Nasdaq surpassed the astonishing price threshold of 5,000. The record high momentum at the time (see the bottom panel of Figure 5-2) confirms that this market behavior was indeed an *inflection*, or the market's final, most powerful price run. The boom was over, just as ABCT indicated it would be, but not very many market participants thought so at the time.

Figure 5-4

Fed Tightening and Subsequent Easing, 1999 to 2001

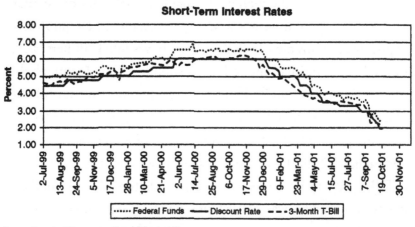

Source: Board of Governors, Federal Reserve System.

Stages 7 and 8 of the new economy bust were as amazing as the boom had been. The stunning bankruptcy of former energy trading giant Enron will possibly become the metaphor for the entire cycle, as Enron was one of the darlings, if not *the* darling, of the new economy. A supposedly unique business model turned a sedentary energy company into a stock market powerhouse. At its peak, Enron stock was selling for more than $80 per share against revenues of more than $100 billion, making it the seventh largest company in the world.[58] But shortly after the Nasdaq hit an inflection point, Enron hit one as well. After suffering substantial losses from several malinvestments, Enron could no longer conceal the fraudulent accounting practices and off-balance-sheet debt that had funded it for so long.[59] Enron's bankruptcy was the largest in the history of the United States at the time. Less than one year after hitting its peak, Enron stock was trading for less than $1 per share, and the crisis threatened to plunge the firm's auditor, Arthur Andersen, into bankruptcy as well.

Andersen consultants allegedly had helped to set up Enron's fraudulent special-purpose entities while Andersen auditors allegedly looked the other way. To make matters worse, Andersen employees later shredded documents after receiving government subpoenas. While Andersen's defense team attempted to shift the blame for this activity solely onto the shoulders of the Andersen partner responsible for the Enron account, David Duncan, it was doubtful that this strategy would be successful. Given the magnitude of the Enron collapse, as well as Andersen's past auditing indiscretions at Sunbeam, Waste Management, and other firms, the risk of economic failure at Andersen was relatively high. That risk increased dramatically in March 2002 when the federal government indicted Andersen for obstruction of justice. In fact, after Andersen was convicted of that charge on

June 15, 2002, partners of the firm pointed to the indictment "as the death knell."[60] The charges against Andersen were unanimously over-turned by the U.S. Supreme Court in 2005; however, by that time the firm had ceased operating.

The subsequent bankruptcy announcement of another new econ-omy icon, Global Crossing, was then the fourth largest such filing in history. Compounding the market's reaction to that bankruptcy was the fact that Andersen was also the auditor for Global Crossing.[61] Thus, market participants sensed an impending accounting melt-down, which in turn generated an irrational despondency that fueled panic-driven selling and increasingly intensive short selling, charac-teristic of a bust. For example, Barry Hyman, the chief market strate-gist of Ehrenkrantz King Nussbaum, was quoted as saying, "The [stock] market is getting irrational in believing the whole accounting issue is in question."[62] Soon the irrational despondency spread to the bond market, as *Wall Street Journal* reporter Gregory Zuckerman noted in an article titled, "Ripples from Enron Accounting Woes Trig-gers Selloff in the Bond Market."[63]

As the fundamental substitutes of the new economy started crum-bling with the market price, market participants began taking a fresh look at traditional fundamental analysis and its most ardent supporter. For example, in November 2002, *Fortune* magazine ran a cover story that read, "The AMAZING Mr. Buffett: The World's Greatest Inves-tor Is Back on Top. Here's What He Thinks Now."[64] However, the new economy did not officially die until January 12, 2003,[65] the day Steve Case tendered his resignation as AOL's chairman of the board. Case had accomplished many things during his tenure as AOL's chairman, not the least of which was the acquisition of Netscape, whose IPO helped to usher in the new economy.

Figure 5-5

Outline of the New Economy Boom and Bust, 1991 to 2002

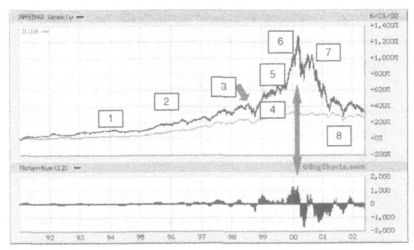

The down-arrow denotes the significant short-term price top made in Stage 3 of the business cycle. The double-sided arrow indicates that the new economy boom and bust occurred on high momentum, which is a typical business cycle characteristic.
Source: BigCharts.com.

To summarize my analysis of the new economy boom and bust, I present a chart denoting each of the eight stages of that business cycle in Figure 5-5.

NEW ECONOMY RECOVERY

As explained earlier, recovery from a business cycle is contingent upon the amount of time it takes the market to purge itself of malinvestments and once again reconcile the fundamentals (revenues, costs, capital, and so on) with market behavior (buying and selling). It was also explained that further interference in the market process would delay business cycle recovery, not jump-start it. In light of the foregoing, the following circumstances increased the risk of a protracted recovery from the new economy.

First, the level of postcycle market interference was substantial; for example, from the March 2000 Nasdaq inflection point, the money supply continued to expand dramatically (see Figure 5-3), while the fed funds rate had been reduced to incredibly low levels (see Figure 5-6).

Given such aggressive postcycle intervention, comprehensive malinvestment liquidation was at best going to be severely delayed, but at least it did occur. For example, as *Wall Street Journal* reporter Greg Ip observed:

> The combination of heavy debts, falling revenue, and skittish investors as well as the rapid obsolescence of yesterday's technology are producing a tide of bankruptcy filings. *Forty percent of the largest filings since 1980 have occurred since the beginning of 2001.* . . . And recovery rates—what lenders can expect to get back after companies are restructured or their assets sold—were an estimated 21 cents on the dollar last year.[66] (Emphasis added.)

Figure 5-6

Fed Funds Rate, December 2000 to December 2001

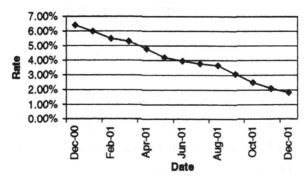

Data source: Board of Governors, Federal Reserve System.

However, at the time, corporate debt was closing in on *$30 trillion,* or roughly triple GDP,[67] and the price/earnings ratio of various stock indexes remained historically high, suggesting that the reflexive feedback loop either had not yet reopened or had not fully reopened.[68] To make matters worse, the U.S. government imposed a 30% tariff on steel, which it fortunately later rescinded, and punitive duties on Canadian softwood, thus provoking a trade war just as it was fighting a very hot war on terrorism.[69]

To ease economic pressures at the time, the Fed resumed expansion of the money supply, as illustrated in Figure 5-7.

Figure 5-7

M3 Growth, 1998 to 2006

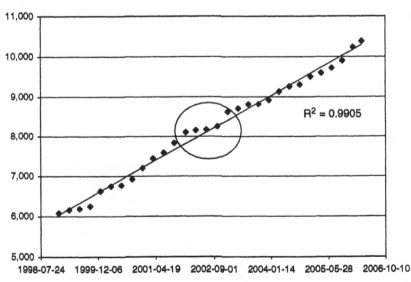

Units in billions. Data displayed are from December 28, 1998, to March 13, 2006, in three-month intervals. In March 2006, the U.S. Federal Reserve (Fed) stopped providing information on the M3 measure. According to a contemporary piece in *The Economist* ("Running on M3: Ignore Money at Your Peril," *The Economist,* March 25, 2006, p. 12): "The Fed claims that M3 does not convey any extra information about the economy that is not already embodied in the narrower M2 measure, so it is not worth the cost of collecting it. It is true that the two Ms move in step for much of the time, but there have been big divergences. During the late 1990s equity bubble, for example, M3 grew faster; over the past year, M3 has grown nearly twice as fast as M2. So it looks odd to claim that M3 does not tell us anything different. The Fed is really saying that it doesn't believe money matters."
Data source: Board of Governors, Federal Reserve System.

The circled data in that figure show that after a period of stabilization, the money supply—as measured by M3—once again started to expand. Such monetary activity is generally undertaken to purportedly ease the economic trauma of business cycle recoveries, as indicated earlier, which frequently result in economic downturns such as recessions (or depressions). Significantly, Austrian economists warn against both continued money supply expansion and increasing government expenditures to mitigate depressions; rather, they argue that if depressions are allowed to resolve on their own, the producers who make up the market will liquidate malinvestments and once again focus on satisfying consumer needs better or more efficiently.[70]

As Figure 5-8 illustrates, government expenditures as reflected by the U. S. national debt have increased tremendously since the new economy bust (as has growth in the money supply).

Figure 5-8

U.S. National Debt, September 1980 to September 2005

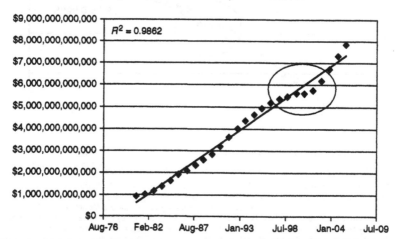

For the years 1980 to 1984, the data provided were rounded in millions. The data displayed are from September 1980 to September 2005.
Data source: Bureau of Public Debt.

Despite the powerful increase in both the money supply and the national debt, the price behavior of the Nasdaq index, which characterized the new economy business cycle, did not exhibit a resumption of boomlike buying, as shown in Figure 5-9.

The Nasdaq index bottomed out in 2002 at around the same time that growth in the money supply was flat (see the circled data in Figure 5-7) and growth in the national debt had stabilized (see the circled data in Figure 5-8). However, the new economy boom did not reignite; therefore, the question arises, what effect, if any, did the government intervention have on market behavior and pricing?

Figure 5-9

New Economy and Post New Economy NASDAQ, 1991 to 2006

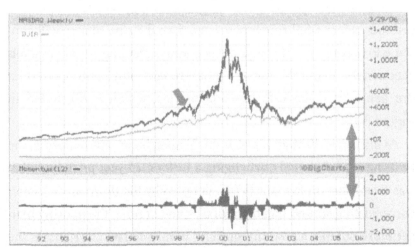

The double-sided arrow points to the fact that while the Nasdaq has diverged somewhat from the DJIA since the new economy bust, it has done so on relatively low momentum. This is significant because boom waves are frequently characterized by powerful momentum.
Source: BigCharts.com.

POST NEW ECONOMY BUSINESS CYCLE ACTIVITY

To recap, the macro-based analytical approach that I used in this chapter contained fundamental elements (reflexive market theory, Austrian business cycle theory, and Graham and Dodd insights), technical elements (Soros's boom-bust model and price chart analysis), and behavioral elements (herd behavior such as irrational exuberance). Traders have long integrated all three forms of analysis in some of their strategies,[71] but such an approach has generally not extended beyond trading. To demonstrate how this approach could be extended to investment,[72] I applied it in real time in April and May of 2006, and documented my findings.[73] The following section is based on those findings.

ABCT holds that when money is pumped into an economy, its effects are generally first felt in the capital markets.[74] If monetary tightening subsequently occurs, the effects of the monetary expansion will resolve after a period of recovery; however, if monetary expansion resumes before a full recovery occurs, then the easy money will continue to make its way through the economy, affecting certain markets accordingly. To put this into the post new economy context, consider the behavior of the U.S. housing market, which is illustrated in Figure 5-10.

As the figure illustrates, just as the Nasdaq boom was maturing, the housing market started challenging a historic 25-year price high that was established in the late 1970s (denoted by the down arrow). After consolidating around that high for a period of time, the housing market broke out into a powerful uptrend in mid- to late 2001, just as the Nasdaq index was retracing all of its gains. This was probably not a coincidence: after capital market–based investments such as those

Figure 5-10

Housing prices, 1970 to 2006

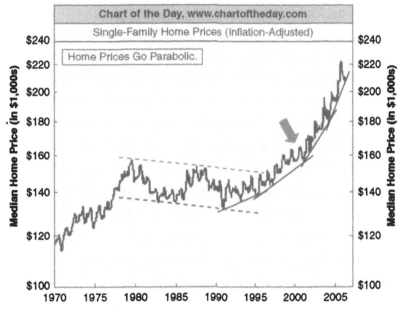

The down arrow denotes price consolidation around the historic high price level formed in the late 1970s. Such consolidation often precedes powerful price breakouts and trends.
Source: Chart of the Day.

reflected by, for example, the Nasdaq index, perhaps no other market is more sensitive to interest-rate manipulation than the real estate market.[75] Nevertheless, during much of the new economy boom, the real estate market in general was selling at relatively low levels. For example, and as noted value investor John Neff—the former manager of the highly successful Windsor Fund—stated in his autobiography:

> Historical [dividend] yield advantages become tougher to dupli-
> cate as bull markets gather steam. But even in steamy 1998 and
> 1999, opportunities did not vanish entirely. Investors comfortable

with real estate investment trusts (REITs) grabbed yields of about 7 percent—quite a striking margin over the 1.4 percent yield by the S&P 500.[76]

Earning a 7% yield while waiting for a value gap to close is an extremely appealing value investing option. Regarding the probability of REIT value gaps closing, as indicated earlier, real estate in general is one of the most interest-rate-sensitive forms of investment. Therefore, following the new economy bust, real estate had a reasonable probability of being affected by continued money supply expansion, as, all things being equal, lower interest rates equate to higher real estate values. Additionally, there is precedent for real estate booms following stock market booms; for example, Graham and Dodd themselves commented on the new era–related real estate boom that topped out in 1931 (or two years after the famous 1929 stock market crash).[77] And as Figure 5-10 illustrates, the real estate market in general started to accelerate following the resumption of the Fed's monetary expansion (see, for example, Figure 5-7). To put this market behavior into context, consider a comparison of the Dow Jones Wilshire Real Estate Securities Index with the DJIA in a format similar to the one that I used to analyze the new economy boom and bust, which is presented in Figure 5-11.

In less than two years, real estate prices as measured by the Dow Jones Wilshire Real Estate Securities Index substantially outpaced the DJIA. However, such price appreciation had "put home-ownership out of reach for more people than at any time in more than a decade."[78]

Additionally, the continued monetary expansion caused prices to begin to inflate. The correlation between the extent of money supply

Figure 5-11

Dow Jones Wilshire Real Estate Securities Index Compared to the DJIA, 2004 to 2006

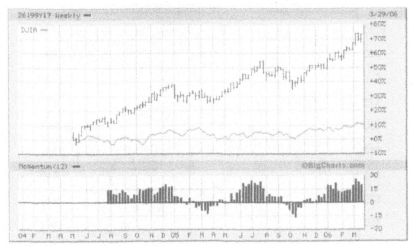

The number 26199Y17 in the upper left-hand corner is the symbol for the Dow Jones Wilshire Real Estate Securities Index. Data before 2004 are unfortunately not available.
Source: BigCharts.com.

expansion and the corresponding extent of price inflation is difficult to measure; however, as Austrian economist Murray Rothbard generally observed, "The larger the increase in money stock, the greater, *ceteris paribus*, will be its impact on prices."[79] The implications of this for overall prices given the nature and extent of the increase in the money supply at the time (see Figure 5-7) seemed significant. For example, consider the price of oil, shown in Figure 5-12, keeping in mind that these data are from 2006.

As the figure illustrates, the price of oil increased dramatically—to a 20-year high—subsequent to the 2001 new economy bust. To put this price run-up into context, compare the price of oil as given by the AMEX Oil Index (XOI) to the DJIA, as shown in Figure 5-13.

Figure 5-12

Oil Prices, 1970 to 2006

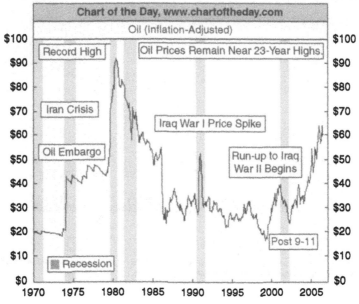

Source: Chart of the Day.

As the figure illustrates, the gap between the DJIA and the XOI that started to form in 1991 was closed by a high-momentum price uptrend. There were two significant aspects of this uptrend:

- It broke out after a relatively long period of consolidation, which is a technical indicator of trend sustainability.[80]
- The highest market price recorded by the XOI during the consolidation occurred in early to mid-2001, or the period of transition from the new economy to post new economy business-cycle activity.

Figure 5-13

AMEX Oil Index Compared to the DJIA, 1991 to 2006

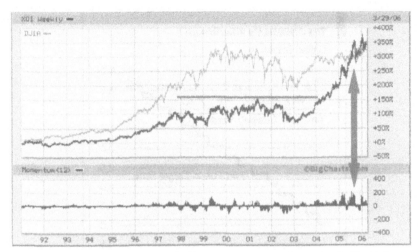

The thick horizontal line denotes a period of long-term price consolidation. The double-sided arrow denotes that the XOI's powerful uptrend occurred on relatively high momentum, which is a typical boom wave characteristic.
Source: BigCharts.com.

Before the real estate boom ended, a number of articles on its sustainability were published,[81] some of which examined the then-recent pattern of fed funds rate increases, which are illustrated in Figure 5-14, to support the hypothesis that the real estate boom was nearing its end.

At that time, the real estate boom in general did seem to be cooling as a result of the higher mortgage rates resulting from higher interest rates.[82] The ending of that boom was to be economically significant, as the real estate market in general served as a production catalyst for many other markets, including the construction trades, building materials such as lumber and copper,[83] and of course home equity finance–driven consumption.

Figure 5-14

Fed Funds Rate Development, 2003 to 2006

Source: "Bernanke ponders his course," The Economist, March 25, 2006, http://www.economist.com/displaystory.cfm?story_id=5662615

However, the fact that money supply inflation—as measured by M3—was accelerating at the time (see Figure 5-7) suggested that governmental support for boom-driven buying still existed. Additionally, default rates, as measured by the U.S. High Yield Default Index, were extremely low, suggesting the absence of the financial distress that is frequently observed during busts and recoveries in general; for example, consider the financial distress experienced in the years immediately following the new economy bust (during 2001 and 2002) noted earlier.[84] Therefore, enough uncertainty concerning the nature and extent of the economy existed at the time to warrant that investors with interest-rate-sensitive investments such as real estate consider ways of protecting the value of those investments.[85] In this regard, real estate investors had the option of hedging their investments via 10 separate real estate indexes offered by S&P;[86] these offerings facilitated relatively routine hedging operations, which was a significant alternative that past real estate investors did not have the benefit of.

In addition to hedging, real estate investors could have considered liquidating investments that were no longer characterized by a favorable value gap. With regard to the advisability of liquidating investments during a boom, legendary money manager Victor Sperandeo has, for example, commented on "the profit potential of riding the governmental bubble in the initial stages of inflation, jumping off early, and being on solid ground when the bubble burst, waiting to pick up the pieces."[87]

In addition to defensive tactics, there were several offensive investment tactics that could have been used during business cycle activity. For example, investors could have considered investments in light of a possible resumption of an oil boom through an analysis of the eight business cycle stages discussed earlier—in other words, buying during the boom stages, liquidating as the boom topped out, and possibly selling short during the bust stages. Additionally, ancillary markets, or other interest-rate-sensitive markets that had not experienced as pronounced a boom or uptrend, could have also been screened for potential investment opportunities. For example, consider the case of gold at the time, as illustrated in Figure 5-15.

The price run-up in gold from late 2001 to 2006 had been to multiyear highs, but on a relative basis, the prices of gold and silver, as reflected by the Phlx Gold and Silver Index (XAU), lagged the DJIA by a fairly wide margin; in other words, and as illustrated in Figure 5-16,

Figure 5-15

Monthly Gold Prices, 1976 to 2006

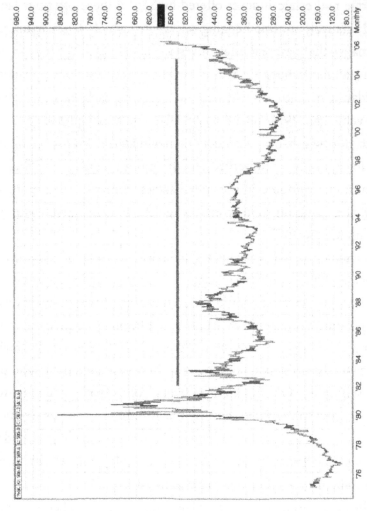

The horizontal bar above the price top formed between 1982 and 1984 denotes an area of price resistance, which is a price level above the market where selling pressure is anticipated.

Source: FutureSource, courtesy of Lingle Investment Group.

Figure 5-16

Phlx Gold and Silver Index Compared to the DJIA, 1991 to 2006

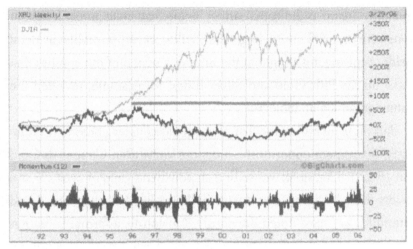

The thick horizontal bar denotes a significant long-term resistance level.
Source: BigCharts.com.

the Phlx Gold and Silver Index had thus far not exhibited the price behavior reflected by the boom waves of the Nasdaq, the Dow Jones Wilshire Real Estate Securities Index, and the AMEX Oil Index.

Of potential interest at the time was that the Phlx Gold and Silver Index was just starting to challenge multiyear highs (in other words, Phlx Gold and Silver Index prices had not yet broken out above the thick horizontal bar shown in Figure 5-16), which could be extremely significant, as investing at new highs can be a very successful strategy,[88] especially during business cycles. In fact, some market participants feel that there is an informational component to multiyear market price highs,[89] a belief that I agree with.

One possible approach to screening for potential investment opportunities in a market environment such as the Phlx Gold and Silver Index's at the time is to use value-based indicators such as low price/earnings ratios, high dividend yields, or other such measures to identify potential investments. An example of how such indicators could be used can be found in the real estate market during the new economy boom. As indicated earlier, before real estate prices broke out to new highs, REITs were, in general, selling at very favorable dividend yields. Applying this insight at the time to a search of the equities that make up the Phlx Gold and Silver Index, for example, revealed the output presented in Table 5-1.

This table identifies one firm that appeared to be a potential value-based investment opportunity: Freeport-McMoRan Copper & Gold Inc. (FCX). That stock was selling at a dividend yield of over 2% and at less than 16 times earnings, which is a key Graham and Dodd threshold, as I have noted previously. Obviously, a formal valuation would be required to determine if that stock was a viable investment, but it did screen well, which is a critical first step.*

Table 5-1

Phlx Gold and Silver Index Equities Screen, April 2006

Ticker	Company Name	P/E	Yield (%)
ABX	Barrick Gold Corporation	38.4	0.79
AEM	Agnico-Eagle Mines Limited	75.3	0.10
AU	Anglogold Ashanti Ltd	NA	0.36
DROO.Y	Drdgold Ltd	0.0	0.00
FCX	Freeport-McMoRan Copper & Gold Inc.	13.3	2.01
GFI	Gold Fields Ltd New	0.0	0.58
GG	Goldcorp Inc New	37.0	0.61
HMY	Harmony Gold Mng Ltd	0.0	0.00
KGC	Kinross Gold Corp	0.0	0.00
MDG	Meridian Gold Inc	0.0	0.00
NEM	Newmont Mining Coporation	62.1	0.77
PDG	Placer Dome Inc.	104.1	0.45

Data source: www.wsj.com.

---

* See the Conclusion for further information on screening and its place in the investment process.

The price per share of Freeport-McMoRan Copper & Gold stock on April 3, 2006, was $61.48. If the stock had been purchased on that date and sold two years later, on April 3, 2008, the sale price would have been $103.69 per share, for a capital appreciation of 68.7% (not including dividends), which illustrates the profit potential of integrating macroanalysis with the Graham and Dodd approach.

Continuing along this line, I expanded my screen to the entire basic materials sector of the market, which includes gold, silver, and oil equities.[90] For example, at the time, I screened that sector for equities selling at relatively high dividend yields and low price/earnings ratios; the partial results of that search are presented in Table 5-2.

The price comparison data in this table show that some of the equities in the exhibit seemed to be value-based investment opportunities; however, the data also show that some were not opportunities, thereby underscoring the obvious importance of valuation in the practice of investment. The table also illustrates the importance that dividends can play in investment analysis. In addition to generating income, dividends can also help to mitigate the effects of adverse price movement.

This screen was generated on the expectation of a boom wave; however, a screen could also be generated in the context of a bust or a recovery. For example, one of the most lucrative forms of investment during recoveries can be found in bankruptcy proceedings. Investors who specialize in such opportunities are popularly known as *vulture investors*.[91] Despite the pejorative nature of this term, distressed investing has been, and continues to be, a lucrative investment option for those with a distress-based circle of competence and the capital resources necessary to leverage that competency over time.

Table 5-2

Basic Materials Sector Screen, April 2006*

Ticker	Company Name	P/E	Yield (%)	Price 4/3/2006	Price 4/3/2008	Price Change	Annualized, Including Yield
PCU	SOUTHERN COPPER C	9.1	13.0	$85.6	$113.2	32.3%	29.1%
FDG	FORDING CDN COAL	7.7	12.6	$37.7	$56.0	48.5%	36.9%
DMLP	DORCHESTER MINLS	14.4	11.8	$26.1	$20.8	−20.5%	1.6%
PGH	PENGROWTH EGY UTS	12.1	11.1	$22.9	$19.3	−15.8%	3.2%
ERF	ENERPLUS RES FD	14.4	10.0	$50.7	$44.0	−13.3%	3.3%
PDS	PRECISION DRILL T	3.0	8.5	$32.7	$22.9	−29.9%	−6.4%
BPL	BUCKEYE PARTNERS	15.8	6.9	$42.4	$47.4	11.6%	12.7%
TCLP	TC PIPELINES LP	12.3	6.8	$33.5	$34.3	2.1%	7.9%
SXL	SUNOCO LOG PTNRS	17.4	6.8	$41.6	$49.8	19.7%	16.6%
MMP	MAGELLAN MIDSTREA	16.3	6.7	$33.1	$42.0	27.0%	20.2%
PAA	PLAINS ALL AMER L	16.4	6.1	$44.6	$48.1	8.0%	10.1%
ETP	ENERGY TRANSFER P	12.2	6.1	$38.8	$47.0	21.1%	16.6%
TNH	TERRA NITR CO COM	6.7	6.0	$20.5	$115.4	463.1%	237.5%
NRP	NATURAL RES PTNRS	15.4	5.8	$52.6	$29.4	−44.1%	−16.2%
YPF	Y P F SOCIEDADE A	15.3	5.6	$53.7	$44.3	−17.6%	−3.2%
ARLP	ALLIANCE RES PTNR	12.5	5.1	$35.8	$35.3	−1.5%	4.4%
PVR	PENN VIRGINIA RES	11.7	4.9	$57.2	$25.5	−55.4%	−22.8%
CPNO	COPANO ENERGY L.L	19.1	4.9	$44.4	$34.5	−22.4%	−6.3%
NL	N L INDS	15.8	4.7	$10.7	$11.7	9.7%	9.5%
OLN	OLIN CP	11.7	3.7	$21.5	$21.3	−0.8%	3.3%
DOW	DOW CHEMICAL	8.8	3.7	$40.6	$38.4	−5.4%	1.0%
PTR	PETROCHINA CO ADS	11.0	3.6	$108.4	$135.5	24.9%	16.1%
WOR	WORTHINGTON INDS.	14.3	3.4	$20.1	$17.3	−13.9%	−3.5%
RDS–B	ROYAL DUTCH SHELL	8.8	3.4	$65.7	$69.8	6.2%	6.5%
FRD	FRIEDMAN INDS INC	12.5	3.4	$9.7	$5.1	−47.9%	−20.6%
EMN	EASTMAN CHEM CO	7.5	3.4	$51.5	$65.2	26.6%	16.7%
SXT	SENSIENT TECH COR	19.2	3.3	$18.0	$30.3	68.5%	37.5%
BP	BP PLC	11.2	3.3	$69.7	$62.5	−10.3%	−1.9%
TOT	TOTAL S.A.	10.6	3.1	$132.3	$76.6	−42.1%	−17.9%
CVX	CHEVRON CORP	9.0	3.1	$58.3	$87.7	50.4%	28.3%
WDFC	WD 40 CO	17.9	2.9	$31.3	$34.1	8.9%	7.3%
PKX	POSCO	4.2	2.6	$65.4	$129.0	97.3%	51.2%
ARJ	ARCH CHEMICALS IN	17.8	2.6	$29.7	$38.6	29.8%	17.5%
REP	REPSOL YPF S.A.	9.2	2.5	$28.4	$36.6	29.1%	17.1%
	Average	12.6	5.7	44.6	49.7	11.4%	11.4%

* Nine stocks from the original listing I evaluated were deleted from this table because of lack of data.
The symbols of those stocks are PWI, PTF, VLI, NBP, LYO, UAPH, NHY, EON, and BF.
Data source: Yahoo! Finance and www.wsj.com.

CONCLUSION

As I write this conclusion in mid-2008, the U.S. real estate boom has ended; for example, the S&P/Case Shiller National Real Estate Index has fallen by 14.1% during the first quarter of 2008, which represents a decline greater than that witnessed during the Great Depression of the 1930s (see Figure 5-17).

Analyzing monetary and fiscal policy during this period of time will be especially important. Even though the U.S. government no longer publishes the M3 measure, which I used throughout this chapter, private research sources continue to publish it. Such sources are frequently subscription-based, but they are well worth the investment. For example, such sources show that M3 growth since the measure was formally discontinued by the Fed continued to increase dramatically

Figure 5-17

Housing Market Decline

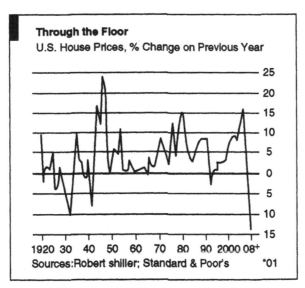

Source: "The Housing Market—Dropping a Brick," *The Economist*, May 31, 2008, p. 34.

Figure 5-18

Commodity Research Index as of June 2008

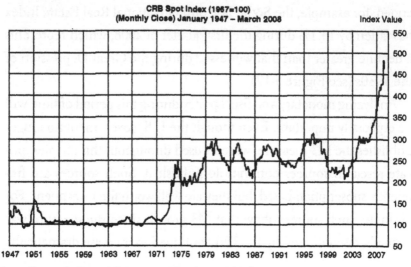

CRB Spot Index (1967=100)
(Monthly Close) January 1947 – March 2008

Source: Commodity Research Bureau; www.crbtrader.com/crbindex/.

into 2008. As a result, it is not surprising that boom behavior has (as of early to mid-2008) shifted to commodities. See, for example, Figure 5-18, which is a price chart of the Commodity Research Bureau Index.

Such remarkable levels of price inflation will have substantial economic consequences; hopefully, the approach presented in this chapter will help you to better assess those consequences, and to identify investment opportunities within them.

APPENDIX 1: WARREN BUFFETT AND EFFICIENT MARKET THEORY

Warren Buffett completed graduate studies in economics at Columbia University in 1951, which was where he met Benjamin Graham.

Despite this history, Buffett has been less than fully supportive of some of Columbia's research efforts; for example, according to biographer Roger Lowenstein:

> Buffett seemed especially resentful about the [efficient market] theory's hold on his alma mater. He was willing to give a lecture at Columbia, and did so every year or two, but refused to donate money to it. John C. Burton, the business school dean, said, "He told me very frankly he didn't think education was enhanced by money and secondly that he didn't think business schools were teaching the things he wanted to support. He was very hostile to the idea of efficient market research."[92]

Regarding Buffett's thoughts on the efficient market theory, financial author Peter Bernstein relates the following:

> Consider this set of coin-tossing possibilities, proposed by Warren [Buffett]. Suppose 225 million Americans all join in a coin-tossing contest in which each player bets a dollar each day on whether the toss of a coin will turn up heads or tails. Each day, the losers turn their dollars over to the winners, who then stake their winnings on the next day's toss. The laws of chance tell us that, after ten flips on ten mornings, only 220,000 people will still be in the contest, and each will have won a little over $1,000. After that, the game heats up. Ten days later, only 215 people will still be playing, but each of them will be worth over $1,050,000.

> [Buffett] suggests that this small group of winners will marvel at their own skills. Some of them will write books on "How I

Turned a Dollar into a Million in Twenty Days Working Thirty Seconds a Morning." Or, they will tackle skeptical professors of finance with "If it can't be done, why are there 215 of us?" But, [Buffett] goes on to point out, ". . . then some business school professor will probably be rude enough to bring up the fact that if [225] million orangutans had engaged in a similar exercise, the results would be much the same—215 egotistical orang-utans with 20 straight winning flips."[93]

APPENDIX 2: A PRACTICAL, REFLEXIVE FUNDAMENTAL PROXY

The purpose of Soros's technical model is to illustrate the eight stages of a business cycle through the graphical depiction of a speculative bubble. The boom and bust waves of a business cycle are character-ized by a *bubblelike* price pattern, and by the divergence between market behavior and the fundamentals. Soros chose stock prices and earnings per share (EPS) to represent market behavior and the funda-mentals, respectively, in his technical model. As discussed in the chapter, an EPS proxy was needed to illustrate the new economy busi-ness cycle because earnings data for the Nasdaq were not readily avail-able. The Dow Jones Industrial Average (DJIA) was chosen as the proxy because

- The blue chip stocks that make up the DJIA are widely con-sidered the value standard because of the ability of the cor-responding blue chip firms to deliver consistently exceptional total returns to shareholders.
- The two indexes have a long-term trending consistency, which is illustrated in Figure 5-19. As can be seen, both

Figure 5-19

Nasdaq Index and Dow Jones Industrial Average, 1973 to 1990

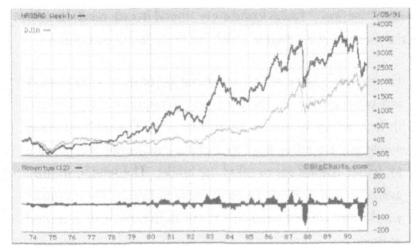

Source: BigCharts.com.

indexes trended over a relatively consistent range from 1978 through 1991. Figure 5-2 shows that this range remained relatively intact until the later part of 1998. At that time, the divergence between the two indexes began to expand as the Nasdaq entered Stages 4 and 5 of the boom. The divergence clearly illustrates capital flowing out of the "old economy" and into the "new economy." Correspondingly, Figure 5-2 illustrates how the divergence collapsed during the subsequent bust.

In sum, the proxy chosen facilitates the analysis of the eight stages of the new economy business cycle, and it served as a framework with which to analyze post new economy market behavior, as demonstrated in the later parts of the chapter.

APPENDIX 3: ENRON

Enron was reportedly short of cash "practically from the day Ken Lay created" the firm.[94] Enron found a way around its cash needs via a financial device called the *prepay*, which has been described as follows:

> Enron would agree to deliver natural gas or oil to an ostensibly independent offshore entity [or special-purpose entity] that was, in fact, set up by one of the lenders. . . . The offshore entity would pay Enron up front for its future deliveries and promise to deliver natural gas or oil to the lender. The lender, in turn, agreed to deliver the same commodity to Enron. The company would pay a fixed price for those deliveries over a period of time.
>
> On paper these looked like separate transactions. But they weren't. The commodity trades in effect canceled each other out, leaving Enron with a promise to pay a fixed return on the money it has received—exactly like a loan with interest![95]

Enron used its cash to boost its earnings and to fund a multitude of projects, many of which were malinvestments. For example, it was reported that Enron dealmakers, "flew around the world, overpaying for power plants in India, Poland and Spain, a water plant in Britain, a pipeline in Brazil, and thousands of miles of Internet cable. Enron accumulated 50 energy plants in 15 countries. Virtually none of them were profitable."[96] Similarly, it was reported that shortly after Jeff Skilling became Enron's CEO in August 2001,

> Enron abandoned a costly bid to become the leading supplier of first-run movies on the Web. Its other bright hope, retail

electricity, was fading. . . . The company's costly power plant in India was mired in political controversy. Enron privately classified 45 percent of its $9 billion in international projects as "troubled" assets.[97]

Furthermore, Enron deals were frequently backed by Enron stock, ensuring a financial collapse if and when the stock collapsed.[98] As George Soros himself observed:

Enron, like many companies, used special purpose entities (SPEs) to keep debt off its balance sheets. But unlike many other companies, it used its own stock to guarantee the debt of its SPEs. When the price of Enron fell, the scheme unraveled, exposing a number of other financial misdeeds the company had committed.[99]

Concluding thoughts on this financial strategy are that it

Worked well for the short term, when Enron needed a quick boost for its quarterly earnings. But as Enron's trading [businesses] expanded, its other businesses underperformed. Its debt and cash needs kept growing, so the company needed to make more and bigger "structured transactions" to keep the game going—pledging increasing amounts of [its] stock. Enron's strategy began to resemble what members of Congress would later call a high-tech Ponzi scheme.[100]

Chapter | 6

A GRAHAM AND DODD–BASED APPROACH TO CATASTROPHE VALUATION

Both individual skill (art) and chance are important factors in determining success or failure.

—*Benjamin Graham and David Dodd*[1]

There is no such thing as a bad risk. There are only bad rates.

—*Jack Ringwalt*
Founder and Former CEO of National Indemnity[2]

INTRODUCTION

Black's Law Dictionary, 6th ed., defines *catastrophe* as, "A notable disaster; a more serious calamity than might ordinarily be understood from the term 'casualty.' Utter or complete failure." Given this definition,

This chapter contains material from the *Journal of Alternative Investments*, © 2005 by Institutional Investor, which is reprinted with permission.

if one were to define a *super catastrophe,* or super cat, as an extreme catastrophic event with a monetary value in excess of $100 million, it would be reasonable to assume that most people would not consider such an event to be a viable alternative investment opportunity.[3] And yet, in some cases, that is exactly what I will argue.

When a super cat strikes, the costs involved can be exorbitant, as Hurricane Katrina in 2005 dramatically showed. While the probability or odds of a hurricane striking the Gulf Coast of the United States can be rather high, not all hurricanes cause the level of damage that Hurricane Katrina did. In fact, estimated probabilities of such super cats can be relatively low, and as a result, events of this kind can present potentially lucrative alternative investment opportunities for those with the requisite resources and valuation methodology to assess them.

In this chapter, I present a methodology for valuing super cats using the 2003 Pepsi Play for a Billion sweepstakes. The background section that follows provides information on the sweepstakes, while the valuation section presents a pricing methodology that combines basic insurance pricing with Graham and Dodd theory in a unique and interesting way. The aftermath and guidelines section describes what happened in the Pepsi Play for a Billion sweepstakes, and presents practical guidelines that can be used to evaluate future alternative super cat–based investment opportunities. The chapter ends with a brief conclusion and overview commentary on the related field of catastrophe bonds.

BACKGROUND

In mid-2003, PepsiCo announced a promotional $1 billion sweepstakes that was the largest promotional event in history. Nevertheless, the basic mechanics of the event were relatively simple: PepsiCo included game pieces on "specially marked 'Play For a Billion' and/or 'Billion-Sweeps.com'" products, such as all the various brands of Pepsi, Mountain Dew, Sierra Mist, Mug Root Beer, Orange Slice, Mr. Green, and Lipton Brisk. Each game piece contained a 10-character alphanumeric code that the contestants could use to enter the sweepstakes. From all of the entries received, PepsiCo would randomly choose 1,000 contestants who would compete, by process of elimination, for a *guaranteed* $1,000,000 prize. The contestant who won that prize would also hold a six-digit number. If that number exactly matched the numbers drawn at random on live television, the contestant would win the $1 billion grand prize.[4] The television show was hosted by personality Drew Carey, and was produced by Diplomatic Productions, which also happened to be the producer for the popular television show *Who Wants to Be a Millionaire?*

PepsiCo planned to spend $15,000,000 advertising the event, in addition to other "extensive promotional tie-ins with the WB Network and its corporate parent, AOL Time Warner."[5] This highly innovative marketing initiative was designed to promote, and increase awareness of, the Pepsi brand.

At the end of the year 2002, PepsiCo had a book value of $9.5 billion,[6] and therefore a loss this large could have affected the firm's value, and possibly even the scope of its operating capabilities. In order to proceed with the sweepstakes, therefore, PepsiCo sought to transfer this risk through the purchase of specialty "prize coverage" insurance, which was brokered through SCA Promotions.

According to reporter Gordon Anderson, "'It doesn't take long to call the roll of companies that would be willing to take part in a super-jumbo case like this,' says [Robert] Hamman [of SCA Promotions].

The only possible U.S. underwriter: Warren Buffett's Berkshire Hathaway."[7]

At the end of the year 2002, Berkshire Hathaway's balance sheet contained $10.3 billion of *cash*; the company was debt free and had a book value of $33.6 billion.[8] Consequently, its ability to assume a super cat risk such as this was without question. This is a significant point because creditworthiness is a central concern for financial institutions in general,[9] and for alternative super cat investors in particular. Therefore, SCA Promotions generally could not have chosen a better financial institution with which to partner on this alternative investment.[10]

To sum up the potential alternative investment opportunity thus far, PepsiCo is the sponsor of the Play for a Billion sweepstakes and is seeking to transfer the risk of having to pay out the $1 billion grand prize. The company approached SCA Promotions to broker the risk transfer, and SCA, in turn, approached Berkshire Hathaway to assume it. Thus the question at this point in the chapter is: at what price would Berkshire Hathaway be likely to be willing to accept the assumption of such an enormous risk; put differently, at what price could this super cat be considered a viable alternative investment opportunity?

I was not provided with any information on this alternative investment other than what is publicly available. Additionally, I was not (and am not) privy to the pricing methodology that either Berkshire Hathaway or SCA Promotions uses to value alternative investment opportunities like this. Nevertheless, by combining basic insurance pricing and Graham and Dodd theory, I will present a method for valuing alternative super cat investments in general, and the Pepsi Play for a Billion sweepstakes in particular.

VALUATION

According to the rules of the Pepsi Play for a Billion sweepstakes, the $1 billion grand prize had a present value of $250 million, as it was structured as a 40-year annuity with a 4.5% interest rate.

The odds of the game were described as follows: "Each Sweepstakes Winner's odds of winning the One Billion Dollar Prize are 1-in-1,000,000, and overall odds that the One Billion Dollar Prize will be awarded in the Event are 1-in-1,000."[11] Some events can present different odds depending on the way one views them. Given the two sets of odds, a question arises regarding which one to use in the valuation or pricing analysis. Rather than choose between the two, I will price the risk at both odds in this chapter, noting that the two prices should relatively reconcile, as they pertain to the same event. This can be considered somewhat analogous to EPV reconciling with NAV in base-case valuation, as explained in Chapters 1 and 2.

Traditional insurance pricing theory calculates *premium,* or the value of risk assumption, as the sum of a risk's expected loss and a risk premium, which is normalized by the amount of homogeneous risks that are assumed. Putting these variables into symbols gives a basic insurance pricing model,[12] which is presented in equation (6-1).

$$Pr = E(L) + (c \times s)N^{1/2}/N \qquad (6\text{-}1)$$

where:

Pr = premium
$E(L)$ = expected loss
c = confidence level (one tail)
s = standard deviation
N = number of homogenous events

Two modifications will be made to this model, labeled equation (6-1), for use in this chapter's valuation:

- First, as only one event is being valued, the N variable will be dropped.
- Second, a volatility factor variable will be added to denote the fraction of the standard deviation that is deemed necessary to generate a margin of safety–based price. This modification is important because Graham and Dodd–oriented investments *require* a margin of safety irrespective of whether they pertain to assets or liabilities.

Regarding the margin of safety, Benjamin Graham noted that it "is always dependent on the price paid. It will be large at one price, small at some other price, nonexistent at some still higher price.[13] . . . It is available for absorbing the effect of miscalculations or worse than average luck."[14] Obviously, worse than average luck is a critical concern in this field, and thus reasonable questions to ask at this point in the chapter are: Could pricing based on a traditional insurance pricing model contain a reasonable margin of safety? And if so, how?

Questions such as these will be addressed later in the chapter, but before proceeding with the valuation, I will apply the previous two modifications to equation (6-1) to produce the pricing model that will be used in this chapter:

$$\text{Premium} = \text{expected loss} + [\text{confidence level} \times (\text{standard deviation} \times \text{factor})] \qquad (6\text{-}2)$$

Pricing at Odds of 1 in 1,000

I begin the valuation of the Pepsi Play for a Billion sweepstakes at odds of 1 in 1,000; pricing at odds of 1 in 1,000,000 will follow. Calculating the expected loss, which is the first pricing variable in equation (6-2), at 1-in-1,000 odds could be accomplished by constructing a simple payout table such as the one illustrated in Table 6-1.

Using the variables contained in that table to estimate the volatility of this event gives a standard deviation of $7,901,740.[15]

Inserting the expected loss and standard deviation into equation (6-2) at confidence levels of 90%, 95%, and 99% and a factor of 1 (which means that 100% of the standard deviation is used in the pricing) gives the premium profile presented in Table 6-2.

Table 6-1

Payout Table at Odds of 1-in-1,000

Probability (p)	Loss (L)	
0.1000%	$250,000,000	= $250,000
99.9000%	$0	= $0
		$250,000 = expected loss [E(L)]

Illustrating the expected loss calculation (0.1% × $250 million) + (99.9% × $0) = $250,000.

Table 6-2

Pricing at Odds of 1 in 1,000 and a Factor of 1

Premium		
90%	95%	99%
$10,364,228	$13,287,872	$18,661,055

For example, the premium at 99% confidence was calculated from Equation (6-2) as follows: $250,000 + [2.33 × ($7,901,740 × 1)] = $18,661,055.

The factors for 90% and 95% confidence levels (one tail) are 1.28 and 1.65, respectively.

Given the super catastrophic nature of this event (its $250 million present value is greater than the $100 million super cat threshold identified earlier), I would argue that pricing at 99% confidence is required. In order to assess the adequacy of the price at this level, $18,661,055, I will use a common insurance measure known as *rate on line* (RoL).

RoL is calculated by dividing the premium for a given risk by the amount of risk, which in this case amounts to $0.07 = $18,661,055/$250 million. A RoL of $0.07 may not seem to be high for an alternative investment like this, but it actually can be considered relatively high. As a result, I will reprice this alternative investment at a factor level of 0.5, which means that one-half of this event's $7,901,740 standard deviation will be used in the pricing. Recalculating the pricing at this factor level, at the same confidence levels, gives the premium profile presented in Table 6-3.

While a factor of 0.5 may at first seem low to some readers, it can be considered quite high; for example, I have evaluated a number of catastrophe bonds with factors considerably lower than 50%, some of which were determined to contain a reasonable margin of safety. (I comment further on catastrophe bonds in this chapter's conclusion.)

Table 6-3

Pricing at Odds of 1 in 1,000 and a Factor of 0.5

Premium		
90%	95%	99%
$5,307,114	$6,768,936	$9,455,527

The premium at 99% confidence was calculated as follows:

$250,000 + [2.33 × ($7,901,740 × 0.5)] = $9,455,527.

The premium at 99% confidence in Table 6-3 is $9,455,527; however, this figure represents the "pure premium" or loss cost of this event. In other words, this price has not yet been loaded for overhead and profit. In practice, insurance actuaries perform detailed statistical analyses to derive overhead and profit factors. In this valuation, I will load the premium by the risk-free rate of interest to derive the final premium. Such a load is appropriate given the odds of the event, meaning that at odds of 1 in 1,000, it is a virtual statistical certainty that no one will win the sweepstakes, which supports the use of the risk-free rate as a loading factor. At the time of this alternative investment, the yield on the 10-year Treasury note, which is frequently used as a risk-free rate, was 3.33%.[16] Adjusting the price or pure premium that I derived by this amount gives a final premium in the amount of $9,770,397 = $9,455,527 × (1 + 0.0333).

Recalculating the RoL at this price gives $0.04 = $9,770,397/$250 million. I will comment on the adequacy of this RoL if my pricing at odds of 1 in 1,000,000 supports it.

Pricing at Odds of 1 in 1,000,000

I begin this valuation the same way I began the previous valuation at odds of 1 in 1,000; namely, by constructing a payout table, which is displayed in Table 6-4.

The $250 million present value of the $1 billion grand prize has an expected loss of only $250 at odds of 1 in 1,000,000. Using the information in this table to calculate standard deviation gives $250,000. Table 6-5 shows the output of inserting these variables into equation (6-2) to calculate the premium for this event at the familiar confidence levels of 90%, 95%, and 99%, and at a factor of 1.

Table 6-4

Payout Table at Odds of 1-in-1,000,000

Probability (p)	Loss (L)	
0.0001%	$250,000,000	= $250
99.9999%	$0	= $0
		$250 = expected loss [E(L)]

Following the same logic as Table 6-1, (0.0001% × $250 million) + (99.9999% × $0) = $250.

Table 6-5

Pricing at Odds of 1 in1,000,000 and a Factor of 1

Premium		
90%	95%	99%
$320,250	$412,750	$582,750

The premium at 99% confidence was calculated as follows:

$250 + [2.33 × ($250,000 × 1)] = $582,750.

At a 99% confidence level, the calculated premium for assuming the risk of this super cat at odds of 1 in 1,000,000 amounts to $582,750, which obviously does not reconcile with the 1 in 1,000 premium of $9,770,397. Furthermore, I am not aware of any alternative investor or insurance company that would be willing to assume super cat–level risk like this for only $582,750, and with good reason. At this premium level, the RoL is only $0.002 = $582,750/$250 million, which is suboptimal to say the least.

Notwithstanding the seemingly paltry premium of $582,750, the slight odds of payout (1 in 1,000,000) means that it is a virtual statistical certainty that no one will win the $1 billion (annuity-based) grand prize. Therefore, if an alternative investor such as Berkshire Hathaway, for instance, assumed the risk of this exact super cat every year into perpetuity, the $582,750, 99% confident premium would have a capitalized value of $9,210,522 = $582,750 × (1/6.33%). The premium was capitalized before taxes as a simple, nongrowth perpetuity at an estimated 6.33% discount rate,[17] which is my estimated cost of capital for Berkshire Hathaway in mid-2003.[18]

While this calculation may at first seem confusing because this super cat is a one-time event rather than a recurring one, I am using the full-capitalized value of the premium—theoretical though it is—on an adjustment basis to help determine the potential viability of this super cat–based alternative investment, where *viable* is defined as risk assumption with a reasonable margin of safety. Think of this adjustment as a kind of super cat risk premium, which is inclusive of super catastrophic levels of risk, overhead, and profit.

Therefore, adding this risk premium of $9,210,522 to the original premium of $582,750 equals a final premium of $9,793,271, which closely reconciles with my 1 in 1,000 premium of $9,770,397.

The RoL for both premiums (meaning, premiums calculated at odds of both 1 in 1,000 and 1 in 1,000,000) is $0.04, which may at first seem somewhat low to some readers. If it does, consider this: on a comparative basis, a $0.04 RoL equates to $40,000 of premium charged for a traditional $1,000,000 commercial general liability (CGL) policy, which can be relatively common on certain insurance accounts. However, there is a substantial difference between this super cat and a traditional CGL insurance policy: an insurance policy usually provides insurance coverage for 365 days, while the Pepsi Play for a Billion sweepstakes provides coverage for only *one* day.

Therefore, given the slight odds of payout (1 in 1,000 or 1 in 1,000,000, depending on which set of odds you use), a RoL of $0.04,[19] and a limited risk assumption period of *one* day, I would argue that assuming the present value risk of the Pepsi Play for a Billion sweep-stakes (or $250 million) is a viable alternative investment. And as reported in the mainstream press, Berkshire Hathaway did alterna-tively invest in this super cat. While it is my understanding that the specific amount of premium that Berkshire Hathaway charged was/is confidential, it has been reported that, "In return for a seven-figure premium (though less than $10 million) [sic], Berkshire [Hathaway] has assumed the risk of a payout."[20],*

The following section comments on the results of the Play for a Billion sweepstakes and provides some general guidelines for future alternative, super cat–based investments.

POSTMORTEM AND GUIDELINES

In a grand act of showmanship before the September 14, 2003, Play for a Billion television show, it was announced that a chimpanzee by the name of Kendall would draw the winning grand prize numbers.[21] Warren Buffett summed up the results of this alternative investment to Berkshire Hathaway shareholders as follows:

> PepsiCo promoted a drawing that offered participants a chance to win a $1 billion prize. Understandably, Pepsi wished to lay off this risk, and we were the logical party to assume it.[22] So we wrote a $1 billion policy, retaining the risk entirely for our own account.[23] Because the prize, if won, was payable over time, our exposure in present-value terms was $250 million. (I helpfully

---

* I have been advised by several people familiar with this deal that my valuation is "very close" to the actual price paid by PepsiCo, which was derived at odds of 1 in 1,000.

suggested that any winner be paid $1 a year for a billion years, but that proposal didn't fly.) The drawing was held on September 14 [2003]. Ajit [Jain] and I held our breath,[24] as did the finalist in the contest, and we were happier than he. PepsiCo has renewed for a repeat contest in 2004.[25]

Thus, the final contestant did not win the $1 billion grand prize, which is the exact outcome that the odds reflected. As a result, the Pepsi Play for a Billion sweepstakes was a successful alternative investment for Berkshire Hathaway. Significantly, it was also a successful business transaction for PepsiCo, as it allowed that firm to advertise and promote its brand in an innovative and unique way, without the risk of the super cat's possible effects on the company's value and operating ability. Given this dual benefit, it is not surprising that this event seemed to mark the beginning of an ongoing business relationship between Berkshire Hathaway and PepsiCo. For example, PepsiCo held another Play for a Billion sweepstakes the following year, the drawing of which was held on September 12, 2004. This event was hosted by personalities Damon Wayans and Tom Bergeron, and as with the 2003 event, the final contestant did not win the grand prize.

Because this form of alternative investment is likely to grow in popularity over the coming years, given the escalating nature of global risk and global risk transfer, the following guidelines may prove useful to future alternative super cat investors.

Ability and Willingness to Pay
*First and foremost, there **must** be an unquestioned ability and willingness to pay any super cat claim immediately.* Because of the amount

of money involved in super cats, those transferring the risk require, appropriately, immediate payment of any claim. For example, if the final contestant in the Pepsi Play for a Billion sweepstakes (in either 2003 or 2004) had won the grand prize, neither PepsiCo nor the grand prize winner—nor anyone else, for that matter—would have doubted for a moment that Warren Buffett was going to pay the claim in a timely fashion.

The universe of financial institutions that are able to assume super cat–level risk is, at the present time, rather small. As a result, creditworthiness is a competitive advantage for Berkshire Hathaway that even extends to its reinsurance arm, Gen Re (this is the same Gen Re that was the subject of Chapter 4's valuation). For example, in the 2002 Berkshire Hathaway, Inc., Annual Report, Buffett stated that because of the financial backing of Berkshire Hathaway,

> General Re, rated AAA across-the-board, is now in a class by itself in respect to financial strength.
>
> No attribute is more important. Recently, in contrast, one of the world's largest reinsurers—a company regularly recommended to primary insurers by leading brokers—has all but ceased paying claims, including those both valid and due. This company owes many billions of dollars to hundreds of primary insurers who now face massive write-offs. "Cheap" reinsurance is a fool's bargain: When an insurer lays out money today in exchange for a reinsurer's promise to pay a decade or two later, it's dangerous—and possibly life-threatening—for the insurer to deal with any but the strongest reinsurer. (p. 9)

The reinsurer mentioned in this quotation was believed to be Gerling Re, but that firm publicly rebutted Buffett's allegations. While it was uncharacteristic of Buffett to go after a competitor in so public a forum, it did underscore the importance he placed on his creditworthiness-based competitive advantage during a time of heightened geopolitical and macroeconomic risk.

Given sufficient demand over time, financial syndicates could form to assume super cat levels of risk, and if demand continues, those syndicates could evolve into a specialized market with clearinghouses that would financially guarantee all risk transfers. Such an evolution would facilitate greater levels of super cat risk transfer.

Well-Defined Risk

The word *risk* can have many different meanings. For example, *Black's Law Dictionary*, 6th ed., lists a number of definitions for risk, including the following, "The element of uncertainty in an undertaking; the possibility that actual future returns will deviate from expected returns." According to popular financial author Peter Bernstein, "The word 'risk' derives from the early Italian *risicare*, which means 'to dare.' In this sense, risk is a choice rather than a fate."[26] A popular risk and insurance textbook, meanwhile, notes that the term "risk is sometimes used in a specific sense to describe variability around the expected value and other times to describe the expected losses."[27] Furthermore, a practically oriented finance book defines risk as "instability; uncertainty about the future; more specifically, the degree of uncertainty involved with a project or investment."[28]

An argument can be made in support of each of these definitions, and yet each of them seems to fall short with respect to super cat risk. For example, equating risk with uncertainty is not entirely accurate because uncertainty cannot be quantified. In other words, if one is uncertain about the nature of an event, one cannot assign odds to that event other than by guessing, and guessing has absolutely no role whatsoever in super cat valuation.

As to risk being a probability-weighted return or payout, in the Pepsi Play for a Billion sweepstakes case, that amounted to either $250,000 or $250, depending on which odds were used, which clearly did not reflect that super cat's risk.

Additionally, while the event's standard deviation at both sets of odds did reflect significant variability around the expected loss, neither measure adequately represented the risk of this super cat:

- At odds of 1 in 1,000, the standard deviation turned out to be too high in a practical sense, thereby necessitating pricing at a factor of 0.5 rather than a factor of 1.
- At odds of 1 in 1,000,000, the standard deviation turned out to be entirely too low, as reflected in an inadequate price of $582,750 with a paltry rate on line of $0.002.[29]

In light of this information, it could be useful to define the term *risk* in the context of alternative super cat investments as the monetary amount that could be lost at any time during the investment. For example, in the case of the Pepsi Play for a Billion sweepstakes, the risk was clearly $250 million.

Well-Defined Time Frame

Time is money; therefore, given any two investments with relatively the same level of profitability, the one that pays out more quickly is generally preferable. Consequently, if an alternative super cat investment has a relatively small exposure window, that benefit should not be overlooked.

Simple, "User-Friendly" Risk Assumption Language

Given the magnitude of a super cat, it is imperative that the scope of risk assumption outlined in a contract is clear and unambiguous to all concerned. Complicated or convoluted risk assumption contract language increases the possibility of miscalculation, which is unacceptable in the field of super cat alternative investments. Additionally, lawyers make a very good living exploiting complicated or convoluted wording when the stakes are much lower than super cat levels. They therefore will not hesitate to initiate litigation in any disputed super cat–related claim, which will only increase costs for all concerned (except the lawyers, of course).[30]

Deep Statistical or Actuarial Expertise

Accurate calculation of the odds is critically important in this form of alternative investment. Therefore, I suggest having the odds calculated, checked, and then double-checked by either statisticians or insurance actuaries, as the mathematical margin of error in this field is zero, without exception.

A Reasonable Margin of Safety

Whether you agree with margin of safety theory for mainstream investments or not (although I certainly hope that you do), given the magnitude of super cat risk, it would be fiscally irresponsible to undertake such alternative investments without a reasonable margin of safety, as "worse than average luck" could very well mean rapid insolvency.

Marketing Expertise

Berkshire Hathaway is presented with opportunities to alternatively invest in super cats like the Pepsi Play for a Billion sweepstakes because of the Warren Buffett brand. While Buffett is a shrewd businessman who makes no bones about buying only at a margin of safety,[31] he is seen as being honest and trustworthy, which is critically important in alternative super cat investments. While this level of trust partly rests on the strength of his firm's balance sheet, much of it is generated by his personal brand.[32] Therefore, any financial institution or financial syndicate that wishes to compete for these types of alternative investments must engender the same level of trust to be successful over time.

It Is Not as Easy as It May Look

The stress involved in risking $250 million on the numerical draws of a monkey, on nationwide television, should not be underestimated. Super cat alternative investments are not for everyone, and they should not be marketed as such. However, for those financial institutions with the requisite resources and psychological makeup, super cat alternative investments could be a lucrative part of a value-creating portfolio.

CONCLUSION AND A WORD ON CATASTROPHE BONDS

This chapter introduced the concept of super cat–based alternative investments by way of the relatively recent Pepsi Play for a Billion sweepstakes. A valuation approach using both a basic insurance pricing model and Graham and Dodd theory was presented, which is significant because both Benjamin Graham and Warren Buffett were/ are heavily involved in insurance operations.

The Pepsi Play for a Billion alternative investment was a success for Berkshire Hathaway (in both 2003 and 2004). This development, as well as the escalating levels of global risk and global risk transfer, could lead to an increased popularity for this type of alternative investment in the future. Toward that end, I presented practical guidelines for future alternative super cat investors to consider.

Before concluding this chapter, I would like to comment on the related field of catastrophe bonds (or "cat bonds" for short). Cat bonds are high-yielding insurance-backed securities that put some or all of the bond's principal and/or coupon payments at risk based on natural perils such as hurricanes or earthquakes. These bonds have emerged over the recent past—especially since the incredibly volatile 2005 hurricane season—as popular forms of alternative investments.

One challenge with cat bond valuation pertains to the estimation of event probabilities, as no one knows the exact probabilities of a hurricane or earthquake. An example of this was the 2005 hurricane season that devastated the U.S. Gulf Coast. After that hurricane season, modeling firms revised their model probabilities upward, which was understandable; however, subsequent hurricane activity in 2006 and 2007 turned out to be remarkably light, suggesting that perhaps the original probabilities had not needed to be revised after all.

Notwithstanding probability estimation issues, cat bonds are frequently evaluated purely quantitatively. This approach has seemingly worked well; for example, since cat bonds were first introduced in the mid-1990s, they have, in general, been very profitable. This trend is not likely to continue as the market continues to develop, meaning that prices and product structures generating economic returns are likely to come under increasing levels of pressure. Furthermore, and as with investments in general, a strictly quantitative approach to catastrophe-based valuation ignores a great deal of qualitative information. As we saw in Chapters 1 through 4, a hallmark of Graham and Dodd valuation is the effective use of both quantitative and qualitative forms of information in the context of one overall framework.

It is my feeling that cat-based investment in general can be improved upon by combining the quantitative approaches currently in use with insurance-based underwriting techniques and margin of safety–based pricing analysis. However, it is important to point out that insurance underwriting is not a panacea; effective insurance underwriters can be as scarce as effective investors or M&A specialists. An example of this is Gen Re's performance after its acquisition by Berkshire Hathaway (discussed in Chapter 4). Gen Re's poor performance occurred despite the firm's long-stated objective to underwrite at a profit. Nevertheless, the linkage of quantitative model output with insurance-based underwriting techniques and margin of safety–based pricing analysis holds great promise in the field of cat-based alternative investments, and will hopefully be explored and developed.

Chapter | 7

FINANCIAL STRATEGY AND MAKING VALUE HAPPEN

The qualitative factors upon which most stress is laid are the nature of the business and the character of the management. These elements are exceedingly important, but they are also exceedingly difficult to deal with intelligently.

—*Benjamin Graham and David Dodd*[1]

I am a better investor because I am a businessman, and a better businessman because I am an investor.

—*Warren E. Buffett*[2]

INTRODUCTION

Sometime in the year 1999, I attended a seminar put on by business guru Tom Peters. I confess that I generally do not attend guru-based

This chapter contains material from *Business Strategy Series,* © 2007 by Emerald Publishing, which is reprinted with permission.

seminars because I am usually very disappointed with the material that is presented, but Peters' presentation that day contained a section that resonated powerfully with me. The title of that section was "the tenth-grade history book," and it went something like this: read any tenth-grade history book and record the names of the people mentioned in it, being careful to "ignore the nuts" (by "nuts" Peters was referring to people like Hitler, Stalin, Mao, and like characters who have plagued humanity through their very existence), and then see who is left. Undertaking this exercise, you are left with names such as George Washington, Thomas Jefferson, Benjamin Franklin, Thomas Edison, Henry Ford, Isaac Newton, and Albert Einstein. Next, Peters observed that even though these are the very people who shaped—and indeed continue to shape—our world, educational institutions generally do not teach students how to be like them.

Thinking about this observation after the seminar, I felt that it also applied to the field of finance. For example, if you ask students studying finance today whom they most admire, you will hear names like Warren Buffett, George Soros, Mario Gabelli, Seth Klarman, and Bruce Kovner. And yet, I do not believe that, in general, modern finance programs teach students to be successful the way these investors have been.

Peters' observation even extends to business training in general. While this may at first seem odd given the popularity of the MBA degree, consider, for example, CEOs such as the late Thomas Watson of IBM and Warren Buffett. Whether modern MBA programs teach students to be successful the way these businessmen were is currently the subject of some debate.[3]

Business is both art and science, meaning that it involves quantitative, qualitative, and behavioral elements, all of which interact continuously, especially in today's rapidly changing business environment. Yet, critical business functions like finance and strategy, for example, are often practiced in separate departments or organizational silos. Even when they are overseen by a common governance structure, finance and strategy are frequently conducted separately, often by disparate professionals with limited interaction. Furthermore, strategic and financial activities are commonly plagued with contrasting goals and different performance metrics, which can exacerbate discipline disconnects, leading to suboptimal decision making and lower levels of organizational performance over time.

As managers seek greater levels of efficiency, they are beginning to adopt a more interdisciplinary approach.[4] For example, Daimler-Chrysler recognized the need for this type of approach after conducting an intensive assessment in 1998; in other words, it realized that it faced a critical "need for a fully integrated management system that combines strategic planning, operational planning, performance management, and human resources management."[5] While this recognition seemed to come too late for Chrysler, similar points of view are becoming more popular in general. For example, a study conducted by *CFO* magazine documented corporate financial practitioners' desire to play a larger role in strategy formulation.[6]

Academics have also begun to integrate disciplines in their research. For example, Robert Kaplan of Harvard Business School has combined strategy and performance management in highly original ways with his work on the Balanced Scorecard.[7] Similarly, William Fruhan—also of HBS—merged strategy and finance in a powerful, yet practical manner.[8] And Paul Schoemaker of the Wharton School has incorporated "the management of uncertainty and paradox" in highly innovative and practical ways in his research.[9]

Discipline integration seems to be gaining momentum as capital markets increasingly look to business managers for integrated approaches to competitive initiatives, risk management, and stakeholder communication. Therefore, there seems to be a broad-based need for a practical interdisciplinary framework such as the one presented in this chapter, which I refer to as *financial strategy*.

Finance generally involves allocating the scarce resources that a firm controls, while *strategy* pertains to formulating a unique customer value proposition. Properly executed, both finance and strategy are predicated upon the ability to *measure* and *manage* outcomes. Financial strategy integrates these disciplines—and the management of the risks that they generate—and by so doing enhances a firm's customer relationships, and bottom line, by allocating scarce resources to targeted value propositions more efficiently over time. Put in a Graham and Dodd context, financial strategy can be thought of both as a way to manage franchises and as a framework to assess franchises.

The critical aspect of financial strategy is not the individual stages of the approach, per se, but the manner in which firms integrate and employ those stages. Consider, for example, Coca-Cola's effective response to the failed introduction of New Coke and Johnson & Johnson's decisive management of the infamous Tylenol tampering incidents of the 1980s.[10] The positive results that each firm achieved— under extremely trying circumstances—were not the result of any one particular discipline, but rather of the integrated manner in which a variety of disciplines were employed in the formulation and implementation of a response and solution. In the following sections, I will describe the individual stages of this approach in more detail.

STRATEGY FORMULATION

Formulating a strategy begins with determining how to better or more economically satisfy customer preferences in unique ways, which is the hallmark of all franchises. The customer focus of this activity is crucial; for example, according to David D'Alessandro, who is the former chairman and CEO of John Hancock Insurance Company, "Pleasing customers should be the CEO's only consideration."[11] Dell operationalized this belief by building a business model around the direct sale of computers to its customers: "Think Customer" is the sign at Dell Building 3.

Strategy formulation involves a series of activities that are undertaken to guide a firm toward a plan for creating value for its customers, while at the same time differentiating itself from its competition. Initial activities in this process include examining the external environment and addressing questions such as, "What customer need(s) are not being fulfilled?" or "How can certain needs be fulfilled more efficiently?" Answers to questions of this type include aspects of both vision and analysis.

A strategic vision is, first and foremost, a creative act that, as noted management professor Henry Mintzberg has cogently explained, is not subject to quantification.[12] Rather, it is an inspirational point of view on how a need can be better or more efficiently satisfied. Operationalizing a vision requires a wide variety of activities, such as analyzing a firm's strengths and weaknesses in comparison with the opportunities and threats of the marketplace. At the conclusion of such activities, long-term objectives can be formulated and then broken down into short-term goals and business plans.

Significantly, resource allocation is usually not addressed during this process, and frequently neither is performance management, which is interesting when you consider that the popular return on investment (ROI) metric is derived by simply quantifying the results of the activities undertaken to execute a strategy in financial terms and then dividing that measurement by the amount of financial resources used by those activities.

RESOURCE ALLOCATION

Once a strategy has been formulated, decisions concerning how best to allocate financial and human resources to implement it must be made. Today, these decisions frequently involve outsourcing arrangements.

Allocating financial resources is conducted via the valuation process. This book has focused on Graham and Dodd–based valuation; however, most valuations conducted in a corporate finance setting involve forecasting future cash flows, which is an activity that many practitioners and academics alike consider the most important function of corporate finance.[13] The process behind this activity is formally known as *capital budgeting* and involves estimating the benefits and costs—or revenues and expenses—of an initiative over time in order to determine if it is economically viable.

Capital budgeting frequently proceeds as follows: The finance department—which, as noted earlier, is often not included in formulating strategy—receives a strategic proposal and is asked to "run the numbers." Financial analysts then go to work constructing highly detailed models illustrating the expected cash flow development of the strategic proposal's expected benefits and costs over time. The most popular methodologies for accomplishing this are net present value (NPV), internal rate of return (IRR), and payback. While the basic mechanics of these methodologies are relatively simple, implementing them effectively can be anything but simple. For example, and as Columbia University professors Bruce Greenwald and Judd Kahn observed:

> In theory, the correct value of a project is the value of future benefits discounted at an appropriate cost of capital, minus future costs, usually discounted at the same cost of capital. The result is mathematically equal to the value of the present and future net cash flows appropriately discounted, the familiar net present value (NPV) of financial analysis. The problem is that although the method is true in theory, it is seriously flawed in practice.[14]

NPV and IRR give practitioners a tremendous amount of flexibility, which is probably one of the reasons why these methodologies are so popular. Another reason for the popularity of these methods is that they are relatively easy to use. However, each methodology requires assumptions that must be made by the person (or people) using them, who is frequently a financial analyst. Just because a financial analyst has read a strategic proposal does not mean that his model will capture the nuances of the strategic benefits and costs development pattern over time. As a result, disconnects can emerge between strategy and finance that can cause the capital budgeting process to degenerate into a numbers exercise instead of what it should be, namely, a quantitative assessment of a strategic initiative (or project). Additionally, this activity involves forecasting an uncertain future, which no one can do accurately because human beings are simply not designed to predict the future.

Similar difficulties are frequently encountered when it comes to allocating human resources to a strategic initiative (or project). For example, how many firms go through a capital budgeting-like process when it comes to staffing an initiative (or project)? Frequently, human resources are allocated for personality reasons, such as likability, bureaucratic or political concerns, or simple availability. While personality and availability are important considerations, the objective of human resource allocation should be to assign the most capable people to an initiative (or project) to ensure its success, not simply to staff it and then hope for results.

To further complicate matters, capital budgeting and human resource allocation are frequently conducted in isolation. Thus, another disconnect between capital budgeting and human resource allocation can emerge; in other words, the human resources chosen to implement a strategy may not be able to deliver the cash flows as modeled by financial analysts. Consequently, value chains rarely proceed from one stage to the next in a smooth, linear fashion, as theory suggests they should. Consider the illustration in Figure 7-1.

Financial strategy approaches resource allocation differently. First, it would include finance personnel in strategy formulation activities, so that they are intimately aware of a strategy's nuances and the expected benefits and costs assumptions. Similarly, strategists would be consulted throughout the capital budgeting process to validate key

Figure 7-1

Value Chains, Theory and Practice

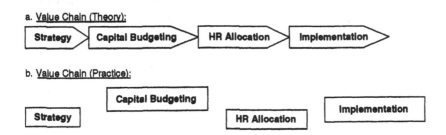

assumptions and to ensure that the financial model is being constructed in a strategically consistent manner.

Given the level of interaction between financial analysts and strategists, the capital budgeting process becomes a logical extension of strategy rather than a separate (and possibly disconnected) task. This dynamic is illustrated in Figure 7-2 and is typical of franchises, which were defined in prior chapters as firms operating with sustainable competitive advantages that are identified in a Graham and Dodd–based valuation by a significant EPV-to-NAV spread.

Figure 7-2

Linking Strategy and Capital Budgeting

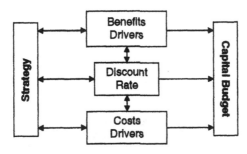

Once the capital budget has been prepared, people must be chosen to generate the expected cash flows. From a financial strategy perspective, the capital budget becomes a tool to use in the human resource selection process. This is logical, inasmuch as people should be selected for an initiative (or project) based on the expectation that their skills will help to make that initiative a success. Therefore, once benefits and costs drivers have been identified and modeled, personnel can be chosen based on their ability to leverage the benefits drivers and mitigate the costs drivers (to the extent possible) to increase the probability of a measurably successful result. This is illustrated in Figure 7-3.

Financial strategy thus aligns human resource selection with the capital budget, which itself is aligned with strategy. This results in a more logical value chain, such as the one illustrated in Figure 7-1a, rather than the disjointed value chain frequently seen in practice (and illustrated in Figure 7-1b). Logical value chains result in consistently greater levels of value creation over time by franchises. Noted examples of this include GEICO and Microsoft.

Figure 7-3

Human Resource Allocation

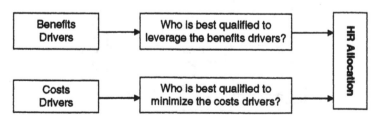

PERFORMANCE MANAGEMENT

Performance management is the process of accessing the relative success (or failure) of the activities undertaken to implement and execute a strategy. Historically, the field of performance management has generally fallen within the purview of managerial accounting, where the focus was, not surprisingly, on financial measures such as ROI,[15] which was discussed earlier. However, performance management has recently emerged as a separate discipline, predominantly because of the success of Robert Kaplan and David Norton's seminal writings on the *Balanced Scorecard (BSC)*.

The BSC introduced a multiperspective framework with which to manage performance based on the argument (correct, in my opinion) that value can be created more efficiently if both lagging and leading measures are tracked across multiple perspectives rather than just from a financial perspective. Four common BSC perspectives are

- Financial
- Customer
- Internal (or operational)
- Learning and growth[16]

The BSC framework has proved to be incredibly popular, and it is also incredibly flexible, as Kaplan and Norton have successfully extended it to the field of strategy.[17] Relatively recent events have supported this strategic extension; for example, corporate failures such as Enron's illustrated the need for strong interactive performance management systems to ensure that business activities are consistent with both a business strategy and all applicable laws and regulations.

As a general rule, performance metrics should flow logically from a valuation or a capital budget. This connection between valuation and performance management means that the measures used to assess performance are based on key leading and lagging indicators that reflect the expected benefits and costs of the strategy being implemented, as quantified in a valuation. For example, assume a five-year strategic initiative (or project) that has a cost or budget of $15,000,000 and a targeted IRR of 25%. Managing the highs and lows of an initiative like this over time can be extremely difficult in practice. Leading and lagging indicators derived from a valuation—such as milestones, benefits realization, periodic ROI measures, sales targets, and other such indicators—can be chosen to help manage the initiative to immediate success or via workarounds that may be required as a result of issues uncovered during the implementation.

Therefore, in a financial strategy context, performance management becomes yet another strategic extension: using a valuation as a strategic guide, key measures can be identified to assess whether the people executing a strategy are succeeding or not, and by what magnitude. Once final performance has been assessed, the financial strategy process begins anew—that is, with the formulation of a new strategy, the allocation of new resources, and the selection of new performance measures.

RISK

Each financial strategy stage generates a risk of loss, which must be carefully identified, assessed, and managed. All things in life, including running a business, rarely proceed without incident. For example, a business strategy may turn out to be wrong; the wrong resources may be allocated to a strategic implementation; the wrong measures may be chosen to assess performance, obfuscating results; and so on. Mistakes such as these can and often do occur, and when they do, value can be destroyed, which is significant because franchises are known for creating value, not destroying it. However, while value creation is the ultimate goal of every firm, it is not the only goal.

Recall that financial strategy begins with a customer focus (strategy formulation), then proceeds to a financial focus (the allocation of shareholder and debtholder funds) and a human resource focus (employees) before ending with a performance focus (management). Applied effectively, each of these focus points should contribute to the firm's value, and if a firm consistently demonstrates efficiency at each point, it will both become a franchise *and* remain one over time. However, the fact that so few firms are franchises demonstrates how difficult it is to accomplish this. One of the reasons for the difficulty is the inescapable presence of risk.

Each of the financial strategy stages contains an element of risk, meaning that each carries with it the possibility of loss. To begin with strategy, the risk associated with it is, logically enough, *strategic risk*, which can be defined as the possibility of destroying customer value or eroding a firm's differentiating characteristics. Consider, for example, Mattel's acquisition of The Learning Company (TLC) in 1999.

In essence, Mattel sought to resolve the performance issues emanating from its core product lines, such as Barbie dolls, GI Joe action figures, and Disney-licensed toys, by growing through acquisition into the interactive toy area. While this may have seemed to be a sensible strategy at the time, the acquisition of TLC was riddled with problems, which no doubt consumed managerial attention.[18] As Mattel's managers were wrestling with the issues of this acquisition, a key competitor—MGA Entertainment via its Bratz toy line—was planning an attack on Mattel's flagship product, Barbie. Between the years 2001 and 2004, the Bratz toy line took over the core market segment of 6- to 13-year-old girls from Barbie in a dramatic fashion.[19] In essence, by seeking to grow beyond its core, Mattel relatively neglected the needs of its existing customers and by so doing provided a key competitor with a strategic opportunity, with value-destroying results.

Resource allocation—the second financial strategy stage—generates a risk of *economic inefficiency*, which "occurs when resources—labor, machines, financial capital, information, even the time of executives—are allocated in an inappropriate manner."[20] This applies to business operations, human resource decisions (hiring, firing, promotions, and so on), M&A deals, joint ventures, vendor selection, capital projects, and other such actions. As an example, consider the case of the Revco leveraged buyout in 1986: it occurred at an acquisition premium of 48%, which arguably reflected undisciplined buying. After the firm went private, internal power struggles emerged that split organizational cohesion and loyalty. As a result, attention was diverted from operational performance and fiscal discipline, resulting in Revco's filing for Chapter 11 bankruptcy only 19 months after going private.[21]

The flip side of performance management—the third stage in the financial strategy process—is *risk management*, which received extensive attention following the 2007 subprime contagion and resulting risk management failures at a number of large financial institutions (such as Bear Stearns, and in 2008 Lehman Brothers). Generally, risk management can be defined as "the identification and assessment of the collective risks that affect firm value, and the implementation of a firm-wide strategy to manage those risks."[22] As an example of poor risk management, consider Quaker Oats's 1994 acquisition of Snapple.

Snapple had been suffering from performance issues in the year prior to its acquisition, which incredibly included a reduction in its earnings per share (EPS) forecast four days after Quaker announced its acquisition. Despite this announcement, Quaker Oats went ahead with its $1.7 billion acquisition; however, it failed to resolve Snapple's performance issues, and as a result, 2½ years later Quaker Oats sold Snapple for just $300 million, thereby taking a $1.4 billion write-off.[23] This result could probably have been avoided if Quaker Oats had assessed and managed the risks of both this acquisition and Snapple's performance more effectively.

FINANCIAL STRATEGY

It is understandable why many business and investment professionals seem to prefer compartmentalized organizational designs, and thus why the disciplines of strategy, finance, performance management, and risk management are managed as separate and distinct disciplines: it is easier to understand and manage the technical aspects of these disciplines when they are taken in isolation. For example, it is easier to allocate capital if the overall process for doing so belongs to the CFO. Similarly, personnel decisions can be easier to make if human resources are managed within the confines of a central human resources department. A silo-based approach also aids in assigning accountability, but its narrow focus can be a substantial disadvantage in times of extreme volatility and change. Additionally, it can be argued that business silos increase agency costs, as managers and employees vie for what is best for their silo (or career), even if it is at the long-term expense of the firm.

The interdisciplinary approach presented in this chapter centers on the fact that the three financial strategy stages are not separate functional disciplines subject to strict compartmentalization, but rather critical parts of one overall process. I would argue that Warren Buffett demonstrates the strength of this type of approach through the results that Berkshire Hathaway has achieved over time.* Nevertheless, many executives continue to rely upon traditional silo-based processes and operations to avoid strategic mishaps; however, such mishaps continue to occur. Consider, for example, those experienced at Disney.

Disney expanded its entertainment-based lines of business with the purchase of ABC, but it was unable to strategically connect network television, sports programming, and theme parks, resulting in lost market value and the resignation of its once-popular CEO, Michael Eisner. Similarly, AOL Time Warner's promise to strategically meld its various business units together to leverage the convergence of communication and entertainment media also suffered failure, leading to the resignation of CEO Steve Case.[24] These examples demonstrate the value that can be destroyed in the absence of an effective integration of strategy, finance, performance management, and the related management of the risks generated over time.

Firms that do achieve a cohesive approach to strategy, resource allocation, performance management, and risk management create value both internally and externally over time. For instance, investors and other stakeholders analyze firms with an eye toward consistency

---

* Buffett rarely receives accolades for his strategic abilities, but I would argue that strategy is actually his core competency; valuation, investment, and M&A are simply the logical outputs of his strategic insights.

and attention to core competencies, and reward actions that build a firm's franchise through a thoughtful, well-articulated vision for profit, sustainability, and growth. Historical examples include GEICO and IBM.

Internally, managers often find that once financial strategy–related information is available throughout a firm, empowered employees respond, increasing efficiency and organizational effectiveness. Harrah's Entertainment, for example, integrated its strategy for enhancing customer service by empowering cashiers with site-specific cash management systems to allocate cash levels properly based on the cashiers' analyses of a day's needs. Using this integrated method of managing strategy and financing, Harrah's has tripled its revenues and profits during the decade preceding the 2007–2008 credit crisis.[25] However, and perhaps even more significant, Harrah's activities provided its executives with valuable information that they could use to plan future strategic initiatives. The connection between strategic, financial, and performance information is a key benefit for Harrah's and a cogent illustration of the power of a financially strategic approach.

Each of the three financial strategy stages is, in a fundamental way, temporally linked:

● Strategy formulation pertains to the future.
● Resource allocation pertains to the employment of presently secured financial and human resources.
● Performance management essentially addresses what happens during the implementation.

This temporal linkage generates substantial information as the financial strategy stages cycle through time. The effective utilization

Figure 7-4

The Financial Strategy Feedback Loop

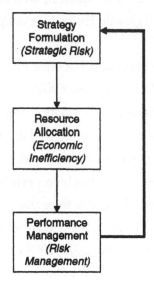

of this information can be considered an example of "double loop" learning, as illustrated in Figure 7-4.[26]

The figure illustrates the *financial strategy feedback loop*, which is the link between strategy and performance management and is therefore a powerful information source. Unfortunately, this information source is rarely tapped or leveraged. Those firms that do leverage it, though, are among the most successful and include Johnson & Johnson and Microsoft.

Microsoft's strategy to gain market share through product bundling and giveaways has generated some regulatory controversy. Beyond the controversy, however, is Microsoft's unquestioned ability to fold marketplace feedback on the needs of its customers into its product development, resource allocation, and strategic planning processes, which has kept it at the forefront of innovation and customer satisfaction in an incredibly competitive industry.

In short, the success of financially strategic firms (or franchises) is based on their ability not just to develop, sustain, and grow a competitive advantage for individual products over time, but to efficiently analyze and act on information regarding potential opportunities and threats, also over time.

CONCLUSION

Financial strategy can broadly be defined as an interdisciplinary approach to more efficiently allocating scarce resources within a firm to satisfy customer preferences better or more efficiently over time. The approach has three primary stages: strategy formulation, resource allocation, and performance measurement, each of which generates a risk of loss, and all of which are temporally linked. For summary and application purposes, the essence of each stage can be represented by the following questions:

- How does the firm satisfy its customers' preferences better or more efficiently over time? How does it differentiate itself from its competition?
  - Is the strategy viable *and* sustainable? What internal weakness or external threat could derail it?*

---

* From the popular, and deceptively simple, SWOT (or strengths, weaknesses, opportunities, and threats) strategic framework.

- What is the most efficient way to fund and staff strategic initiatives?
  - Is the valuation consistent with the assumptions of the strategy it quantifies?
  - Is the firm staffed appropriately to implement its strategy?
- Were strategic implementation activities successful? Why or why not?
  - Were strategic risks identified, assessed, and managed in a timely manner? Why or why not?

The key insight of the financial strategy approach is that the interaction of strategy, resource allocation, performance management, and risk management can generate more value over time than any of the disciplines taken in isolation. This is not to imply that specialized skills in these disciplines are no longer necessary; such skills are and will remain incredibly important. However, the perspective required for success at the managerial level is frequently far broader than any one discipline can provide. For example, while Warren Buffett is best known as a value investor and Sandy Weill as a deal maker, the results that each of these men achieved were built on the successful application of a variety of disciplines over time. To put this observation into the context of financial strategy, consider the illustration presented in Figure 7-5.

Each intersection in the figure illustrates a basic financial strategy interface. These interfaces can generate substantial amounts of information that senior managers can leverage and capitalize on to create value over time. Both Buffett and Weill, for example, instinctively capitalized on such information throughout their successful careers.

Figure 7-5

Financial Strategy Interaction

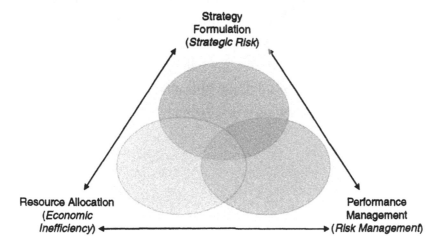

However, this type of information is perhaps best leveraged on an organizational rather than an individual basis.

The financial strategy feedback loop is the information and learning component of the approach, and it essentially involves the recording and application of the knowledge acquired in prior financial strategy stages. By so doing, this feedback loop addresses questions such as

- What has been learned from prior cycles?
- How can that knowledge be used to enhance current strategy formulation, resource allocation, performance management, and risk management efforts?

The efficiency of learning organizations is widely known, as are the exemplary results generated by such organizations—for example,

GEICO and Watson's IBM. While relatively few firms have been able to match these results and become franchises over time, I am confident that more financially strategic firms will produce similar results in the future, thereby creating ample opportunities for the value investors of the future, so long as they are able to identify them. The process of investment opportunity identification, or screening, is one of the topics that I address in the conclusion following this chapter.

CONCLUSION

A general definition of intrinsic value would be "that value which is justified by the facts—e.g., assets, earnings, dividends, definite prospects."

—*Benjamin Graham and David Dodd[1]*

Value investing, the strategy of buying stocks at an appreciable discount from the value of the underlying businesses, is one strategy that provides a road map to successfully navigate not only through good times but also through turmoil. Buying at a discount creates a margin of safety for the investor—room for imprecision, error, bad luck or the vicissitudes of volatile markets and economies.

—*Seth A. Klarman[2]*

INTRODUCTION

Every now and then, when I pick up a popular business magazine, I come across an article that reports on some new quantitatively oriented trader who has come up with a system that processes fundamental information "in a manner similar to Graham and Dodd, except much more *rigorously*." In this context, *rigorous* usually means heavily mathematical. When I read things like this, I simply shake my head and put the magazine down. As I have demonstrated in this book, applied value investing is about identifying what you know and what you do not know, and then taking steps to quantify what you do know in a conservative yet rigorous manner so that a disciplined valuation can be formulated. This type of approach tends to optimally leverage business judgment—which usually is very costly to obtain—over time, and can be practically applied within the confines of a few broad rules:

- Do not invest outside of a well-defined circle of competence.
- Identify your own investment opportunities and value them conservatively within a disciplined framework.
- Invest only with a reasonable margin of safety. Transactions without a margin of safety are speculations, as Benjamin Graham stressed in his writings and as the noted modern value investor Seth Klarman also stresses in his.[3]

In short, applied value investing is a discipline, not a system, and therefore mathematics is a tool, not a solution. One way of illustrating this is by examining the analytical layers of the approach as illustrated in Figure C-1.

In the following sections of this Conclusion, I discuss some of the key aspects of each layer of analysis illustrated in the figure. I then close this book with commentary on additional information sources for those who are interested in exploring this subject further.

SCREENING

Several quantitative variables have become associated with applied value investing over the years, including assets selling at

- Low market-to-book ratios
- Low price-to-cash flow, price-to-earnings, or price-to-sales ratios
- High dividend yields

Figure C-1

Layered Analysis

Screening

- *Quantitative*—low market-to-book, low price-to-earnings, high dividend yield, and so on.
- *Qualitative*—business cycle analysis, franchise-based research, special situations (such as bankruptcies, spin-offs, and restructurings) analysis, and so on.

Initial Valuation

- *Conservative*
  - *Net Asset Value (NAV) Adjustments.*
  - *Earnings Power Value (EPV) Assumptions—earnings-based inputs.*
  - *Franchise Value (FV) Analysis—identifying competitive advantage.*
  - *Growth Value (GV) Analysis—evaluating the logic of growth.*
- *Initial margin of safety assessment.*

Validations

- *Net Asset Value (NAV) Adjustments*—appraiser, auditor, consultant, and/or expert input on select balance sheet adjustments.
- *Earnings Power Value (EPV) Assumptions*—targeted executive discussion items.
- *Franchise Value (FV) Analysis*—financial strategy–based inquiries and corresponding questions for executive management.
- *Growth Value (GV) Analysis*—do consistent strategic themes support growth initiatives?

Final Valuation

- *Margin of safety assessment.*

There are many other quantitative variables that can be developed mathematically, depending on the objectives of an investor, portfolio manager, or M&A specialist.[4] However, it is important to remember that whatever form a quantitative analysis may take, in a Graham and Dodd context it is only a screen, or the first layer of the analytical process. Quantitative screens are not systems, no matter how mathematically "rigorous" they may be. Consider Benjamin Graham's thoughts on this topic:

> In forty-four years of Wall Street experience and study I have never seen dependable calculations made about common stock values, or related investment policies, that went beyond simple arithmetic or the most elementary algebra. Whenever calculus is brought in, or higher algebra, you could take it as a warning signal that the operator was trying to substitute theory for experience, and usually also to give to speculation the deceptive guise of investment.[5]

This quotation is an excerpt from an address that Graham gave in the year 1958, and yet as I edit this Conclusion in 2008, I am amazed at how current Graham's insight is. For example, the role that the abuse of higher mathematics played in the credit crises of 2007–2008 vividly illustrates how little investors in general, and Wall Street in particular, seem to have learned in the last fifty years.[6]

Screens can also be qualitative in nature. For example, a qualitative screen could be based on business cycle analysis, as shown in Chapter 5. Another qualitative screen could involve franchises, which admittedly can be difficult to identify, especially early on, meaning right after a franchise has been formed, when it is just starting to generate economic returns.

A friend of mine conducted an informal but interesting study on franchises. Essentially, he went back in history and discovered that a number of well-known franchises were profiled in popular magazines such as *Time* somewhat before their stocks were widely recognized on the market. The results of this study are private (meaning that they are not being published), but its example illustrates how qualitative and publicly available information could potentially be used to screen for franchise-based opportunities.[7]

Qualitative sources could also be used to identify special situation–based value investment opportunities, such as bankruptcies, spin-offs, and restructurings, which are reported on in newspapers, on the Internet, and in specialty publications.[8]

In practice, I generally recommend the use of both quantitative and qualitative screens. While this practice can generate a great deal of information, it has a natural filter in the circle of competence; in other words, one's circle of competence will determine how much information needs to be generated to efficiently identify possible investment opportunities for further consideration in an initial valuation.

INITIAL VALUATION

An initial valuation is a working hypothesis of value that is based on research and applied business insight. An initial valuation is used to assess whether a screened potential investment opportunity could contain a reasonable margin of safety, and thus qualifies as a candidate for more in-depth levels of analysis. In the following subsections, I highlight key initial valuation considerations by level of value along the modern Graham and Dodd continuum.

Net Asset Value

Valuation as described in this book begins with balance sheet analysis and net asset value (NAV). The discipline of reconstructing a balance sheet, line by line, on a reproduction basis helps to level-set assumptions, and by so doing helps to ground a valuation in the facts, as noted, for example, by Graham and Dodd in the quote that opens this Conclusion.

Most balance sheet adjustments are fairly straightforward; for example, the mechanics of adjusting receivables, inventory, land, and even reserves can be fairly obvious (this is not to say that deriving these adjustments is easy, only that the approaches to deriving them are fairly well known). The goodwill adjustment, however, can be somewhat complex because it is intangible.

In a modern Graham and Dodd context, goodwill frequently encompasses a blended adjustment of a wide range of intangible assets. Not only can the scope of this adjustment be incredibly wide, but the basis for it—a multiple of the selling, general, and administrative expense—is extremely subjective. Frankly, this adjustment is the only part of the modern Graham and Dodd approach that I feel needs to be further developed. One step in the development process could involve mapping the components of intangible assets that are included in the goodwill category. Consider the example presented in Figure C-2.

The figure presents a "strategy map," based on the seminal work of Robert Kaplan and David Norton, that illustrates the basic components of the goodwill category. I made several adaptations to the original diagram. First, I grayed out the "Revenue Growth Strategy" boxes because growth is assessed in the final level of value along the continuum, not at the NAV level. I also identified key

Figure C-2

Goodwill-Based "Strategy Map"

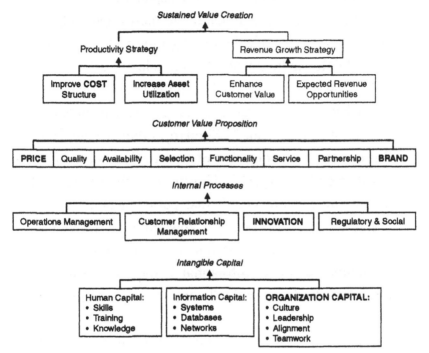

Adapted from Robert Kaplan and David Norton, "Measuring the Strategic Readiness of Intangible Assets," *Harvard Business Review*, February 2004, p. 4. The "Revenue Growth Strategy" category in the upper right corner of the exhibit has been intentionally grayed out.

intangible assets in bold capital letters. Working from the top of the diagram down:

● *Cost* is the first variable identified. Low-cost products can generate substantial goodwill over time, as we saw in Chapter 3 with GEICO. Other well-known examples include Progressive Insurance, Wal-Mart, and Target.

● *Price* is the second variable because increased customer value should equate to pricing power. Microsoft is a contemporary example of this, while Gen Re in the 1960s to early 1980s is a historical example (as noted in Chapter 4).[9]

- *Brand* is the next, and arguably the most important, intangible asset. For example, bestselling author and former CEO David D'Alessandro stated, "'Will it help or hurt the brand?' is the most useful of all mantras in the marketplace. It is the prism through which every business decision, major or minor, can and should be made."[10] Similarly, value investor Thomas Russo noted that an objective of modern Graham and Dodd–based practitioners is to "find businesses selling at reasonable prices with superior brands that possess genuine competitive advantage."[11] For example, powerful brands were identified in Chapter 2 as a substantial part of my Sears valuation. As another example, substantial brand value would also likely be reflected in virtually any valuation of Johnson & Johnson.

- Every firm strives to be *innovative*, but very few firms are able to be consistently innovative over time. Apple is an example of a successful innovation-based firm, as are Microsoft and IBM. GEICO has also been incredibly innovative with respect to its highly entertaining marketing campaign, as noted in Chapter 3.

- Next to brand, *organizational capital* may be the most important intangible asset. An example of this is Goldman Sachs's and JPMorgan Chase's performances in 2007 following the subprime contagion compared to that of many other financial institutions.[12] Obviously, there can be numerous factors behind these firms' relative success, but I would argue that most of those factors probably emanate from their organizational capital base, which is what seems to have inspired Warren Buffett to invest in Goldman Sachs (on a distressed basis) in 2008.[13]

Decomposing goodwill into discrete categories like this facilitates more focused levels of analysis, which can range from simple ratio-based analysis to more intensive forms of statistical and private market value–based analyses, depending on the complexity of the valuation at hand. This type of approach seems more consistent with the underlying philosophy of Graham and Dodd–based valuation than simply aggregating all of a firm's intangible assets into one subjective, multiple-based adjustment.

Earnings Power Value

Estimating sustainable operating earnings or earnings before interest and taxes (EBIT) is fundamental to earnings power valuation and can be somewhat complex. There are a variety of ways to approach this estimation, samples of which were provided in Chapters 1 through 4 of this book. There is no one way to make this estimate, which is one of the reasons why the circle of competence is so important: investors or analysts must know which approach is right for the particular firm they are valuing at the particular time they are valuing it.

As noted in prior chapters, most valuations end after EPV because most firms are not franchises. However, when EPV is substantially greater than NAV, the firm being valued may be a franchise, and therefore requires further analysis.

Franchise Value

Franchise valuation can present a variety of significant challenges. First, franchises are inherently intangible and thus inherently difficult to value. Furthermore, many franchises have finite life spans; for example, academic studies suggest that there is a general franchise life span, or competitive advantage horizon, of approximately five to ten years.[14] A dramatic example of a finite franchise life span, and the risks it can generate, was presented in the Chapter 4 valuation of Gen Re.

Franchise analysis is rooted in strategy, which can seem simple—especially with the benefit of hindsight—but in practice can be inordinately confusing and complex. Fortunately, base-level franchise considerations seem to be relatively clear:

- A track record of *economic returns,* which can be defined as a return on capital (ROC) greater than the weighted-average cost of capital (WACC) or a return on equity (ROE) greater than the cost of equity, over time.[15]
- A very clear strategy, or some unique way in which a firm creates value for its customers. Uniqueness is very important in franchise valuation because without it there is no franchise; in other words, if the firm you are valuing is similar to other firms in its industry, it is not a franchise. Needless to say, not many valuations will pass this litmus test.
- An executive team that is focused on both implementing the strategy *and* perpetuating it over time.

Evaluation of the second and third of these items is likely to require substantial strategic-based research and analysis, which can be highly specialized and somewhat involved. As this is not a strategy book, I will identify strategic references that could be consulted for further information in the Resources section.

Growth Value

Growth is the final level of value along the modern Graham and Dodd value continuum, and it is the most intangible level of value. Growth is also one of the most difficult ways to earn a superior return over time. The reasons why involve macro-based, market, and micro-based considerations.

Macro-based considerations are the easiest to explain: when markets are booming, growth-based strategies tend to do spectacularly well, and they can be fairly easy to implement. An obvious recent example is the Nasdaq index during the "new economy" boom of the late 1990s, as profiled in Chapter 5. The "buy on dips and then hold on" and "buy the latest technology IPO" approaches did very well while the Nasdaq was booming. An incident that I witnessed one day provides a dramatic example of this.

On the train to work one morning, I sat directly across from two very nice ladies who appeared to be average, middle-class workers in their late fifties to early sixties. Part of their discussion that morning went something like this:*

"Did you read that Warren Buffett is not investing in technology stocks because he doesn't understand them?"

"Oh, my."

"Yes, I know. He's really missing out. What a shame. He was once so successful. Too bad he hasn't kept up with the times. My technology stocks are up over 100% already this year, and I see a lot of upside—so much so that I plan to retire soon."[16]

---

* For clarification purposes, I was not eavesdropping on this conversation; however, as I was directly across from these individuals, it was impossible not to hear their conversation, given how loud they were speaking.

The poignancy of this moment—which occurred as the Nasdaq was nearing its top in early 2000 (and therefore, as of 2008, the person who made the comment about retiring soon is probably still hard at work)—is impossible to capture in writing, but it illustrates my point: when markets are booming, even the most basic growth strategies can generate exceptional returns for practically anyone who employs them.[17] Of course, those returns will end when a bust ensues, as it invariably will, but it could take years for that to occur.

Market dynamics also tend to limit growth opportunities. Growth inherently reflects increasing levels of demand, but the economic profit generated from that demand is a signal that will attract the attention of competing firms, which will try to capture some of that profit through innovative products, services, or cost offerings of their own. Still other competitors will try to anticipate shifting demand and therefore concentrate on emerging opportunities that can erode or eliminate base demand. Such disruptive change-oriented strategies have been written about extensively and can destroy established growth initiatives.[18]

From a micro-based level, growth creates value only if it occurs within a franchise. Managing a franchise requires focused discipline on delivering a unique value proposition; however, growth often requires substantial innovation. Balancing these two aspects—namely, focused management on the one hand and innovative strategy formulation and execution on the other—can be extremely difficult over time. Firms that are able to balance the two, though, can create substantial value over time.

Margin of Safety

To sum up, once an initial valuation has been prepared, a preliminary determination can be made as to whether an investment seems to contain a reasonable margin of safety. A rule of thumb is that the margin of safety should be at least 30 to 33%, and preferably much larger. If a valuation meets this rule, the next step is to validate the initial adjustment and calculation assumptions.

NAV ADJUSTMENTS

The extent to which independent appraisers, experts, auditors, and other such professionals are retained to validate an initial NAV adjustment is contingent upon the scope and scale of a particular valuation and the way individual value investors practice their craft. For example, as Roger Lowenstein observed in his introduction to the sixth edition of Graham and Dodd's *Security Analysis,* "while some investors rely strictly on the published financials, others do substantial legwork. Eddie Lampert, the hedge fund manager,* visited dozens of outlets of auto-parts retailer AutoZone before he bought a controlling stake in it."[19]

In other words, whether an investor or analyst engages in "legwork" or just concentrates on the financials and other information sources (as Warren Buffett seems to do) depends on his individual approach to value investing. However, the option of retaining experts is one of the dynamics that makes the modern Graham and Dodd approach seemingly ideal for corporate M&A, as it enables corporations to leverage their organizational capital (see Figure C-2) or the vast stores of industry-specific knowledge within their workforce, including outside expert contacts.

---

* This is the same Eddie Lampert who purchased Sears, the valuation of which was the topic of Chapter 2.

For example, in the Sears valuation presented in Chapter 2, the two key adjustments that would have required independent expert input were the real estate adjustment and the goodwill adjustment. The scope of both of these adjustments—$804 million in the case of real estate and $10.12 billion in the case of goodwill—required substantial research to ensure that the adjustments were neither too aggressive nor too low. Had another retailer expressed an interest in Sears, it could have used its own property managers to appraise the value of Sears' real estate holdings, and possibly consulting firms that it had worked with to help appraise the value of Sears' goodwill. This is not to imply that the aforementioned Graham and Dodd–based guideline of being "approximately right rather than absolutely wrong" no longer applies; rather, it reflects the fact that there are degrees of being approximately right, and that all practical efforts should be made to be as approximately right as possible, without falling under a delusion of certainty.

Delusions of certainty can have a strong appeal, somewhat akin to a siren song. For example, the hedge fund Long-Term Capital Management (LTCM) found this out the hard way in 1998. Despite having two Nobel Prize–winning economists on its staff, along with a former member of the Federal Reserve, Ivy League finance professors, and celebrated bond traders, LTCM failed disastrously, and by so doing seemingly threatened the short-term viability of the global monetary system.[20] LTCM's failure has been attributed to a myopic fixation on quantitative models based on historical distribution and correlation assumptions that were expected to accurately represent the future.[21] This was a very clear delusion of certainty, although some members of LTCM still seem not to recognize it as such.[22]

In sum, NAV adjustments should be based on sound professional judgment and validated with select expert input to the extent that this is desirable or possible. As no valuation will be 100% accurate, all adjustments should be made *conservatively*.

EPV ASSUMPTIONS

The most significant EPV assumption pertains to how operating earnings (or EBIT) is estimated. There are a number of ways of making this estimation, as noted earlier. Validating the estimate could involve a review of a target's or an investment's operating and financial plans in addition to probing discussions with the executive team. In this regard, Regulation FD (Fair Disclosure) governs communication between a firm and its stockholders (current and future), and as I am not a lawyer, I will not comment on the extent of communication that this regulation allows (you should consult with an attorney who is knowledgeable in this area). Whatever level of communication you are able to secure with a firm and its executives is important and could mean the difference between a successful investment and an unsuccessful one. I note that direct corporate communication is an option that is available only to professional investors and corporate M&A specialists, which, once again, makes the modern Graham and Dodd approach seemingly ideal for corporate M&A.

FRANCHISE VALIDATION

Perhaps nowhere is assumption validation more important than with franchise valuation. Validation of a franchise naturally flows from the output from validating EPV assumptions, inasmuch as a franchise is identified by a substantial EPV-to-NAV spread.

The focus of franchise validation is a firm's strategic plan and corresponding discussions with its executive team. I presented sample lines of inquiry that could form the basis for this activity at the end of Chapter 7. To put such inquiries into context, here are the broad objectives of the franchise validation process:

- To clearly identify a firm's strategy and the risks that could jeopardize it
- To gain a level of comfort that the strategy is viable over time, which means at least the next five to ten years
- To become convinced that a firm's management is committed to both defending *and* perpetuating its franchise over time

If any of these objectives is not achieved, then, in general, you should not pay for a franchise because it is likely that no franchise exists. While this may seem fairly obvious, in practice validating a franchise can be extremely difficult and complex. Even Warren Buffett, for example, has found it difficult at times, most especially with the Gen Re acquisition that was profiled in Chapter 4. Frankly, if Buffett could sustain a substantial franchise risk–generated loss, then anyone can.

GROWTH VALUATION

I have stressed the intangibility of growth throughout this book, and therefore you may be tired of reading about it by now. I did this because growth-based assumptions have consistently resulted in higher valuations, which generate higher prices for investments and acquisitions, which, in turn, generate higher levels of risk over time. Consider Graham and Dodd's comments on the subject:

> It follows that *once the investor pays a substantial amount for the growth factor,* he is inevitably assuming certain kinds of risks; *viz.,* that the growth will be less than he anticipates, that over the long pull he will have paid too much for what he gets, that for a considerable period the market will value the stock less optimistically than he does.[23] (Italics original.)

Mitigation of growth-based risk requires strong business logic—strategic, financial, and operational—before growth-based initiatives should be undertaken. If this logic is not readily apparent, then growth should not be paid for (and growth initiatives should not be undertaken).

Perhaps the quintessential Graham and Dodd–based example of successful growth initiatives is the GEICO acquisition, which was profiled in Chapter 3 and which I recommend that you study carefully. I am not the first to recommend the study of GEICO. For example, hedge fund manager Eddie Lampert reportedly studied the GEICO acquisition intensely,[24] which obviously paid off, as he subsequently acquired Kmart and, as profiled in Chapter 2, Sears at prices consistent with a margin of safety.

After your study of GEICO, I recommend that you revisit Chapter 4 and the Gen Re acquisition so that you have a balanced understanding of both the potential benefits and the potential risks of franchise-based growth initiatives.

FINAL VALUATION

After all adjustments and estimates have been validated, checked, and rechecked, a final valuation can be constructed and the margin of safety assessed. For a stock purchase, the process of accomplishing this is fairly straightforward: the offer price on the market is compared with the valuation. With an acquisition or side deal, however, pricing can become the subject of negotiation.

Negotiation can be a complex endeavor, but, like strategy, it often looks relatively easy to the uninitiated. Negotiating is not easy, especially when it involves substantial amounts of money.

Before a negotiation commences, a formal negotiating strategy should be prepared. A wide variety of books have been written about negotiation and how to formulate a negotiation strategy. One of the best books on these topics that I have read is titled *Getting to Yes*. Here is what the authors of that book say about developing a negotiating strategy:

> First, in almost all cases, strategy is a function of preparation. If you are well prepared, a strategy will suggest itself. If you are well versed in the standards relevant to your negotiation, it will be obvious which ones to discuss and which ones the other side might raise. If you have thoroughly considered your interests, it will be clear which ones to mention early on and which ones to bring up later or not at all. And if you have formulated your [best alternative to a negotiated agreement] in advance, you'll know when to walk.[25]

Applied value investing is all about preparation; therefore, if you follow the framework conservatively level by level, research all adjustments and estimates intensely, check and cross-check them vigorously, and consider each investment's margin of safety carefully, you will be well prepared to negotiate from a position of value.

CONCLUSION

Applied value investing begins with identifying and developing a well-defined circle of competence and adopting a margin of safety–based mindset. These two characteristics are fundamental to the successful application of the approach in either an investment or an M&A context over time. Once these characteristics are established, the disciplined application of the valuation framework will help you to achieve your goals, if you apply it well.

One benefit of the framework is that it facilitates the constant checking and rechecking of assumptions and estimations. For example, EPV serves as a check on NAV; independent experts can be retained to check the initial NAV assumptions; conversations with management and due diligence activities can validate earnings, franchise, and growth-based assumptions; and so on. Once again, the aim of Graham and Dodd–based investing is to be "approximately right rather than absolutely wrong," but that does not mean that all practical efforts should not be taken to be as approximately right as possible. In fact, an effective value investor is likely to understand the economics, value drivers, and risk drivers of a company he is valuing as well as, and in some cases actually better than, a company's officers.[26] This is an important point because at times, value investing can be portrayed as a somewhat less-than-rigorous discipline.

For example, consider the following comment that was reported in a popular newspaper article on Warren Buffett's investment in

Goldman Sachs in September of 2008: "Mr. Buffett is famous for making quick investment decisions based on his gut. For the Goldman deal, he says, 'I didn't see a book. I just made a judgment.' The quality of Goldman's management team and its franchise, he says, sealed the deal for him."[27]

Upon reading this comment, one could reasonably infer that Buffett really did make a $5 billion investment, which is a significant investment even for him, "based on his gut." However, that same article noted that Goldman approached Buffett before the September deal, and here is how he described what happened: "'They [Goldman Sachs] had sounded me out in the past, as everyone else had,' Buffett says. The previous offer, he says, was 'nothing I would say "yes" to.'"[28]

To help put the apparent disparity of these two paragraphs into context, consider the following: Warren Buffett includes "acquisition criteria" in every Berkshire Hathaway annual report and on Berkshire Hathaway's Web site. Here is a reproduction of those criteria, which essentially represent Buffett's investment opportunity screen:

1. Large purchases (at least $50 million of before-tax earnings),
2. Demonstrated consistent earning power (future projections are of no interest to us, nor are "turnaround" situations),
3. Businesses earning good returns on equity while employing little or no debt,
4. Management in place (we can't supply it),
5. Simple businesses (if there's lots of technology, we won't understand it),
6. An offering price (we don't want to waste our time or that of the seller by talking, even preliminarily, about a transaction when price is unknown).

The larger the company, the greater will be our interest: We would like to make an acquisition in the $5-20 billion range. *We are not interested, however, in receiving suggestions about purchases we might make in the general stock market.*[29] (Italics original.)

The universe of firms qualifying for these criteria is finite, which is as it should be, because that is the purpose of a screen—to limit potential investment opportunities. Therefore, it would not surprise me to learn that Buffett had valued all the firms within his screened universe before he was contacted by any of them, and that he consistently updates his valuations as circumstances warrant. That way, he can just make a judgment "based on his gut" regarding any deal when the time is right. This is not meant to imply that Buffett misled his interviewer in the newspaper article quoted; rather, it is meant to point out that there is very likely a significant difference between how you and I might define a "gut" decision and how a 50+ year Graham and Dodd veteran defines one.

The lesson here is that disciplined and conservative valuation and the research, checking, rechecking, and cross-checking of assumptions that go with it are the keys to long-term success in applied value investing, as well as—in general—in most other professions. And here is the best part: if you love doing this, it won't even seem like work.

I wish you well on your value investing journey.

RESOURCES

The primary sources for Graham and Dodd–based investment are the six editions of *Security Analysis* that were published by McGraw-Hill, which is also the publisher of this book:

- The first edition, published in 1934
- The second edition, published in 1940
- The third edition, published in 1951
- The fourth edition, published in 1962
- The fifth edition, published in 1988
- The sixth edition, published in 2008

If you have not read these books yet, then I recommend that you start with the sixth edition: it is an update of the 1940 edition with superb commentary from Seth Klarman, Bruce Greenwald, Roger Lowenstein, James Grant, and others.

Following *Security Analysis*, the next best reference is Benjamin Graham's *The Intelligent Investor*. The editions of this book that are in print include the original 1949 edition, a 1973 edition, and a recent 2003 edition.

After Benjamin Graham's books, the four most important value investing books, in my opinion, are

- Bruce Greenwald, Judd Kahn, Paul Sonkin, and Michael van Biema, *Value Investing: From Graham to Buffett and Beyond* (New York: Wiley, 2001).
- Bruce Greenwald and Judd Kahn, *Competition Demystified: A Radically Simplified Approach to Business Strategy* (New York: Portfolio, 2005), which is predominantly a strategy book, but is obviously written from a Graham and Dodd perspective, given who the authors are.
- Seth Klarman, *Margin of Safety: Risk-Averse Investment Strategies for the Thoughtful Investor* (New York: HarperBusiness, 1991). The author is one of the most successful value investors practicing today, and his book on the subject is superb.
- Joel Greenblatt, *You Can Be a Stock Market Genius: Uncover the Secret Hiding Places of Stock Market Profits* (New York: Fireside, 1997). Don't be fooled by the title of this book; it is an excellent work that was written by an exceptionally talented value investor. That said, I would not recommend any other book with a title like this one's.

In addition, if you have the opportunity to attend Bruce Greenwald's value investing course at Columbia University—either the full-time or the executive version—I strongly recommend that you take it.

Numerous books have been written about Warren Buffett, but *the* book is arguably Roger Lowenstein, *Buffett: The Making of an American Capitalist* (New York: Broadway, 1995). After you read that book, I strongly recommend that you read Lowenstein's *When Genius*

Failed: The Rise and Fall of Long-Term Capital Management (New York: Random House, 2000), which is an absolute classic.

Several non-Graham and Dodd–related books that I recommend reading are

- Robert Bruner, *Deals from Hell: M&A Lessons That Rise above the Ashes* (Hoboken, N.J.: Wiley, 2005).
- Paul Carroll and Chunka Mui, *Billion Dollar Lessons: What You Can Learn from the Most Inexcusable Business Failures of the Last 25 Years* (New York: Portfolio, 2008). You can really appreciate a good deal only when you know what a bad one looks like, and it is much better to acquire that knowledge through books like these rather than through actual experience.
- Stuart Gilson, *Creating Value through Corporate Restructuring: Case Studies in Bankruptcies, Buyouts, and Breakups* (New York: Wiley, 2001), especially Chapter 6 on "vulture investing," which as an academic paper won the author the 1996 Graham and Dodd award.
- Peter Lynch, *One Up on Wall Street: How to Use What You Already Know to Make Money in the Market* (New York: Simon & Schuster, 1989).
- Peter Lynch, *Beating the Street* (New York: Simon & Schuster, 1994 [1993]). Lynch is not a Graham and Dodder, but he is a fellow traveler and one of the most successful mutual fund managers in history.
- Howard Schilit, *Financial Shenanigans: How to Detect Accounting Gimmicks and Fraud in Financial Reports*, 2nd ed. (New York: McGraw-Hill, 2002), which is especially helpful for financial statement analysis.

For more information on financial strategy, see the original book by William E. Fruhan, Jr., *Financial Strategy: Studies in the Creation, Transfer, and Destruction of Shareholder Value* (Homewood, Ill.: Irwin, 1979). Robert S. Kaplan and David P. Norton have published a number of seminal multi-discipline-based writings, including

- *The Balanced Scorecard: Translating Strategy into Action* (Boston: HBS Press, 1996).
- *The Strategy-Focused Organization: How Balanced Scorecard Companies Thrive in the New Business Environment* (Boston: HBS Press, 2001), which is my favorite book of the five that I have listed here. If you are interested in franchise valuation, this is a particularly important book to study.
- *Strategy Maps: Converting Intangible Assets into Tangible Outcomes* (Boston: HBS Press, 2004).
- *Alignment: Using the Balanced Scorecard to Create Corporate Synergies* (Boston: HBS Press, 2006).
- *The Execution Premium: Linking Strategy to Operations for Competitive Advantage* (Boston: HBS Press, 2008).

Turning to strategy, the best place to start is with Liam Fahey and Robert Randall, eds. *The Portable MBA in Strategy* (New York: Wiley, 2001). Robert Randall is also the editor of the journal *Strategy & Leadership*, which is both extremely good and very practical, so I strongly recommend it. Another strategy resource is the book *Competition Demystified*, cited earlier, which can be compared to Michael Porter, *Competitive Strategy: Techniques for Analyzing Industries and Competitors* (New York: Free Press, 1980).

Finally, I strongly recommend former Windsor Fund manager John Neff's autobiography, *John Neff on Investing* (New York: Wiley, 1999), which Neff coauthored with writer S. L. Mintz.

A WORD ON ECONOMICS

The field of mainstream economics today is, in many ways, extremely troubled. Readers of this book probably do not need me to outline the reasons why this is the case.[1] Here are some economics-related resources that I have found useful, and that may be of interest.

An excellent general introduction to economics is Thomas Sowell, *Basic Economics: A Common Sense Guide to the Economy*, 3rd ed. (New York: Basic Books, 2007).

In Chapter 5, I refer extensively to the Austrian School of economics in my analysis of the "new economy" boom and bust. More information on Austrian business cycle theory (ABCT) can be found in

- Richard Ebling, ed., *The Austrian Theory of the Trade Cycle and Other Essays* (Auburn, Ala.: Ludwig von Mises Institute, 1996), which is a very practical introduction.
- Murray Rothbard, *America's Great Depression* (Auburn, Ala.: Ludwig von Mises Institute, 2000 [1963]). As you read this book about the "new era" of the 1920s and 1930s, you will find amazing parallels with current, post new economy times. That said, one must remember that history does not repeat itself exactly, but that it often rhymes, as it is currently doing. For example, consider the following parallel between the credit crisis of 2008 and the Panic of 1907: "'What Buffett is doing [meaning, investing in firms like Goldman Sachs and

General Electric in 2008] is similar in ways to what [financier J. P.] Morgan did in 1907,' said Richard Sylla, an economist and financial historian at the Stern School of Business at New York University. 'It's what you might call profitable patriotism.'"[2] However, a far more interesting parallel, which was identified by Howard Marks in the recently published sixth edition of Graham and Dodd's *Security Analysis*, pertains to real estate mortgages in the 1920s and the 2000s.[3]

● Ludwig von Mises, *The Theory of Money and Credit* (Indianapolis, Ind.: Liberty, 1980 [1912]), which is the book that introduced ABCT.
● Roger Garrison, *Time and Money: The Macroeconomics of Capital Structure* (New York: Routledge, 2001), which is a modern treatment of ABCT.

The first two of these books are easily accessible to lay readers, while the last two are considerably more advanced and technical.

A bit of historical trivia: there is a link of sorts between value investing and Austrian economics. Warren Buffett's father, Howard, was a U.S. congressman and a member of what is known as the "Old Right," which was a political movement (it no longer exists, but Congressman and former presidential candidate Ron Paul of Texas is attempting to resurrect it) that espoused limited to no governmental intervention in markets (or decisions and activities involving buying and selling), extremely low levels of government spending, noninterference in foreign entanglements, low taxes, and so on. Howard Buffett is mentioned in the late Austrian economist Murray Rothbard's book *Man, Economy and State* (Auburn, Ala.: Ludwig von Mises Institute, 2004 [1962]), pp. xxv and lxxxi–lxxxii. I strongly recommend this book to those who may be interested in economics, but note before you buy it that it is 1,000 pages in length.

An excellent general overview on the new era boom and bust of the 1920s is Tom Nicholas, *Trouble with a Bubble*, HBS Case Services, #9-808-067, April 3, 2008.

A superb work of economic forecasting is Peter Warburton, *Debt & Delusion: Central Bank Follies That Threaten Economic Disaster* (Princeton, N.J.: WorldMeta View, 2005 [1999]), which predicted the credit crises of 2007–2008 years beforehand.[4]

The field of behavioral economics is also generating a great deal of interesting material as of late, which will not come as a surprise to value investors, inasmuch as Graham and Dodd wrote about "the irrational behavior of the market" in 1934[5] and described "the market [as] a *voting machine*, wherein countless individuals register choices which are the product partly of reason and partly of emotion."[6] (Italics original.) Three current and noteworthy books on behavioral economics are

- Robert Shiller, *Irrational Exuberance*, 2nd ed. (New York: Currency, 2005).
- Dan Ariely, *Predictably Irrational: The Hidden Forces That Shape Our Decisions* (New York: Harper, 2008).
- Richard Thaler and Cass Sunstein, *Nudge: Improving Decisions about Health, Wealth, and Happiness* (New Haven, Conn.: Yale, 2008).

In closing, I generally recommend that you ignore economic material that is either written or presented by economists who shill for a newspaper, television show, government/political party, financial institution, or consulting firm. Peter Lynch, the famed former manager of the Fidelity Magellan Fund, was probably thinking of such material when he famously said, "If you spend 13 minutes a year on economics, you've wasted 10 minutes."[7]

ENDNOTES

PREFACE

1. Benjamin Graham, *The Intelligent Investor* (New York: Harper & Row, 1973 [1949]), p. 286.
2. As quoted in Robert Hagstrom, *The Warren Buffett Way: Investment Strategies of the World's Greatest Investor* (New York: Wiley, 1994), p. 97.
3. Value investing is the popular name by which the Graham and Dodd approach is known, and as a result I use the two names interchangeably in this book.
4. The only possible exception could be the Gen Re acquisition profiled in Chapter 4, as I was an employee of that firm when Buffett acquired it; however, I was not involved in the acquisition itself while an employee, and the valuation presented is based on public information that was subjected to thorough legal review prior to its initial publication in the *Journal of Alternative Investments*.
5. See, for example, George Soros, *The Alchemy of Finance* (Hoboken, N.J.: Wiley, 2003 [1987]).
6. There are important exceptions to this statement, including the works of Robert S. Kaplan and William E. Fruhan, Jr., which I discuss in Chapter 7.

   A significant institutional exception occurred in 2006, when the Yale School of Management instituted a new integrated-based business curriculum. Yale's approach holds great promise, and I hope it will develop successfully. One risk to its success is that there are currently insufficient outlets in which to publish integrative research, a situation that I hope will soon be rectified. Srikant Datar, David Garvin, and James Weber, *Yale School of Management*, HBS Case Services, #9-308-011, February 29, 2008, p. 15.

7. I am a graduate of the executive version of Greenwald's value investing course at Columbia University, which is where I heard him make this statement.

8. Others have made this observation as well. See, for example, David Abrams, "The Great Illusion of the Stock Market and the Future of Value Investing," in Benjamin Graham and David Dodd, *Security Analysis*, 6th ed. (New York: McGraw-Hill, 2008 [1934]), p. 627.

9. Risk in this context refers to the margin of safety, which is a core value investing principle that is explained in forthcoming chapters.

CHAPTER 1

1. Benjamin Graham, *The Intelligent Investor* (New York: Harper & Row, 1973 [1949]), p. 286.

2. Benjamin Graham and David Dodd, *Security Analysis*, 3rd ed. (New York: McGraw-Hill, 1951 [1934]), p. 480.

3. Austrian economist Murray Rothbard has insightful comments on the concept of intrinsic value relative to the well-established subjective theory of value in *Man, Economy, and State* (Auburn, Ala.: LvMI, 2004 [1962]), pp. 316–317.

4. Graham (1973 [1949]), p. 281.

5. This quote is from Warren Buffett and is found in the 1984 Berkshire Hathaway Annual Report, located at www.berkshirehathaway.com/letters/1984.html.

6. Graham (1973 [1949]), pp. 281–282.

7. Benjamin Graham and David Dodd, *Security Analysis*, 2nd ed. (New York: McGraw-Hill, 1940 [1934]), p. 68. Note also Graham and Dodd (1951 [1934]), pp. 44–45.

8. Bruce Greenwald, Judd Kahn, Paul Sonkin, and Michael van Biema, *Value Investing: From Graham to Buffett and Beyond* (New York: Wiley, 2001), p. 145.

9. A possible exception involves distressed investing (which is popularly known as "vulture investing"). For more information, see Stuart Gilson,

Creating Value through Corporate Restructuring: Case Studies in Bankruptcies, Buyouts, and Breakups (New York: Wiley, 2001), Chapter 6. Emerging markets may present cigar butt–like opportunities for those with the knowledge required to identify them.

10. For example, see Roger Lowenstein's narrative on Warren Buffett's thoughts around this period of time in *Buffett: The Making of an American Capitalist* (New York: Broadway, 1995), pp. 154–161.

11. Bruce Greenwald, "Deconstructing the Balance Sheet," in Benjamin Graham and David Dodd, *Security Analysis*, 6th ed. (New York: McGraw-Hill, 2008 [1934]), p. 539.

12. This includes M&A; for example, and as *University of Virginia* financial economist Robert Bruner observed, "the key strategic driver of profitability has less to do with focus and relatedness and more to do with knowledge, mastery, and competencies. What does your company know? What is it good at doing?" From Robert Bruner, *Deals from Hell: M&A Lessons That Rise Above the Ashes* (Hoboken, N.J.: Wiley, 2005), p. 39.

13. Berkshire Hathaway Annual Report, 1996; www.berkshirehathaway.com/letters/1996.html. Similarly, Benjamin Graham (1973 [1949], p. 287) noted that an intelligent investor should limit "his ambition to his capacity and [confine] his activities within the safe and narrow path of standard, defensive investment. To achieve *satisfactory* investment results is easier than most people realize; to achieve *superior* results is harder than it looks."

14. Greenwald et al. (2001), p. 56.

15. Comparing PPE to revenue can be a useful analytical exercise, as Bruce Greenwald showed in Graham and Dodd (2008 [1934]), pp. 545–546.

16. Graham and Dodd (1940 [1934]), p. 22.

17. Berkshire Hathaway Annual Report, 1993; www.berkshirehathaway.com/letters/1993.html.

18. Greenwald et al. (2001), pp. 61–62.

19. See, for example, Seth Klarman, *Margin of Safety: Risk-Averse Investment Strategies for the Thoughtful Investor* (New York: HarperBusiness, 1991), p. 125.

20. For a practical introduction to option pricing, see Aswath Damodaran, *Investment Valuation: Tools and Techniques for Determining the Value of Any Asset*, 2nd ed. (New York: Wiley, 2002), Chapter 5. Those who are enamored with option-pricing models are encouraged to read Nassim Nicholas Taleb, *The Black Swan: The Impact of the Highly Improbable* (New York: Random House, 2007).

21. Form 10-K of Delta Apparel Corporation, 2002, p. F-15.

22. Greenwald et al. (2001), pp. 39–40.

23. I did not find detail in net interest commentary that I felt was sufficient so I formulated the estimate subjectively.

24. Berkshire Hathaway Annual Report, 1992; www.berkshirehathaway.com/letters/1992.html.

25. John Neff and S. L. Mintz, *John Neff on Investing* (New York: Wiley, 1999), p. 71. This book had the misfortune of being published in 1999, when the "new economy" boom was roaring, and therefore it did not receive the level of attention that it should have. See Chapter 5 for more information on the "new economy."

26. For further information, see, for example, "Warren Buffett and Goldman Sachs—Tucking In," *The Economist*, September 27, 2008, p. 86; and "GE—Buffett to the Rescue," *The Economist*, October 4, 2008, p. 68.

27. "GE—Buffett to the Rescue," p. 68. See David Einhorn, *Fooling Some of the People All of the Time: A Long Short Story* (Hoboken, N.J.: Wiley, 2008), pp. 39–40 and 122 for interesting commentary on GE Capital's former CEO, Gary Wendt.

28. According to Benjamin Graham, the margin of safety "is always dependent on the price paid. It will be large at one price, small at some other price, nonexistent at some still higher price. . . . It is available for absorbing the effect of miscalculations or worse than average luck." Graham (1973 [1949]), p. 281.

29. Thomas Sowell, *Knowledge and Decisions* (New York: Basic Books, 1996 [1980]), p. 85.

CHAPTER 2

1. Benjamin Graham, *The Intelligent Investor* (New York: HarperBusiness, 1949), p. 38.
2. Benjamin Graham and David Dodd, *Security Analysis*, 3rd ed. (New York: McGraw-Hill, 1951 [1934]), p. 39.
3. See, for example, Robert Eccles, Kersten Lanes, and Thomas Wilson, "Are You Paying Too Much for That Acquisition?" *Harvard Business Review*, July–August 1999, pp. 136–146. Note also Paul Carroll and Chunka Mui, *Billion Dollar Lessons: What You Can Learn from the Most Inexcusable Business Failures of the Last 25 Years* (New York: Portfolio, 2008).
4. Alfred Rappaport, "10 Ways to Create Shareholder Value," *Harvard Business Review*, September 2006, p. 71.
5. For more information on the Kmart acquisition, see Stuart Gilson and Sarah Abbott, *Kmart and ESL Investments (A)*, HBS Case Services, #9-209-044, August 14, 2008.
6. This section, and much of the background information on Sears in this chapter, draws heavily on Sanjay Sood and Rajiv Lal, *Sears, Roebuck and Co.*, Stanford Business School Case Services, #M-278, October 1997.
7. Richard Sears was no longer with the firm at this time—he resigned in 1913 over creative differences and passed away the following year.
8. On the importance of managerial attention, see, for example, Robert Simons and Antonio Davila, "How High Is Your Return on Management?" *Harvard Business Review*, January–February 1998, pp. 71–80.
9. Paul Stowell and David Stowell, *Kmart, Sears, and ESL: How a Hedge Fund Became One of the World's Largest Retailers*, Kellogg Business School Case Services, #KEL133, 2005.
10. Readers who are not familiar with basic financial accounting are strongly encouraged to explore that subject further. An excellent resource is David Hawkins, *Corporate Finance Reporting and Analysis: Text and Cases* (New York: Irwin/McGraw-Hill, 1998 [1971]).

11. Sears Form 10-K, 2005, p. F-6. For more information on this adjustment, see Chapter 1.

12. Ibid., p. F-11.

13. Stowell and Stowell (2005).

14. Sood and Lal (1997).

15. For more information on customer captivity, see Bruce Greenwald and Judd Kahn, *Competition Demystified* (New York: Portfolio, 2005).

16. Bruce Greenwald, Judd Kahn, Paul Sonkin, and Michael van Biema, *Value Investing: From Graham to Buffett and Beyond* (New York: Wiley, 2001), pp. 61–62.

17. Sears Form 10-K, 2005, p. F-5; calculations are the author's.

18. Ibid., p. 29.

19. Ibid., p. F-13.

20. Ibid., Footnote 10; calculations are the author's.

21. Ibid., p. F-6; calculations are the author's.

22. Benjamin Graham and David Dodd, *Security Analysis* (New York: McGraw-Hill, 1934).

23. Sears Form 10-K, 2005, p. F-5.

24. I did not find detail in net interest commentary that I felt was sufficient so I formulated the estimate subjectively.

25. Source: http://research.stlouisfed.org/fred2/series/GS10/22; calculations are the author's.

26. Graham and Dodd (1934), p. 453, note that 16 times expected earnings "is as high a price" as should generally be paid for an investment.

27. Private-market value is a concept that was introduced by money manager and celebrated Graham and Dodd practitioner Mario Gabelli; it is defined as "the value an informed industrialist would pay to purchase assets with similar characteristics"; www.gabelli.com/news/articles/regselby_123099.html.

28. Gary McWilliams and Gregory Zuckerman, "Lampert Admits Flubs, Sees Sears Turnaround," *Wall Street Journal,* January 30, 2008.

29. Kris Hudson, "Sears Would Face Soft Real-Estate Sector," *Wall Street Journal,* January 23, 2008; and Gretchen Morgenson, Michael Barbaro,

and Geraldine Fabrikant, "Saving Sears Doesn't Look Easy Anymore," *New York Times*, January 27, 2008.

30. Ibid.

31. For information on initiative execution, see Robert Kaplan and David Norton, *The Execution Premium: Linking Strategy to Operations for Competitive Advantage* (Boston: HBS Press, 2008).

CHAPTER 3

1. Benjamin Graham, *The Intelligent Investor* (New York: Harper Business, 1949), p. 93.

2. Benjamin Graham and David Dodd, *Security Analysis*, 6th ed. (New York: McGraw-Hill, 2008 [1934]), p. 368.

3. Arthur Levitt, Jr., "Foreword," in Robert Bruner, *Deals from Hell—M&A Lessons That Rise Above the Ashes* (New York: Wiley, 2005), p. x.

4. For an excellent summary, see Roger Lowenstein, *Buffett: The Making of an American Capitalist* (New York: Broadway, 1995), pp. 195–202.

5. Aetna C & S was subsequently purchased by Travelers, which is where the business is managed today (2009). For disclosure purposes, I am a policyholder of both GEICO and Travelers.

6. Bruce Greenwald, Judd Kahn, Paul Sonkin, and Michael van Biema, *Value Investing: From Graham to Buffett and Beyond* (New York: Wiley, 2001), p. 85.

7. Source: www.berkshirehathaway.com/letters/2005.html.

8. For more information, see Lowenstein (1995), pp. 133–135.

9. Ibid., p. 195.

10. GEICO Form 10-K, 1994; dollars in thousands.

11. See Joseph Calandro, Jr., and Thomas O'Brien, "A User-Friendly Introduction to Property and Casualty Claim Reserving," *Risk Management and Insurance Review* 7, no. 2 (2004), 177–187 for information on reserve analysis.

12. Greenwald et al. (2001), pp. 61–62.

13. GEICO Form 10-K, 1994; dollars in thousands.

14. The amount of GEICO's outstanding shares was approximately 67.9 million of which Buffett owned 50.4%, per Robert Bruner, *Warren E. Buffett, 1995*, Darden School of Business Case Services, #UVA-F-1160, 1998 (1996), p. 11.

15. GEICO Form 10-K, 1994, Note J.

16. Benjamin Graham and David Dodd, *Security Analysis* (New York: McGraw-Hill, 1934), p. 453.

17. Bruce Greenwald and Judd Kahn, "All Strategy Is Local," *Harvard Business Review*, September 2005, pp. 94–104.

18. For more information, see Michael Treacy and Fred Wiersema, *The Discipline of Market Leaders: Choose Your Customers, Narrow Your Focus, Dominate Your Market* (Cambridge, Mass.: Perseus, 1997 [1995]).

19. Berkshire Hathaway Annual Report, 1993; www.berkshirehathaway.com/letters/1993.html. Buffett's comments on GEICO's moat, but only from the cost side, are in the Berkshire Hathaway Annual Report, 1986, www.berkshirehathaway.com/letters/1986.html.

20. Berkshire Hathaway Annual Report, 1992; www.berkshirehathaway.com/letters/1992.html. Furthermore, as in the quote at the beginning of this chapter, Benjamin Graham himself stated, "The stock of a growing company, if purchasable at a suitable price, is obviously preferable to others."

21. For more information on this margin of safety approach, see Greenwald et al. (2001), pp. 108 and 137.

22. Berkshire Hathaway Annual Report, 1995; www.berkshirehathaway.com/letters/1995.html.

23. The source of the premium figure is GEICO's 1994 Form 10-K.

24. Suzanne Vranica, "How a Gecko Shook Up Insurance Ads," *Wall Street Journal*, January 2, 2007, p. B1.

25. Benjamin Graham, *The Intelligent Investor* (New York: Harper & Row, 1973 [1949]), p. 61.

26. Tom Copeland, Tim Koller, and Jack Murrin, *Valuation: Measuring and Managing the Value of Companies*, 3rd ed. (New York: Wiley, 2000 [1990]), p. 452.

27. Those interested in background information on the CAPM can refer to any number of finance sources, such as Aswath Damodaran, *Investment Valuation: Tools and Techniques for Determining the Value of Any Asset,* 2nd ed. (New York: Wiley, 2002), Chapter 4.

28. Bruner (1998 [1996]), p. 11.

29. Berkshire Hathaway Annual Report, 1993; www.berkshirehathaway.com/letters/1993.html. Similarly, financial economist Robert Shiller observed, "If one tries too hard to be precise, one runs the risk of being so narrow as to be irrelevant." Robert Shiller, *Irrational Exuberance* (New York: Doubleday, 2005 [2000]), p. xxi. For more information on Buffett's thoughts, see Lowenstein (1995), pp. 315–322.

30. Gabelli indicated that his approach to discount-rate estimation was subjective and judgment-based. He did not discuss the specifics of his approach.

31. Seth Klarman, *Margin of Safety: Risk-Averse Investment Strategies for the Thoughtful Investor* (New York: HarperBusiness, 1991), p. 113. Note also Klarman's comments in "The Timeless Wisdom of Graham and Dodd" in Graham and Dodd (2008 [1934]), p. xxxviii.

32. Equity cash flows can be used in place of dividends. For more information, see Timothy Luehrman, *Note on Valuing Equity Cash Flows,* HBS Case Services, #9-295-085, 1994.

33. See, for example, John Graham and Campbell Harvey, "How Do CFOs Make Capital Budgeting and Capital Structure Decisions?" *Journal of Applied Corporate Finance* 15, no. 1 (Spring 2002), 12–13.

CHAPTER 4

1. Benjamin Graham, *The Intelligent Investor* (New York: Harper & Row, 1973 [1949]), p. 61.

2. Benjamin Graham and David Dodd, *Security Analysis,* 6th ed. (New York: McGraw-Hill, 2008 [1934]), p. 80.

3. The Berkshire Hathaway press release for this deal can be found at www. berkshirehathaway.com/news/jun1998.html.

4. All figures are taken from Berkshire Hathaway annual reports, found at www.berkshirehathaway.com.

5. General Re Corporation Annual Report, 1997, p. 36.

6. *Black's Law Dictionary*, 6th ed., (St. Paul, Minn.: West Publishing Co., 1990) p. 1288.

7. For information on economic profit, see, for example, Bennett Stewart, *The Quest for Value: A Guide for Senior Managers* (New York: HarperBusiness, 1999 [1991]).

8. See Michael Treacy and Fred Wiersema, *The Discipline of Market Leaders: Choose Your Customers, Narrow Your Focus, Dominate Your Market* (Cambridge, Mass.: Perseus, 1997 [1995]), for more information on this strategy.

9. R. L. Bornhuetter and R. E. Ferguson, "The Actuary and IBNR," *Proceedings of the Casualty Actuarial Society* 59 (1972), 181–195.

10. See, for example, Sarah Hibler, "Major Reserve Deficiencies Remain," *National Underwriter*, September 8, 2003, p. 8.

11. See Joseph Calandro, Jr., and Thomas O'Brien, "A User-Friendly Introduction to Property and Casualty Claim Reserving," *Risk Management and Insurance Review* 7, no. 2 (2004), 177–187, for further information on reserve analysis.

12. General Re Corporation Annual Report, 1997, footnote 13, p. 54.

13. Ibid., footnote 10, p. 51.

14. See David Hawkins, *Retiree Benefit Note Analysis*, HBS Case Services, #9-104-065, 2004, for information on pension liability analysis.

15. *Retrocession* is the term used to describe reinsurance for reinsurance companies.

16. Bruce Greenwald, Judd Kahn, Paul Sonkin, and Michael van Biema, *Value Investing: From Graham to Buffett and Beyond* (New York: Wiley, 2001), pp. 61–62.

17. General Re Corporation Annual Report, 1997, p. 35.

18. According to Berkshire's press release, www.berkshirehathaway.com/ news/jun1998.html:

> First, this transaction removes constraints on earnings volatility that have caused General Re, in the past, to decline certain attractive business and, in other cases, to layoff substantial amounts of the business that it does write. Because of both its status as a public company and its desire to maintain its AAA credit rating, General Re has, understandably, been unable to operate in a manner that could produce large swings in reporting earnings. As part of Berkshire, this constraint will disappear, which will enhance both General Re's long-term profitability and *its ability to write more business*. (Emphasis added.)

19. General Re Corporation Annual Report, 1997, p. 35.
20. Board of Governors, Federal Reserve System.
21. Benjamin Graham and David Dodd, *Security Analysis* (New York: McGraw-Hill, 1934), p. 453.
22. Recall that we deducted interest on cash in note (2E) in the narrative. It makes no sense to capitalize the interest earned on cash, since that amount equals the amount of cash on the balance sheet.
23. Options were not expensed in this valuation, as at the time of this acquisition, option expensing was not the issue that it is today. Were options to be expensed in this valuation, earnings would have decreased by $16 million. General Re Corporation Annual Report, 1997, footnote 12, p. 54.
24. The press release can be found at www.berkshirehathaway.com/news/ jun1998.html.
25. Berkshire Hathaway Annual Report, 2002; www.berkshirehathaway.com/ letters/2002pdf.pdf.
26. Berkshire Hathaway Annual Report, 2001; www.berkshirehathaway. com/2001ar/2001letter.html.

27. Hibler (2003).
28. Berkshire Hathaway Annual Report, 2002.
29. Ibid.
30. Lisa Howard, "HIH Debacle: A Litany of Ineptitude," *National Underwriter,* July 14, 2003, pp. 21–22.
31. Shaheen Pasha, "General Re SEC Notice Puts Scrutiny on Finite-Risk Pdts," *Wall Street Journal,* December 30, 2004; www.wsj.com.
32. www.naic.org/topics/topic_finite_re.htm. See the appendix to this chapter for a more detailed definition of finite risk.
33. Kevin Kingsbury, Amir Efrati, and Karen Richardson, "General Re's CEO Steps Down Amid Pressure from Prosecutors," *Wall Street Journal,* April 14, 2008; http://online.wsj.com/article/SB120818287782312719.html.
34. On Buffett's timing for acquiring Gen Re, see, for example, *IBNR Weekly,* Dowling & Partners, #31, August 12, 2001.
35. Berkshire Hathaway Annual Report, 1997; www.berkshirehathaway.com/letters/1997.html.

Our rate of progress in both investments and operations is *certain* to fall in the future. For anyone deploying capital, nothing recedes like success. My own history makes the point: Back in 1951, when I was attending Ben Graham's class at Columbia, an idea giving me a $10,000 gain improved my investment performance for the year by a full 100 percentage points. Today, an idea producing a $500 million pre-tax profit for Berkshire adds *one* percentage point to our performance. It's no wonder that my annual results in the 1950s were better by nearly thirty percentage points than my annual gains in any subsequent decade. Charlie's experience was similar. We weren't smarter then, just smaller. At our present size, any performance superiority we achieve will be minor. . . .

Though we are delighted with what we own, we are not pleased with our prospects for committing incoming funds. Prices are high for both businesses and stocks. That does not mean that the prices of either will fall—we have absolutely no view on that matter—but it does mean that we get relatively little in prospective earnings when we commit fresh money. (Emphasis original.)

Gen Re's losses drove its cost of float up extremely high; in other words, its "underwriting loss" was higher than market rates for money. According to Buffett, "An insurance business has value if its cost of float over time is less than the cost the company would otherwise incur to obtain funds. But the business is a lemon if its cost of float is higher than market rates for money." Furthermore, because its cost of float was so high, the Gen Re acquisition became a "turnaround situation," which is something Buffett has publicly stated that he has no interest in. See, for example, the 2002 Berkshire Hathaway Annual Report, cited previously.

36. Thanks to value investor and UConn Professor Pat Terrion for bringing this argument to my attention.
37. Graham and Dodd (2008 [1934]), p. 106.
38. Robert Bruner, *Deals from Hell: M&A Lessons That Rise Above the Ashes* (Hoboken, N.J.: Wiley, 2005).
39. Benjamin Graham, *The Intelligent Investor* (New York: Harper & Row, 1973), p. 281.
40. Bruner (2005), pp. 346–347.
41. Ibid., p. 90.
42. Ibid., Chapter 14.
43. Ibid., pp. 67–75.
44. Berkshire Hathaway Annual Report, 1998; www.berkshirehathaway.com/news/jun1998.html.
45. Joseph Calandro, Jr., Scott Lane, and Ranga Dasari, "A Practical Approach for Risk-Adjusting Performance," *Measuring Business Excellence* 12, no. 4 (2008), pp. 4-12.

46. For more information, see Nassim Nicholas Taleb, *Fooled by Randomness: The Hidden Role of Chance in Life and in the Markets*, 2nd ed. (New York: Random House, 2005 [2004]), and Nassim Nicholas Taleb, *The Black Swan: The Impact of the Highly Improbable* (New York: Random House, 2007).

47. For more information, see Dan Ariely, *Predictably Irrational: The Hidden Forces That Shape Our Decisions* (New York: HarperCollins, 2008), and Richard Thaler and Cass Sunstein, *Nudge: Improving Decisions about Health, Wealth and Happiness* (New Haven, Conn.: Yale University Press, 2008).

48. See the valuation presented in Chapter 3 of this book.

49. "Accounting for the Abuses at AIG," *Knowledge@Wharton*, April 20, 2005; http://knowledge.wharton.upenn.edu/article.cfm?articleid=1180.

50. For further information, see, for example, the federal government's press release: "SEC Charges One AIG and Four Gen Re Executives for Aiding in AIG Securities Fraud"; www.sec.gov/news/press/2006-15.htm and accompanying documents.

51. For more information, see, for example, "Recorded Conversations Erased Reasonable Doubt for Jury in Finite Re Trial," *BestWire Services*, March 3, 2008.

52. Kevin Kingsbury, Amir Efrati, and Karen Richardson, "General Re Chief Quits Post—Exit Is Seen as Bid to End Fraud Probe at Berkshire Unit," *Wall Street Journal*, April 15, 2008; http://online.wsj.com/article/SB120818504357212797.html.

53. For the definition of a Wells notice, see http://en.wikipedia.org/wiki/Wells_notice.

54. Paul Carroll and Chunka Mui present an alternative approach that is well worth reviewing in *Billion Dollar Lessons: What You Can Learn from the Most Inexcusable Business Failures of the Last 25 Years* (New York: Portfolio, 2008).

55. An excellent resource on performance management is Andy Neely, Chris Adams, and Mike Kennerley, *The Performance Prism* (London: FT Prentice Hall, 2002).

CHAPTER 5

1. Benjamin Graham, *The Intelligent Investor* (New York: HarperBusiness, 1949), p. 31.

2. Benjamin Graham and David Dodd, *Security Analysis*, 6th ed. (New York: McGraw-Hill, 2008 [1934]), p. 83.

3. See, for example, Graham (1949), p. 37.

4. Benjamin Graham, "Stock Market Warning: Danger Ahead!" *California Management Review*, Spring 1960, pp. 34–61.

5. Richard Brealey and Stewart Myers, *Principles of Corporate Finance*, 6th ed. (Boston: Irwin McGraw-Hill, 2000), p. 358.

6. Ibid, p. 362.

7. See appendix 1 at the end of the chapter for more information on Buffett's thoughts on EMT.

8. George Soros, *The Alchemy of Finance: Reading the Mind of the Market* (New York: Wiley, 1994 [1987]), p. 47.

9. George Soros, *Soros on Soros: Staying Ahead of the Curve* (New York: Wiley, 1995), and Soros (1994 [1987]), p. 42.

10. This is my interpretation, not Soros's. In fact, he uses the term *reflexivity* to describe both the market feedback loop *and* boom-bust behavior, which even he admits is confusing. George Soros, *The Alchemy of Finance: Reading the Mind of the Market* (New York: Wiley, 2003 [1987]).

11. Benjamin Graham and David Dodd stress the importance of price discrepancies numerous times in their classic *Security Analysis* (New York: McGraw-Hill, 1934). Note also Bruce Greenwald, Judd Kahn, Paul Sonkin, and Michael van Biema, *Value Investing: From Graham to Buffett and Beyond* (New York: Wiley, 2001), p. 3, and John Neff and S. L. Mintz, *John Neff on Investing* (New York: Wiley, 1999), p. 63. Austrian economist Ludwig von Mises also comments on price discrepancies in *Human Action* (Auburn, Ala.: Ludwig von Mises Institute, 1998 [1949]).

12. Soros (1994 [1987]), pp. 58–60, presents three examples of past boom-bust cycles to support his model. Interestingly, Graham and Dodd (1934,

p. 2) present a chart of the business cycle that occurred in the U.S. stock market during the 1920s that is remarkably similar to Soros's model. Robert Shiller adopts a similar format in his classic study, *Irrational Exuberance* (New York: Random House, 2005 [2000]).

13. Soros (1995), p. 73.
14. Mark Gimein, "George Soros Is Mad as Hell," *Fortune*, October 27, 2003, p. 139.
15. Roger Garrison, "The Austrian Theory of the Business Cycle in the Light of Modern Macroeconomics," *Review of Austrian Economics* 3, no. 1 (1990), 7.
16. Mises (1998 [1949]), pp. 546–547, 556, and Murray Rothbard, "Economic Depressions: Their Cause and Cure," in Richard Ebeling (ed.), *The Austrian Theory of the Trade Cycle and Other Essays* (Auburn, Ala.: Ludwig von Mises Institute, 1996 [1978]), p. 86.
17. Buying a stock as it makes a new high is an entry tactic that many successful traders such as William O'Neil advocate. See, for example, O'Neil's *How to Make Money in Stocks* (New York: McGraw-Hill, 1995 [1988]), p. 25.
18. This is my interpretation, not Soros's.
19. Robert Shiller, "Bubbles, Human Judgment and Expert Opinion," Cowles Foundation Discussion Paper No. 1303, May 2001, p. 3.
20. This is also my interpretation, not Soros's. Benjamin Graham and David Dodd describe this phenomenon as "a sort of pseudo-analysis to support the delusions of the period"; *Security Analysis*, 6th ed. (New York: McGraw-Hill, 2008 [1934]), p. 61. And Seth Klarman summarized it as follows: "If a historically accepted investment yardstick proves to be overly restrictive, the path of least resistance is to invent a new standard." Seth Klarman, *Margin of Safety: Risk-Averse Investment Strategies for the Thoughtful Investor* (New York: HarperBusiness, 1991), p. 74.
21. Graham and Dodd (1934), p. 365. Mises (1998 [1949]), p. 546, notes that a consequence of credit expansion "is that it falsifies economic calculation and accounting. It produces the phenomenon of imaginary

or apparent profits." Likewise, F. A. Hayek observed that money supply expansion, "upsets the reliability of all accounting practices and is bound to show spurious profits much in excess to true gains." F. A. Hayek, "Can We Still Avoid Inflation?" in Richard Ebeling (ed.), *The Austrian Theory of the Trade Cycle and Other Essays* (Auburn, Ala.: Ludwig von Mises Institute, 1996 [1978]), p. 95.

22. Henry Hazlitt, *Economics in One Lesson* (San Francisco: Laissez Faire Books, 1996 [1946]), p. 158.

23. Misconceptions play a significant role in boom market behavior, as Soros (2003 [1987]), p. 30, observed.

24. Graham and Dodd (1934), p. 54.

25. Ibid., p. 312. To sum up, market participants replace fundamental analysis with fundamental substitute analysis because of the belief that traditional fundamental analysis is incapable of capturing the drivers of the new economic condition. Therefore, it is replaced with financial substitute analysis that participants believe is capable of capturing those drivers. Once again, this is my interpretation, not Soros's. Shiller (2005 [2000]) has two chapters on the topic of "new era thinking," which are superb.

26. Dramatic P/E expansion has long been known as a good technical indicator of a boom, even in mainstream academia. For example, the dramatic P/E expansion of the mid- to late 1990s convinced Robert Shiller that the new economy was a boom. That belief evolved into writing the book *Irrational Exuberance*, cited in note 12, which was published in March 2000, just as the new economy boom topped out. Justin Fox, "Is the Market Rational?" *Fortune*, December 9, 2002.

27. As Soros (2003 [1987]), p. 8, explains, "People base their actions not on reality but on their view of the world, and the two are not identical."

28. Alan Greenspan, "The Challenge of Central Banking in a Democratic Society," Remarks to the Annual Dinner and Francis Boyer Lecture of the American Enterprise Institute for Policy Research, Washington, D.C., December 5, 1996.

29. Charles Mackay, *Extraordinary Popular Delusions and the Madness of Crowds* (New York: Harmon Books, 1980 [1841]), pp. xix–xx.

30. Hazlitt (1996 [1946]), pp. 177–178.

31. Thanks to Rob Lingle for passing this riddle along. It is attributed to Ed Seykota, one of the traders profiled in Jack Schwager, *Market Wizards: Interviews with Top Traders* (New York: New York Institute of Finance, 1989).

32. George Soros, *The Crisis of Global Capitalism: Open Society Endangered* (New York: PublicAffairs, 1998), p. 52.

33. Mises (1998 [1949]), pp. 409, 420.

34. Frank Shostak, "Irrational Exuberance?" *Daily Articles*, Ludwig von Mises Institute, May 5, 2000.

35. While ABCT is clear that the central bank reversal will cause the boom to end, the exact moment at which it will end is impossible to predict. For example, Soros (2003 [1987]), p. 35, indicated that he lost money in the new economy "by short selling Internet stocks too soon." Rather than trying to time the exact moment of the market turn, one could strategically screen a boom-bust cycle for investment opportunities, as I explain later in the chapter.

36. For further information on value gaps in general, see William E. Fruhan, Jr., "Corporate Raiders: Head 'Em Off at Value Gap," *Harvard Business Review*, July-August 1988, pp. 63–69.

37. Greenwald et al. (2001), pp. 155–159.

38. My interpretation, not Soros's.

39. As Austrian economist Ludwig von Mises indicated:

The longer the period of credit expansion and the longer the banks delay in changing their policy, the worse will be the consequences of the malinvestments . . . and as a result the longer will be the period of depression and the more uncertain the date of recovery and return to normal economic activity.

"The 'Austrian' Theory of the Trade Cycle," in Richard Ebeling (ed.), *The Austrian Theory of the Trade Cycle and Other Essays* (Auburn, Ala.: Ludwig von Mises Institute, 1996 [1978]), p. 34. Similarly, Soros (2003 [1987]), p. 33, observed, "The magnitude of the bust tends to be proportionate to the boom that preceded it."

40. Rothbard (1996 [1978]).
41. According to John Murphy, *Technical Analysis of the Futures Markets* (New York: New York Institute of Finance, 1986), p. 277: "Momentum measures the rate of change of prices as opposed to the actual price levels themselves." Strong momentum is a sign of powerful (or sustainable) buying or selling, while low momentum is a sign of weak (or unsustainable) buying or selling.
42. Bob Woodward, *Maestro: Greenspan's Fed and the American Boom* (New York: Simon & Schuster, 2000), p. 15.
43. Ibid., p. 118.
44. In January 1994 the fed funds rate was 3.05%, and by May 1995 it had risen to 6.01%. Board of Governors, Federal Reserve System.
45. Woodward (2000), p. 160.
46. Murphy (1986), pp. 67–68.
47. Soros (2003 [1987]), p. 23, commented, "Investors valued top-line revenue growth disregarding that the business models could be sustained only as long as companies could sell stock at inflated prices."
48. See, for example, Alberto Moel and Peter Tufano, "When Are Real Options Exercised? An Empirical Study of Mine Closings," Harvard Business School working paper, 2000.
49. See, for example, Michael Mauboussin, "Get Real: Using Real Options in Security Analysis," *Frontiers of Finance*, Credit Suisse First Boston, June 23, 1999.
50. Graham and Dodd (1934), pp. 11–12.
51. Ibid., p. 313.

52. The similarities between the business cycles of the 1920s and the 1990s from both an academic and a practical perspective are striking. Comparing Murray Rothbard, *America's Great Depression* (www.mises. org/rothbard/agd.pdf, 2000 [1963]) and Graham and Dodd (1934) to current economic events reveals many similarities between the two business cycles, even though 70 years separate them. Note also in this regard Shiller (2005 [2000]).

53. "The Tech Boom: Valuation Inflation, A Flood of Day Traders and Other Excesses," *Knowledge@Wharton*, November 7, 2001; http:// knowledge.wharton.upenn.edu/index.cfm?fa=viewArticle&id=461.

54. Warren Buffett and Carol Loomis, "Mr. Buffett on the Stock Market," *Fortune*, November 22, 1999.

55. Greenwald et al. (2001), pp. 134–135. Soros (2003 [1987]), p. 30, observed that during the new economy, "stocks were valued at a multiple of revenues, not earnings, and growth was financed by selling stock, not by following sound business plans."

56. Alex McMillan, "Buffett Hits a Bumpy Road: The Technophobe Sees His Stock Tumble," *Money*, January 20, 2000.

57. From June 1999, the progression of the fed funds rate is 4.76%, 4.99%, 5.07%, 5.22%, 5.20%, 5.42%, 5.30%, 5.46%, 5.73%, 5.85%, 6.02%, 6.27%, and 6.27%. Board of Governors, Federal Reserve System.

58. Fortune 500, *Fortune*, www.fortune.com.

59. See Appendix 3 at the end of Chapter 5 for further information.

60. Cassell Bryan-Low, "Andersen Staff Works to Tie Up Loose Ends," *Wall Street Journal*, June 16, 2002; www.wsj.com.

61. Leon Lazaroff, "Global Crossing Sinks Into Ch. 11," *The Deal.com*, January 28, 2002.

62. Stephen Taub, "Wall Street Flees Accounting Challenged Companies," *CFO.com*, January 30, 2002.

63. Gregory Zuckerman, "Ripples from Enron Accounting Woes Triggers Selloff in the Bond Market," *Wall Street Journal*, February 6, 2002; www. wsj.com.

64. Andy Serwer, "The AMAZING Mr. Buffett: The World's Greatest Investor Is Back on Top. Here's What He Thinks Now," *Fortune*, November 11, 2002.
65. Stephen Taub, "Case of the Blues? AOL Chairman to Resign," *CFO.com*, January 13, 2003.
66. Greg Ip, "The Rise and Fall of Intangible Assets Leads to Shorter Company Life Spans," *Wall Street Journal*, April 4, 2002; www.wsj.com.
67. Peter McKay, "The 'Sell' Side: These Analysts Freely Criticize and Win Praise," *Wall Street Journal*, April 4, 2002; www.wsj.com.
68. On March 28, 2002, the P/E ratios for the S&P 500 and Dow Jones Industrial Average were 31.14 and 28.16, respectively. On January 2, 2003, the P/E ratios for the two indexes were relatively unchanged at 33.78 and 23.23, respectively. Source: BigCharts.com.
69. Robert Bartley, "Meanderings on Money," *Wall Street Journal*, May 20, 2002; Arthur Laffer, "Keep the Dollar Strong," *Wall Street Journal*, May 20, 2002; and Llewellyn Rockwell, "Sustainable Growth," *Free Market*, June 2002.
70. As Austrian economist Murray Rothbard (1996 [1978], p. 85) explained:

> The "depression" is . . . the necessary and healthy phase by which the market economy sloughs off and liquidates the unsound, uneconomic investments of the boom, and reestablishes those proportions between consumption and investment that are truly desired by the consumers. The depression is the painful but necessary process by which the free market sloughs off the excesses and errors of the boom and reestablishes the market economy in its function of efficient service to the mass of consumers.

71. See, for example, the comments of Michael Marcus in Schwager (1989), p. 27.

72. There is a significant difference between trading and investing. See, for example, the first chapter of the 1973 edition of *The Intelligent Investor*, which opens with a discussion titled, "Investment versus Speculation." Benjamin Graham, *The Intelligent Investor* (New York: Harper & Row, 1973 [1949]).

73. Joseph Calandro, Jr., "A Perspective on Post New Economy Business Cycle Behavior," May 18, 2006; http://mises.org/journals/scholar/calandro.pdf.

74. Rothbard (2000 [1963]), p. 79.

75. Shiller (2005 [2000]), pp. 78–80, observed the existence of cross-feedback between the equity and real estate markets.

76. Neff and Mintz (1999), p. 72.

77. See, for example, Graham and Dodd (2008 [1934]), pp. 215–217.

78. Ruth Simon, "Housing Affordability Hits 14-Year Low; Higher Prices, Rising Rates Hurt Buyers as Creative Loans Lose Some of Their Punch," *Wall Street Journal*, December 22, 2005; www.wsj.com.

79. Murray Rothbard, *Man, Economy, State with Power & Market* (Auburn, Ala.: Ludwig von Mises Institute, 2004 [1962]), p. 813.

80. O'Neil (1995 [1988]). For a trading perspective, see, for example, Curtis Faith, *Way of the Turtle* (New York: McGraw-Hill, 2007).

81. See, for example, Robert Shiller, "Long-Term Perspectives on the Current Boom in Home Prices," *Economists' Voice*, March 2006; www.bepress.com/ev.

82. At the time of this writing in the year 2006, 30-year mortgage rates are up on average 0.4 percent over the prior year. See Ruth Simon, "The New Rules of Real Estate," *Wall Street Journal*, March 28, 2006; www.wsj.com.

83. Dean Baker, "The Menace of an Unchecked Housing Bubble," *Economists' Voice*, March 2006; www.bepress.com/ev.

84. Mariarosa Verde, Paul Mancuso, and Eric Rosenthal, "U.S. High Yield Default Rate 3.1% in 2005," Fitch Ratings, February 28, 2006. According to Bruce Greenwald and Judd Kahn, *Competition Demystified: A Radically*

Simplified Approach to Business Strategy (New York: Portfolio, 2005), p. 111:

After the [new economy] mania subsided, it became obvious how excessive those predictions were about the rate at which online commerce would supplant traditional shopping. The expectation that the newly hatched, Internet-only retailers would displace their brick-and-mortar competitors also proved mistaken. The bankruptcy courts were soon littered with the remaining assets of failed B-to-C (business to consumer) innovators. There were some significant survivors, Amazon most prominent among them, but their path to profitability proved considerably longer than the proponents of the new economy thesis had anticipated.

85. An example of this uncertainty can be found, for instance, in personal bankruptcies: while first quarter 2006 personal bankruptcies were historically low, the number of personal bankruptcies filed since November 2005 has actually increased fourfold. SmartPros, "After Plunge, Personal Bankruptcies Rising," April 7, 2006; http://accounting.smartpros.com/x52507.xml.

86. Karen Tally, "S&P Will Launch Indexes to Track Housing Prices," *Wall Street Journal,* March 23, 2006; www.wsj.com.

87. Victor Sperandeo and T. Sullivan Brown, *Trader Vic: Methods of a Wall Street Master* (New York: Wiley, 1991), p. 110.

88. O'Neil (1995 [1988]) and Faith (2007).

89. For example, Larry Hite (a founder of Mint Investment Management Company) observed that:

When a market makes a historic high it is telling you something. No matter how many people tell you why the market shouldn't be that high, or why nothing has changed, the mere fact that the price is at a new high tells you something has changed. (Schwager, 1989, p. 188.)

90. The components of the *basic materials* sector of the market are agricultural chemicals, aluminum, major diversified chemicals, copper, gold, independent oil and gas, industrial metals and minerals, major integrated oil and gas, nonmetallic mineral mining, oil and gas drilling and exploration, oil and gas equipment and services, oil and gas pipelines, oil and gas refining and marketing, silver, specialty chemicals, steel and iron, and synthetics.

91. For further information, see Stuart Gilson, "Investing in Distressed Situations: A Market Survey," *Financial Analysts Journal*, November-December, 1995, pp. 8–27, and J. Ezra Merkin, "Blood and Judgment," in Graham and Dodd (2008 [1934]), pp. 265–288.

92 Roger Lowenstein, *Buffett: The Making of an American Capitalist* (New York: Broadway Books, 1995), p. 319.

93. Peter Bernstein, *Capital Ideas: The Improbable Origins of Wall Street* (New York: Free Press, 1993 [1992]), pp. 142–143.

94. Bathany McLean and Peter Elkind, "Partners in Crime," *Fortune*, October 27, 2003, p. 81.

95. Ibid. See also Peter Behr and April Witt, "Visionary's Dream Led to Risky Business," *Washington Post*, July 28, 2002a.

96. Behr and Witt (2002a).

97. Peter Behr and April Witt, "Dream Job Turns into a Nightmare," *Washington Post*, July 29, 2002b.

98. Ibid.

99. Soros (2003 [1987]), p. 30.

100. Behr and Witt (2002a).

CHAPTER 6

1. Benjamin Graham and David Dodd, *Security Analysis*, 6th ed. (New York: McGraw-Hill, 2008 [1934]), p. 61.

2. As quoted in Roger Lowenstein, *Buffett: The Making of an American Capitalist* (New York: Broadway, 1995), p. 134. Note also Graham and Dodd's comment that, "Almost any security may be a purchase at some real or prospective price, and an indicated sale at another price." Benjamin Graham and David Dodd, *Security Analysis*, 3rd ed. (New York: McGraw-Hill, 1951 [1934]), p. 23.

3. For the purpose of this discussion, an alternative investment is an investment instrument other than straight debt, equity, or real estate. Examples include options, futures, and, as presented here, super cats.

4. Source: http://sweepstakes.yahoo.com/billionsweeps/static/rules.html.

5. Gordon Anderson, "Pepsi's Billion-Dollar Monkey," April 10, 2003a; www.azfamily.com.

6. Source: www.wsj.com.

7. Anderson (2003a).

8. Berkshire Hathaway, Inc., Annual Report, 2002, p. 26.

9. Scott Mason, "The Allocation of Risk," in *The Global Financial System: A Functional Perspective* (Boston: HBS Press, 1995), pp. 153–195.

10. Possible exceptions to this statement at the time were the American International Group (AIG); General Electric (GE), which had a reinsurance division at the time; and Citigroup.

11. See the rules referenced in note 4. The odds could be verified given complete disclosure of the sweepstake specifics using one of the various combinations of n objects taken r at a time.

12. James Whalen and Scott Mason, *The Global Property and Casualty Insurance Industry*, HBS Case Services, #9-296-033, 1996 [1995].

13. Graham's comments pertain to mainstream investment purchases. Simply invert the comments for risk assumption purposes; for example, and to paraphrase Graham: The margin of safety is always dependent on the price *quoted*. It will be large at one price, small at some other price, nonexistent at some still *lower* price.

14. Benjamin Graham, *The Intelligent Investor* (New York: Harper & Row, 1973 [1949]), p. 281.
15. The calculation for standard deviation is
    $$s = \{p_1[L_1 - E(L)]^2 + p_2[L_2 - E(L)]^2\}^{1/2}$$
    where s = standard deviation
    p = probability
    L = loss
    $E(L)$ = expected loss
16. Board of Governors, Federal Reserve System.
17. As explained in prior chapters, Graham and Dodd practitioners generally do not use beta-based measures when estimating the cost of equity. Therefore, I estimated Berkshire Hathaway's cost of capital—Berkshire is debt free, so the cost of equity equals the cost of capital—at 6.33%, which is slightly less than two times the 10-year Treasury note yield of 3.33% in June 2003.
18. As discussed in prior chapters, Graham and Dodd practitioners calculate a firm's earnings power value (EPV) by capitalizing expected sustainable earnings as a simple, nongrowth perpetuity.
19. In practice, the final premium could fluctuate anywhere from a low of $9,210,522 to a high of $9,793,271, depending upon the negotiation process.
20. Anderson (2003a).
21. Gordon Anderson, "Pepsi's $1B Chimp Arrives," September 4, 2003b; www.money.cnn.com/2003/09/04/pf/saving/pepsi_monkey_game.
22. Buffett has long held an interest in volatile super cat–like investments. For example, Berkshire Hathaway insured the $252 million baseball contract between Alex Rodriguez and the Texas Rangers in the year 2000. For specifics, see Randolph Cohen and Jason Wallace, *A-Rod: Signing the Best Player in Baseball*, HBS Case Services, #9-203-047, 2003.
23. In other words, Berkshire Hathaway did not transfer (or hedge) any of the risk to a reinsurer, meaning that if someone won the grand prize, Berkshire would pay the $250 million without any contribution from any other financial institution.

24. Ajit Jain is the CEO of National Indemnity, and he is Buffett's lead catastrophe and super cat underwriter.

25. Berkshire Hathaway, Inc., Annual Report, 2003, p. 12.

26. Peter Bernstein, *Against the Gods: The Remarkable Story of Risk* (New York: Wiley, 1998 [1996]), p. 8.

27. Scott Harrington and Gregory Niehaus, *Risk Management and Insurance*, 2nd ed. (Boston: McGraw-Hill, 2004 [1999]), p. 2.

28. A. A. Groppelli and Ehsan Nikbakht, *Finance*, 3rd ed. (New York: Barron's, 1995 [1986]), p. 485.

29. Admittedly, standard deviation is a less than perfect measure, but I understand this and I am very careful when and how I use it. For an incisive case study on what can happen when one is not careful with statistical models, see Roger Lowenstein, *When Genius Failed: The Rise and Fall of Long-Term Capital Management* (New York: Random House, 2000). For strong practical arguments against standard deviation in general, and economic uses of it in particular, see Nassim Nicholas Taleb's *Fooled by Randomness: The Hidden Role of Chance in Life and in the Markets*, 2nd ed. (New York: Random House, 2005) and *Black Swan: The Impact of the Highly Improbable* (New York: Random House, 2007).

30. Note, for example, the following article on credit default swap litigation: Janis Sarra, "Recent U.S. Litigation on Credit Default Swaps," December 2006; www.insol.org/emailer/december2006_downloads/CreditDefaultSwaps.doc.

31. For example, and as Buffett noted in the 1984 Berkshire Hathaway Annual Report, "Simply put, we feel that if we can buy small pieces of businesses with satisfactory underlying economics at a fraction of the per-share value of the entire business, something good is likely to happen to us—particularly if we own a group of such securities"; www.berkshirehathaway.com/letters/1984.html.

32. For more information on brands, see, for example, David D'Alessandro, *Brand Warfare: 10 Rules for Building the Killer Brand* (New York: McGraw-Hill, 2001), pp. 47–48. D'Alessandro is the former CEO of an insurance company (John Hancock).

CHAPTER 7

1. Benjamin Graham and David Dodd, *Security Analysis*, 6th ed. (New York: McGraw-Hill, 2008 [1934]), p. 83.
2. As quoted by Robert Lenzer, "Warren Buffett's Idea of Heaven: 'I Don't Have to Work with People I Don't Like,'" *Forbes*, October 18, 1993, p. 43.
3. See, for example, Paul Schoemaker, "The Future Challenges of Business: Rethinking Management Education," *California Management Review* 50, no. 3 (Spring 2008), pp. 120–139.
4. Mary Crossan, Jeffrey Gandz, and Gerard Seijts, "The Cross-Enterprise Leader," *Ivey Business Journal*, July/August 2008, #9B08DT03.
5. CFO Publishing Corp., "Best Practices from Leading CFOs," *CFO*, April 2000, p. 95.
6. CFO Publishing Corp., "Finance Seeks a Seat at the Strategy Table: A Report Prepared by CFO Research Services in Collaboration with Geac," July 2004; www.cfo.com.
7. See, for example, Robert Kaplan and David Norton, *Strategy Maps: Converting Intangible Assets into Tangible Outcomes* (Boston: HBS Press, 2004), and Robert Kaplan and David Norton, "Strategic Management: An Emerging Profession," *Balanced Scorecard Report*, May-June 2004, pp. 4–7.
8. William Fruhan, *Financial Strategy: Studies in the Creation, Transfer, and Destruction of Shareholder Value* (Homewood, Ill.: Irwin, 1979).
9. See, for example, Paul Schoemaker, *Profiting from Uncertainty: Strategies for Succeeding No Matter What the Future Brings* (New York: Free Press, 2002), and George Day and Paul Schoemaker, *Peripheral Vision: Detecting Weak Signals That Will Make or Break Your Company* (Boston: HBS Press, 2006).
10. For more information on the Tylenol episodes see, for example, Richard Tedlow and Wendy Smith, *James Burke: A Career in American Business* (A), HBS Case Services, #9-389-177, October 20, 2005, and Richard Tedlow and Wendy Smith, *James Burke: A Career in American Business* (B), HBS Case Services, #9-390-030, October 20, 2005.

11. David D'Alessandro, *Brand Warfare: 10 Rules for Building the Killer Brand* (New York: McGraw-Hill, 2001), p. 171.

12. Henry Mintzberg, "The Fall and Rise of Strategic Planning," *Harvard Business Review*, January-February 1994, pp. 107–114.

13. Richard Ruback, "Know Your Worth: Critical Valuation Errors to Avoid," *Faculty Seminar Series* (Boston: HBS Publishing, 2004).

14. Bruce Greenwald and Judd Kahn, *Competition Demystified: A Radically Simplified Approach to Business Strategy* (New York: Portfolio, 2005), p. 323. Note also Seth Klarman, *Margin of Safety: Risk-Averse Investment Strategies for the Thoughtful Investor* (New York: HarperBusiness, 1991), p. 119, and Paul Carroll and Chunka Mui, *Billion Dollar Lessons: What You Can Learn from the Most Inexcusable Business Failures of the Last 25 Years* (New York: Portfolio, 2008), p. 229.

15. For more information, see Thomas Johnson and Robert Kaplan, *Relevance Lost: The Rise and Fall of Management Accounting* (Boston: HBS Press, 1987).

16. These perspectives were presented as "a template not a straight jacket," meaning that perspectives could change depending on the unique needs of a particular firm. This dynamic is unfortunately often forgotten by many practitioners who use the Balanced Scorecard. Robert Kaplan and David Norton, *The Balanced Scorecard* (Boston: HBS Press, 1996), p. 34.

17. See note 7 and Robert Kaplan and David Norton, *The Strategy-Focused Organization: How Balanced Scorecard Companies Thrive in the New Business Environment* (Boston: HBS Press, 2001).

18. Robert Bruner, *Deals from Hell: M&A Lessons That Rise Above the Ashes* (New York: Wiley, 2005), Chapter 11.

19. George Day and Paul Schoemaker, "Scanning the Periphery," *Harvard Business Review*, November 2005, pp. 135–148.

20. Schlomo Maital, *Executive Economics: Ten Essential Tools for Managers* (New York: Free Press, 1994), p. 44.

21. Bruner (2005), Chapter 6.

22. Lisa Meulbroek, "The Promise and Challenge of Integrated Risk Management," *Risk Management and Insurance Review* 5, no. 1 (2002), p. 55.

23. Bruner (2005), Chapter 10.
24. Ibid., Chapter 12.
25. CFO Publishing Corp. (2004).
26. Chris Argyris, "Teaching Smart People How to Learn," *Harvard Business Review*, May-June 1991, pp. 5–15.

CONCLUSION

1. Benjamin Graham and David Dodd, *Security Analysis*, 3rd ed. (New York: McGraw-Hill, 1951 [1934]), p. 16.
2. Seth A. Klarman, *MIT Remarks*, October 20, 2007, www.designs. valueinvestorinsight.com/bonus/bonuscontent/docs/Seth_Klarman_ MIT_Speech.pdf, p. 7.
3. Benjamin Graham, *The Intelligent Investor* (New York: Harper & Row, 1973 [1949]), Chapter 1, and Seth Klarman, *Margin of Safety: Risk-Averse Value Investing Strategies for the Thoughtful Investor* (New York: HarperBusiness, 1991), Chapter 1.
4. For more information, see, for example, Tweedy, Browne Company, "What Has Worked in Investing," 1992; www.tweedy.com/library_docs/ papers/what_has_worked_all.pdf.
5. Graham (1973 [1949]), p. 321. Klarman (1991, p. 17) notes, "The financial markets are far too complex to be incorporated into a formula. Moreover, if any successful investment formula could be devised, it would be exploited by those who possessed it until competition eliminated the excess profits."
6. I note that Roger Lowenstein, *When Genius Failed: The Rise and Fall of Long-Term Capital Management* (New York: Random House, 2000), pp. 234–235, was incredibly prescient in this regard.
7. Peter Lynch has interesting comments in this regard in *One Up on Wall Street* (New York: Simon & Schuster, 1989).
8. For further information, see Klarman (1991) and Joel Greenblatt, *You Can Be a Stock Market Genius: Uncover the Secret Hiding Places of Stock Market Profits* (New York: Fireside, 1997).

9. For information on pricing, see, for example, Thomas Nagle and Reed Holden, *The Strategy and Tactics of Pricing: A Guide to Profitable Decision Making*, 3rd ed. (Upper Saddle River, N.J.: Prentice Hall, 2002 [1987]). An interesting article on pricing is "The Irrationalities of Product Pricing," *Wall Street Journal*, September 22, 2008; http://online.wsj.com/article/SB122160024323844777.html#printMode.

10. David D'Alessandro, *Brand Warfare: 10 Rules for Building the Killer Brand* (New York: McGraw-Hill, 2001), p. 176.

11. Thomas Russo, "Globetrotting with Graham and Dodd," in Benjamin Graham and David Dodd, *Security Analysis*, 6th ed. (New York: McGraw-Hill, 2008 [1934]), p. 720.

12. Interestingly, JPMorgan Chase's CEO, Jamie Dimon, endorsed the recently published sixth edition of Graham and Dodd's *Security Analysis*, which was the only endorsement from a businessperson listed in the book.

13. Susan Pulliam, Kate Kelly, and Matthew Karnitschnig, "Buffett Drove Hard Bargain with Goldman," *Wall Street Journal*, September 25, 2008; http://online.wsj.com/article/SB122226055484170915.html.

14. Krishna Palepu, Paul Healy, and Victor Bernard, *Business Analysis & Valuation: Using Financial Statements*, 2nd ed. (Cincinnati, Ohio: South-Western College Publishing, 2000), Chapter 10, and Benjamin Esty, *Note on Value Drivers*, HBS Case Services, #9-297-082, April 7, 1997, p. 6.

15. For more information, see William E. Fruhan, Jr., *Financial Strategy: Studies in the Creation, Transfer, and Destruction of Shareholder Value* (Homewood, Ill.: Irwin, 1979), and Bennett Stewart, *The Quest for Value: A Guide for Senior Managers* (New York: HarperBusiness, 1999 [1991]).

16. Klarman (1991, p. 103) noted that value investors in general were criticized during the late 1980s because they "avoided participating in the fully valued and overvalued securities" of the time, which crashed (inevitably) in 1990.

17. Benjamin Graham arrived "at a 'law' about human nature that cannot be repealed and is unlikely to be modified to any great extent. This law says that people without experience or superior abilities may make a lot

of money fast in the stock market, but they cannot keep what they make, and most of them will end up as net losers." Benjamin Graham, "Stock Market Warning: Danger Ahead!" *California Management Review*, Spring 1960, p. 41.

18. The seminal work on disruption is Clayton Christensen, *The Innovator's Dilemma* (New York: HarperBusiness, 2000 [1997]), which builds on the theory of "creative destruction" propounded by the late economist Joseph Schumpeter. For more information on Schumpeter and his theory see Thomas McCraw, *Prophet of Innovation: Joseph Schumpeter and Creative Destruction* (Cambridge, Mass.: Belknap Press of Harvard University Press, 2007).

19. Roger Lowenstein, "The Essential Lessons," in Graham and Dodd (2008 [1934]), p. 58.

20. This is disputed, but what is beyond dispute is that LTCM's failure would have generated substantial market disruption. Whether LTCM should have been allowed to fail—the Federal Reserve orchestrated its bailout—is a political question that is beyond the scope of this book.

21. For more information, see Lowenstein (2000). An alternative view can be found in Donald MacKenzie, *An Engine, Not a Camera: How Financial Models Shape Markets* (Cambridge, Mass.: MIT Press, 2006).

22. See, for example, the comments of Myron Scholes in William Breit and Barry Hirsch, eds., *Lives of Laureates: Eighteen Nobel Economists* (Cambridge, Mass.: MIT Press, 2005 [1986]), p. 247.

23. Graham and Dodd (1951 [1934]), p. 399.

24. Robert Berner and Susann Rutledge, "The Next Warren Buffett?" *BusinessWeek*, November 22, 2004; www.businessweek.com/magazine/content/04_47/b3909001_mz001.htm.

25. Roger Fisher, William Ury, and Bruce Patton, *Getting to Yes: Negotiating Agreement without Giving In*, 2nd ed. (New York: Penguin, 1991 [1981]), p. 170.

26. A fairly dramatic example of this can be found in David Einhorn, *Fooling Some of the People All of the Time: A Long Short Story* (Hoboken, N.J.: Wiley, 2008).

27. Pulliam et al. (2008).

28. Ibid.

29. Source: www.berkshirehathaway.com/2000ar/acq.html.

RESOURCES

1. For more information, see Nassim Nicholas Taleb's *Fooled by Randomness: The Hidden Role of Chance in Life and in the Markets*, 2nd ed. (New York: Random House, 2005 [2004]), and *The Black Swan: The Impact of the Highly Improbable* (New York: Random House, 2007). Note especially pages 280–282 in *The Black Swan* regarding Taleb's comments on Myron Scholes and Robert Merton, who were the two Nobel Prize winners involved with LTCM. Regarding LTCM, refer to endnotes 19 to 21 of the Conclusion.

   There are many causes for the troubled state of mainstream economics, but a key one is its failure to address and understand the "real world," which unfortunately is not a new phenomenon. Consider, for example, the following extended quote from a recent biography of economist Joseph Schumpeter (who passed away in 1950):

   Oddly enough, references to actual companies were not common in the professional writings of economists at the time [the late 1930s] and are almost nonexistent today. Rigorous historical analysis of firms and industries has become the purview of business history. Before the appearance of [Joseph Schumpeter's book] *Business Cycles* [that was published in 1939], business history had been in existence for only a few years, and much of its practice was confined to case studies done for classes at Harvard Business School.

   The source of the above quote is Thomas McCraw, *Prophet of Innovation: Joseph Schumpeter and Creative Destruction* (Cambridge,

Mass.: Belknap Press of Harvard University Press, 2007), p. 253. Case studies—especially Graham and Dodd–based case studies—can produce substantial economic insight, as I hope I have demonstrated in this book. However, this assumes that economics is defined as the late British economist Lionel Robbins defined it; namely, as a method for studying the allocation of scarce resources that have alternative uses.

2. Steve Lohr, "Like J. P. Morgan, Warren E. Buffett Braves a Crisis," *New York Times*, October 5, 2008; www.nytimes.com/2008/10/06/business/06buffett.html?_r=1&scp=1&sq=shades%20of%201907&st=cse&oref=slogin. For information on the Panic of 1907, see, for example, Robert Bruner and Sean Carr, *The Panic of 1907: Lessons Learned from the Market's Perfect Storm* (Hoboken, N.J.: Wiley, 2007).

3. Howard Marks, "Unshackling Bonds," in Benjamin Graham and David Dodd, *Security Analysis*, 6th ed. (New York: McGraw-Hill, 2008 [1934]), p. 140. See also pages 183–189 and 215–217 of the same source for some of Graham and Dodd's new era–related real estate commentary.

   Another interesting parallel exists with respect to the structured finance instruments involved in the 2007–2008 credit crises and the junk bond crisis of 1989–1990. For further information on the junk bond crisis, see, for example, Seth Klarman, *Margin of Safety: Risk-Averse Value Investing Strategies for the Thoughtful Investor* (New York: HarperBusiness, 1991), Chapter 4.

4. See also the review by Robert Blumen, "Debt & Delusion," *Daily Article*, August 11, 2004; www.mises.org.

5. Benjamin Graham and David Dodd, *Security Analysis* (New York: McGraw-Hill, 1934), p. 21.

6. Ibid., p. 70.

7. "Betting on the Market—Pros: Peter Lynch, *FRONTLINE*; www.pbs.org/wgbh/pages/frontline/shows/ betting/pros/lynch.html.

INDEX

ABOUT THE AUTHOR

Joseph Calandro, Jr., is the enterprise risk manager of a global financial services firm. Previously he was a financial management consultant who worked on a variety of valuation, financial strategy, and risk management engagements. He was also a part-time finance professor at the University of Connecticut, where he taught value investing and risk management in the school's MBA program. Joe has published widely across disciplines in a variety of journals, including the *Journal of Alternative Investments, Strategy & Leadership*, the *Risk Management & Insurance Review*, and *Measuring Business Excellence*, and he has presented papers at conferences held in the United States, the United Kingdom, and Canada.

Lightning Source UK Ltd.
Milton Keynes UK
UKHW02n2123140618
324263UK00016B/297/P